Praise for *Street Warrior*

"I've known Ralph Friedman for almost forty years, since the first day he walked into Big Joe's Tattoo Shop. He looked more like a biker than a cop. We were on opposite sides of the fence, but we always respected each other! He's the toughest Jew I know, who has more tattoos than I do."
—Chuck Zito, actor/stuntman/bodyguard and former Hells Angel

"*Fugeddabutitt!* If I knew about Detective Ralph Friedman when I was raising hell in New York during the '70s and '80s, I may have dialed back my lifestyle. Friedman's memoir is a rapid-fire page-turner, told with compassion and gut-wrenching reality. It's a walk through the South Bronx in an era that some people would like to forget."
—Gianni Russo, actor, *The Godfather*

"Friedman used his fists, guns, and other available weapons to arrest, wound, and sometimes kill suspects, winning a host of medals for valor in the process. . . . His restlessness for action never abated, to the point where he placed himself in personal peril multiple times. A swashbuckling book that is likely to elicit extreme reactions of applause or disapproval depending on the reader's personal opinions about law enforcement."
—*Kirkus Reviews*

"The toughest crime fighter in the history of NYC didn't leap tall buildings or drive a Batmobile. He was a real-life, tough-as-nails detective, the closest thing to a caped crusader New York ever had. Meet Ralph Friedman, Super-Cop."
—Steven Jay Griffel, bestselling author of the David Grossman series

"It was a different job and a turbulent time, and Ralph Friedman defined the word *Detective*. *Street Warrior* should be required reading for anyone who wants to understand the real world of street policing. Read this book and be awed. An amazing story told by a legendary NYPD detective."
—Joseph D. Pistone, author of *Donnie Brasco: My Undercover Life in the Mafia*

"The explosive, riveting, and incredible street action of a legendary crime fighter—who is also the most highly decorated NYPD detective in New York City history." —Captain Tom Walker (Ret.), author of *Fort Apache*

"All the violence, crime, and chaos of 1970s New York City instantly come to life in this gripping detective story. *Street Warrior* is a true-crime rarity. This gritty firsthand account of an unstoppable NYPD cop will have you rooting for the good guys the whole time!"

—Pat Dixon, host of *NYC Crime Report*

"This book is as fearless as the cop who wrote it and the cops he worked with. Readers will be grateful such men exist. It should be required reading for judges, mayors, and their police chiefs who handcuff our police."

—Charles Brandt, bestselling author of *I Heard You Paint Houses*

"Detective Friedman took me to a place in New York that I had only heard of, either from the newspapers or television news. He told the real story. Great book, a cop's cop and truly a hero."

—Bill Katzing, U.S. Department of Justice (Ret.)

"I enjoyed these true-to-life New York experiences. Funny and gritty, this book is a great example of why we respect those honorable men in blue."

—Aida Turturro, actress, *The Sopranos*

"*Street Warrior* brings to life the axiom 'truth is stranger than fiction.' If I read this book as a novel, I would have put it down as incredulous partway through. But I have known Ralph Friedman for thirty years and was aware of the legendary status of this superman of a cop longer than that. Any one chapter of this cannot-put-down book would represent the pinnacle of most top cops' careers. A must-read, it will change the way you view policing forever."

—Captain Douglas Greenwood, NYPD (Ret.)

"I loved this book. Could not put it down. Mr. Friedman's exploits were an adrenaline rush with many comic moments sprinkled in between. It gives you a newfound respect for the incredibly difficult job police officers face every day, but even more so back in the '70s. Cannot wait for the movie!"

—James Biberi, actor, *Drive, Analyze That*

STREET WARRIOR

RALPH FRIEDMAN
with Patrick Picciarelli

STREET WARRIOR

THE TRUE STORY OF THE
NYPD'S MOST DECORATED DETECTIVE
AND THE ERA THAT CREATED HIM

St. Martin's Press
New York

STREET WARRIOR. Copyright © 2017 by Ralph Friedman and Patrick Picciarelli. Foreword copyright © by Tom Walker. All rights reserved. Printed in the United States of America. For information, address St. Martin's Press, 175 Fifth Avenue, New York, N.Y. 10010.

www.stmartins.com

Unless otherwise noted, all insert photographs courtesy of the author.

The Library of Congress Cataloging-in-Publication Data is available upon request.

ISBN 978-1-250-10690-2 (hardcover)
ISBN 978-1-250-10691-9 (e-book)

Our books may be purchased in bulk for promotional, educational, or business use. Please contact your local bookseller or the Macmillan Corporate and Premium Sales Department at 1-800-221-7945, extension 5442, or by e-mail at MacmillanSpecialMarkets@macmillan.com.

First Edition: July 2017

10 9 8 7 6 5 4 3 2 1

This book is dedicated to all the men and women of the NYPD,
past, present, and future, fighting for justice—
be it in a court of law or at the end of a nightstick.

FOREWORD

As the former commander of the 41st Precinct (Fort Apache) in the South Bronx, I was well aware that the word "legend" wasn't an overused term in the area. A legend, if it came to the Bronx, was most likely suited in a Yankee uniform. But that belief was to be challenged by a young man in a blue uniform by the name of Ralph Friedman.

When you read this book, you must understand something critical. We weren't playing on green grassy fields; we were playing on bloody, potholed streets. In 1971 the New York Police Department engaged in 314 shootouts. Ninety-three hoodlums were killed and 221 were wounded. We lost 15 police officers and had hundreds wounded. This is the environment in which Ralph Friedman found himself. He would be stabbed, bitten, assaulted, and shot at too many times to count. There wasn't much of a change in the city until Rudy Giuliani became mayor.

Legends grow incrementally as time goes by. After Ralph left Fort Apache, his reputation grew with each new Bronx assignment. I could tell you of his physical strength and agility, his incredible arrest records, his gut-wrenching involvement in fifteen unbelievable gun shootings, or the drama of his private life. But that's best left for you to read.

I'd rather tell you one story that convinced me that Ralph would become a legendary police officer. In March 1974, a man was exchanging gunfire with two uniformed officers. When Ralph arrived on the scene, he immediately jumped onto the hood and then the roof of a Cadillac. Ralph leaped onto the culprit and, after a furious battle, was able to subdue, disarm, and arrest him. And so for me began the legend of Ralph Friedman, aka Superman.

Captain Tom Walker, NYPD (Ret.)
Bronx, New York
2017

Prologue

November 1, 1972 —
Confines of the 41st Pct., the Bronx

My problem—if you can categorize it as a problem—was my affinity for the part of police work that involves locking up bad guys and the resulting satisfaction versus spending a lot of time in court as an outcome of making those arrests.

I lived to work the street. And after two years in the New York City Police Department, I was living my dream being part of the 41st Precinct's Anti-Crime Unit. The Four-One, located in the South Bronx, was known as Fort Apache and was just about what you would expect of the Wild West in its heyday. Being assigned to the Four-One was the best on-the-job training any cop could get, and I'd arrived there right out of the police academy. I'd learned more in two years than I could've learned in a lifetime in any other command, making enough quality arrests before I was twenty-three to get an Anti-Crime slot, and I relished every minute of it.

The court thing, however, bugged me. I never looked forward to the hours—sometimes days—of boredom that was the norm for cops taking their arrests through the system. On one particular day, I'd been switched from my normal tour of 6 PM to 2 AM to a day tour so I could go to court on an old case, and I was relieved when it turned out to be a short visit. I returned to the command around noon and was told to team up with police officer Kal Unger, who had also returned from court, and we hit the street.

Kenny Mahon was my regular partner, but since my squad was working the night tour, I was paired with Kal for the remainder of the 8 AM to 4 PM day shift. He was about my age, maybe a year older, with sandy hair and a dry sense of humor. We'd worked together in the past, but not very often. He was a great cop, but that was a given if you made it to Anti-Crime.

Anti-Crime cops worked in plainclothes and used their own vehicles most of the time, along with confiscated cabs, milk trucks, Con Ed vans, and anything else with wheels we could get our hands on. I even used my motorcycle on occasion. We patrolled like the uniforms only didn't normally pick up 911 calls for service. Our job was to arrest offenders, and we were good at what we did. We didn't delude ourselves into thinking that the bad guys didn't know who we were; how long does it take to "make" a cop who works in the same command every day and drives the same vehicles? To overcome the recognition factor, we often took to the roofs or struck quickly before the alert went out that 5-0 was around.

Today, we were in Kal's Volkswagen Beetle.

"Got any place special you wanna go, Ralph? You hungry?" Kal said as he eased the bug into traffic. The engine whined like a lawn mower, and my first thought was that I hoped we didn't get into a car chase.

This was the standard question. The beginning of a tour was a cop's time. Traditionally, it meant coffee or a quick bite to eat before you got down to the business of fighting crime. Not too many dining choices in the Four-One, however. A cop ate in local restaurants at his own risk—you never knew when a cop-hating short-order cook would include a surprise in your sandwich—and I'd made sure I had lunch in a clean place outside court that catered to the court crowd. Realistically, Kal's question was rhetorical; we both wanted to get right to it and lock someone up.

"Nah, just go," I said.

The first hour was typical. The portable radio never stopped spewing out calls; the Four-One was a busy place. Assaults, burglaries past and burglaries in progress, numerous disputes, the usual knifings, blatant drug deals, and other general mayhem—all this in an area of 2.5 square miles. A tour in Fort Apache was like ten tours anywhere else.

The people in the Four-One were mostly Hispanic, with some African Americans and a smattering of white faces (older folks who'd lived in the neighborhood since birth, when the area was actually upper middle class). Now the area was steeped in poverty, drugs, and a crime rate so horrific that a week without at least three homicides was newsworthy.

The afternoon sped along. Kal and I backed up uniformed units on radio calls, harassed a few street punks we knew weren't really doing much (but certainly would commit at least one felony before the day was over), and asserted our authority, sometimes overreaching it. This was the South Bronx in the '70s, when "PC" meant "police commissioner" and the term "political correctness" had not yet entered the lexicon widely. In the Four-One, if a police officer wasn't feared and respected, he would get chewed up and spit out, which usually meant an assignment elsewhere in the city where local kids didn't set their parents on fire for fun.

It was a very cool and exceptionally sunny day, the glare bouncing off the windshield with laser-like annoyance. The neighborhood streets, while somewhat crowded, didn't contain the teeming humanity that would've been present during the summer months. In the humidity festival that is New York during July and August, the South Bronx natives spill onto the streets in an effort to escape the stifling heat of the tenements and high-rise projects. Street gambling, drinking, and hanging out on building stoops were usually a precursor to violence. The higher the temperature, the hotter the tempers flared, and assaults and homicides were sure to follow. You knew autumn arrived in the South Bronx when the domino games moved indoors and the homicide rate began to dip to very high, down from extremely high.

Soon after we'd lost count of how many times we'd driven every street in the command, and with our stomachs growling louder than the car's motor, we contemplated a trip to a neighboring precinct, where we wouldn't get poisoned grabbing something to eat. In the middle of our food fantasy—two of cops' favorite topics are food and sex—the radio run that would change our lives came over the portable: "A signal 10-31, 992 Fox Street, top floor. Units to respond?"

A 10-31 was the code designation for a burglary in progress, a job that obviously required immediate attention. We were a few blocks away from the location. I nodded to Kal and keyed the radio. "Four-One Anti-Crime in plainclothes will take that, Central." Vocalizing that we were in civvies might save us from getting shot by a unit from another command that was passing through without knowing who we were; although two white men in military fatigue jackets and jeans (the unofficial uniform of Anti-Crime cops) waving guns should have been a strong hint that we were the good guys.

"Anything further, Central?" I asked.

The dispatcher came back: "Anonymous call of a male entering the location via the roof. Nothing further."

"Nothing further" left open myriad possibilities: Was the bad guy armed? (Most burglars aren't because it raises the degree of the crime, and, as such, the jail sentence, but maybe this burglar hadn't read the penal law.) A description of the bad guy would've been nice, but we didn't have that either. Or was the job just bullshit, called in by some local asshole to see how many cops would respond for nothing? Bogus calls were an official sport in the South Bronx.

The bottom line was that we had to be careful, and so out came the guns. I'd never worked in another precinct and thus didn't know how cops elsewhere operated; in the Four-One, the very least you did was have your hand on your firearm for *every* call you responded to. The proverbial cat stuck in a tree would be no exception. You never knew what to expect, even from the most mundane of calls.

Kal pulled up a few doors away from the Fox Street address off Westchester Avenue. Parking directly in front of a destination address is ill advised in case of a setup. Hard to believe, but there are people who don't like cops and who think ambushing a few sounds like a fun time.

We were the first unit to arrive. The area had a smattering of civilians on the street, some watching the passing parade from a window perch, most not giving us a second glance as we exited the car and ran for number 992. Constant police activity was so common in the South Bronx that the sight of two white men with guns drawn would not have been a rarity.

We knew other cops were on the way, but we didn't know how long it would take for them to arrive. A burglary-in-progress call usually dictated no sirens to avoid warning the bad guys. Flashing roof lights on radio cars and speed balls on the dashboards of unmarked vehicles were a good tactical alternative because they're silent, and we wouldn't hear them until they had already arrived. That said, we were working in the South Bronx, where lights and sirens on police vehicles are a suggestion, not a law, to yield right-of-way. Typical responses from drivers were streams of curses and invectives involving your mother. Drivers did what they wanted to do; only fire department vehicles got respect . . . sometimes.

As we raced toward the entrance to the building, Kal and I kept glancing up at the rooftops. If this call was an ambush, death would most likely come from above. Even if it wasn't a planned execution, many youths in the area liked to toss stuff off rooftops at responding cops, usually bricks, which often were "preloaded" on roofs in anticipation of the inevitable visit by cops. I've seen everything raining down from above. Including commodes. It was bad enough being brained by a brick, but to suffer the indignity of getting crushed by a toilet bowl was the ultimate embarrassment. If you survived, which was highly doubtful, you'd be called Shithead for the rest of your career.

The building was typical for the area: prewar (*which* war was always the question—some tenements were over a hundred years old), narrow, sometimes with a short cement stairway leading to the door. Buildings varied in condition from serviceable to not fit for human habitation. This one was somewhere in-between. What most of these structures had in common was the overpowering odor of urine throughout the building. Why tenants would pee in their own hallway rather than wait to get into their apartments always mystified me. Maybe they were marking their territory.

Kal was the first in through the door leading from the street. The smell hit us like we got bitch-slapped by a tree limb. After hundreds of times in these broken-down buildings, you'd figure I'd be used to it, but, as with the aroma of a ripe dead body, you never acclimate. Who the hell can live like this? Peeling paint, broken door locks, crud on the floors so deep you can shovel it off. Be it ever so crumbled there's no place like home, I suppose.

We raced up the stairs as quickly as our feet could carry us. Need I say that these buildings had no elevators? And even if they did, they probably wouldn't work.

"Why are these fucking jobs always on the top floor?" Kal asked as he took the stairs two at a time.

As we hit the top-floor landing, we heard the first scream. Loud and shrill, it came from a female, and she sounded terrified. The hallway was dimly lit with no windows, common with these types of buildings, and the building housed five apartments per floor. The scream focused our attention toward the apartment at the far end of the narrow hallway. The door frame on the apartment was splintered, leaving the door pushed in and off one of its hinges.

I was out of breath and my heart was pounding as Kal and I flanked the frame for a moment and listened for something— anything—that might give us an edge when we entered. Just then we heard another piercing howl, and we knew trying to formulate a tactical plan might not be in the best interest of the victim, who sounded as if she was getting tortured. Our presence was required inside—now.

We busted through what remained of the door, side by side. What met us was total darkness, inky blackness. Blind as a bat, I couldn't see a damn thing. Entering the building from bright daylight didn't help, but at least the dimness of the hallway should've helped our eyes adjust. It didn't. Later I'd find out that the apartment's windows were covered in heavy blankets, sheets, and curtains that effectively blocked out all light.

The dark was disorienting; we had left our flashlights in the car because we were working what was left of the day tour. We both yelled "Police!" several times just as another shriek blasted from somewhere in front of us.

We took a few cautious steps forward, trying to identify exactly where the screams were coming from. I was hoping my eyes would get used to the darkness, but that didn't happen.

Something moved, a sound to our right. Kal said, "What the fuck?" and the shooting started.

Muzzle blasts lit up the area. We'd passed through a short foyer adjacent to the living room and were now standing in a hallway that led to the rear of the apartment. There was a black male three feet in front of us, shirtless, gun extended, firing rapidly. Kal went down almost immediately, firing his revolver as he pitched forward. The noise of the gunfight in a confined space was ear-shattering, and I felt as if an ice pick was being shoved into my brain.

I had my gun extended and was firing rounds at the guy who was shooting at us. The room was caught up in a strobe-like miasma of light, screams, and curses.

The gunman tried to get by me, but I grabbed his shoulder and we struggled, grunting and swearing, although our voices sounded muffled given the affect the gunshots had on my hearing. Everything was happening very quickly, yet it felt like slow motion. I was fighting for my life, nearly deaf from the gunshots, and wondering if I'd been hit.

The shooter was about my height, medium build. A river of adrenaline was pumping through me, and I knew that if I didn't put him down, I was gonna die. I heard the approaching cavalry—the job now a rapid response "shots fired," allowing for flashing lights and sirens all the way—or thought I did. The troops were coming, and I hoped they'd arrive in time. As we fought, I pressed my gun against the gunman's chest, hoping that I still had ammo, and fired.

I heard the welcoming sound of a boom, no empty chamber click. The gunman went down like a dropped anchor. I found out later that he'd been hit a few times, but my last round got him square in the heart. The three of us had fired a total of eighteen rounds in what couldn't have been more than a ten-second gun battle in a space the area of a medium-size closet.

I was too pumped to feel fright or exhaustion. I dropped to the floor and grabbed Kal; he was unconscious. I didn't see much blood—shit, I still didn't see much of anything. His fatigue jacket had absorbed most of it from several gunshots.

The apartment began filling with cops. The covers on the windows were being ripped down and everyone was talking, yelling. Sunlight streamed through the windows.

I was practically sitting on the dead gunman who was shoulder to shoulder with Kal. Now I could see that there was actually blood everywhere.

"My partner, he's hit!" I hollered.

Cops kneeled down. I heard exclamations of "Oh, shit!," "He's shot fucking bad!" More cops were pouring into the apartment.

I tried to lift Kal and what seemed like a dozen hands joined the effort. Other cops pushed aside responding officers to make a path. We hoisted him in the air and raced down the stairs. There was no time to wait for an ambulance; seconds counted. Kal was going to be transported by radio car.

Someone had the presence of mind to call the dispatcher to have additional units clear the streets that lead to Jacobi Medical Center, which was over a mile away. Jacobi was where you took injured cops; they had excellent trauma teams. Department cars would block traffic at intersections in a race to get Kal immediate care.

We hit the street running, Kal seemingly lifeless in our grasp. The neighborhood denizens packed the street and were eerily quiet. Now was not the time to taunt the police. While they knew they could get away with almost anything right now, we would return and wouldn't be in a good mood.

Kal was placed as gently as possible on a cop's lap in the back of a marked car and the driver gunned it, lights and siren on overload. But there was a problem.

When time—seconds—meant the difference between life and death for Kal (if he wasn't already dead), numerous responding radio cars had blocked the street, and the operators were everywhere but in their cars. I heard the driver of the car Kal was in, whose name has been lost to me by the span of years, say "Fuck this!" before he began to ram the radio cars out of the way.

I watched the car disappear down the street, now joined by a phalanx of escorting vehicles. I wished I were leaving with him, but knew I wasn't going anywhere; a platoon of bosses would be on the scene shortly to interview me. As I reentered the building, two uniforms were supporting a woman who looked to be about thirty down the stairs. One cop was calling for an ambulance. She was banged up pretty badly, but otherwise seemed in decent shape. I figured she was the source of the screams we'd heard upstairs, and, when the gunfire started, she must've dove for cover in another room in the apartment.

I was being pulled in many directions. Questions came from everywhere. I didn't even know most of the brass who responded to the scene. Things got blurry; I was operating automatically, giving answers, taking accolades, recounting the shooting from various perspectives, and responding to the same questions from different sources over and over. I had lost track of time. I either remained on Fox Street for a few hours, or perhaps fifteen minutes. Pick one.

All I cared about was Kal. I needed to get to the hospital. My mind and heart were racing and I was beyond ramped up.

A deputy inspector pulled me aside.

"Ralph, the mayor wants to talk to you."

I was taken aback. Was I going to City Hall? That was a world away in a far-off land called Manhattan. The Bronx was one of the five boroughs, but it might as well have been in an alternate universe, such was the disparity in socioeconomic conditions. Why did the mayor want to talk to me at all? The DI saw the confused look on my face.

"He's coming to you, Ralph; you're not going to him. Get in the car." He directed me to his department auto, and we sped to Jacobi Hospital.

I made a conscious effort to decompress during the ride, but it didn't work. I was hypervigilant, and my blood pressure must've been through the roof. Aside from the obvious reason to go to the hospital, perhaps having a few hundred doctors available wasn't a bad idea.

The idea of talking to the mayor didn't thrill me. I'm a private person and most comfortable around the people I know and respect. The short list was family and cops, the terms being interchangeable. In the ensuing years, I became accustomed to press conferences, award ceremonies, and media types, but I was never at ease. I wanted to do my job and fade away, and then repeat the process the next day. This, unfortunately, was not the reality.

The streets surrounding the hospital were strewn with numerous NYPD vehicles, all illegally parked. I heard the wash of a helicopter's blades and turned to see a chopper hovering above Pelham Parkway, a six-lane roadway that was apparently being turned into a helipad.

The driver of the car I was in parked on the sidewalk, and I was led past at least a hundred uniforms of varying ranks and jobs: transit cops, housing cops, off-duty cops, cops in uniforms I didn't recognize—all there to give blood and anything else that was required. When a cop is shot, you circle the wagons, and unconditional support comes from everywhere. The word gets out quickly.

Jacobi Hospital had a media room where doctors and other interested parties give updates on high-profile cases. I was sequestered there, a small area with a miniscule stage, a podium, and a few dozen folding chairs in neat lines.

"The mayor's coming in shortly, Ralph," the DI told me.

How do you respond to that? "Wonderful," I said. "How's Kal doing? I want to see him."

"Soon. Do your thing with Lindsay first."

Mayor John Lindsay came breezing in with an entourage. I recognized one of his minions as the deputy commissioner of public information (DCPI), the liaison between the press and the NYPD.

The mayor approached me with an extended hand. "How're you doing, Ralph? You okay? Anything I can do for you?" He was grim and had a look of concern on his face that seemed genuine; with politicians, you never know what's real from what's bullshit.

John Lindsay was an imposing figure. He was tall and slim, impeccably dressed, and had an aura that commanded attention. One of the reasons he'd won the mayoralty was a promise to appoint 3,500 new cops to the force, no mean feat for the times. It was the height of the Vietnam War, and police work was as establishment as you could get. It was not a job young men were lining up to apply for. It was the age of the hippie movement and all the antigovernment rhetoric that went with it. But he'd pulled it off: the city got its cops, and he got Gracie Mansion.

"I'm okay, sir . . . my partner. I don't know how he's doing. I'd like . . ."

The mayor spoke to an aide over his shoulder. "Get an update on the injured officer. Now, please." People began to move.

We talked for maybe five minutes, and I got the distinct impression I was being sized up. The DCPI was paying rapt attention to everything I said.

"You performed heroically, Ralph . . . you and Officer Unger. You'll be recognized for it." He looked to the DCPI who nodded. "I'll be leaving now, just wanted to come and personally thank you for a job well done. You'll be apprised of Officer Unger's condition shortly. Good luck." We shook hands and he was gone along with his crew.

A captain quickly took his place. "Ralph, listen up. There's going to be a press conference in about five minutes. You're the lead. The reporters will want to talk to you . . . ask you questions. You up for it?"

Now I realized the main reason for the Q and A I'd just had with the mayor. While he was sincere in his concern about my welfare, his DCPI was weighing if I was wrapped tight enough to answer questions from the press without falling apart or saying something that would embarrass the job or, worse, the mayor.

I was in a place of high clarity and said so, still on an extreme adrenaline rush with no signs it was going to abate anytime soon. The captain took my word for it and called for a cop to admit the press, or as he so eloquently put it, "Let the bloodsuckers in."

With the rush of reporters came cameramen and lights, lots of lights. As the captain nodded toward the podium, a sergeant from the Four-One materialized by my side. He said to the captain,

"A minute, Cap? Got an update on Kal." He didn't wait for permission.

In a conspiratorially soft voice he leaned closer to me. "Kal's in bad shape. They're pumping blood into him by the gallon. He took a bullet to the heart . . . a sac or something." The sergeant looked confused. "The doc talked medical shit; all I heard was a round to the heart. He's holding his own. They're doing everything that can be done."

I felt myself beginning to break down, but I shook the feeling off. "Okay, Sarge. Keep me in the loop. Please?"

He said, "You bet," and was gone.

I fielded questions for about five minutes. This wasn't my first experience with reporters, but this was my first time as the center of attention with no way to escape. I felt like a nun in a whorehouse: a sea of faces in front of me, all shouting questions, and me staring just above their heads. Trying to make eye contact with each of them would've put me over the edge.

Most questions were relevant to the incident, but no one tried to bait me with questions about the use of deadly force. I thought it wise to give as many yes and no answers as possible, thinking whatever I say can come back to bite me in the ass. A boss on the job once said to me, "You can never get in any trouble keeping your mouth shut." Words to live by.

I knew I'd been justified in my actions, but I didn't entirely trust the media not to edit my responses for ratings. While I was expected to answer questions, I wasn't obligated to elaborate, and I didn't.

One reporter got close to forbidden territory when she asked, "Have you ever shot anyone before, Officer Friedman?"

I had, but I wasn't about to go there. Expecting the question, I had my answer ready: "I hurt someone's feelings once." That shut her up, and a boss moved in to end the interview before the reporter asked for clarification of my wiseass answer. I'd be all over the local evening news.

I stayed at the hospital for another few hours. Kal wound up getting seventy-two pints of blood, most coming from cop volunteers after the hospital's supply of Kal's blood type ran out. A doctor told me that Kal made medical history by taking that much blood in three hours. He had five other gunshot wounds that, while not as severe, were also life-threatening. He'd be in the hospital for two months.

The guy I'd killed was one Charles Williams. He had a rap sheet of assorted priors—as did many of the inhabitants of the Four-One. Williams lived with his wife and kids directly across Fox Street from where the shooting took place. The woman whom he'd assaulted was his girlfriend. Williams would divide his time between his wife and his girlfriend, unbeknownst to his family. Apparently, the girlfriend said or did something to piss him off because he was in the process of beating her to death when Kal and I intervened. Aggravated because we'd interrupted him, he took out his rage on me and Kal—one of many mistakes he'd made that day.

Kal was recovering from surgery and his future was touch and go. One doctor told me that he believed it was a miracle Kal had survived the initial trauma of the shooting, let alone making it through the surgical procedure. As the day meandered into night, cops from the Four-One, plus a smattering of others from commands throughout the city who knew Kal, hunkered down in the hospital to await any change in his condition. No one was going home; we'd sleep where we sat, whether it be in chairs or stretched out on the cold, hard floor. Cops can sleep anywhere; we were seasoned from the two-day marathons that sometimes made up the arrest and arraignment process.

The frenetic pace of the day caught up with everyone; it was as if the 41st Precinct cops were balloons and someone came along and stuck us with pins. The energy and anger we harbored since the shooting had dissipated into exhaustion and quiet reflection. While cops littered the hallways, most were silent, some nodding out as the evening wore on. The solitude gave me time to think.

There's not a cop or member of the military alive who hasn't thought about what it would be like to take a human life. It's something that runs through a cop's mind often. I never dwelled on it; I just felt that one day it might happen. Nothing prepares you for it. You come up with possible scenarios as to *how, who, why,* but conjecture doesn't come anywhere near reality.

We were in the midst of the Vietnam War, and I'd spoken to a number of enlisted friends who'd sweated the day they would experience combat. Would they freeze? Would they prove themselves? Would they be satisfied with the way they handled whatever was thrown at them? Cops are no different; only the battlefields change. I've known cops and soldiers who were forever changed the day they killed. Some experience psychological problems; others drink. Flashbacks are common. Marriages are destroyed. The forward momentum of life becomes intolerable. The malady of post-traumatic stress disorder wasn't even recognized in 1972.

I viewed my actions as totally justified, and as such my conscience was clear. I didn't intend on killing Charles Williams. Police officers are trained to *stop* a threat, to recognize the imminent danger and erase it by no longer having it exist. You keep firing until the threat is stopped. Williams had been shot numerous times before my shot to his heart ended his life. Had he fallen to the floor or just dropped his weapon and given up, he'd have survived.

I don't believe humans are designed to kill each other. We're a higher form of animal and should only kill for food. Society dictates we live in harmony, but this isn't always possible. In places like Fort Apache, day-to-day survival depends on a warrior mind-set, not only for the cops but also for the civilians. I hoped that my first experience taking a human life would be my last. Realistically, I knew this to be wishful thinking and I'd be proved right . . . three more times.

Charles Williams was dead, but he would be a part of my life for a while. My killing of Williams was declared a homicide by the Bronx district attorney. This is procedure whenever a cop kills someone. The question, of course, is whether the homicide was *justified*. There would be a grand jury hearing, during which I would have to validate my use of deadly force.

Three weeks later, it was deemed just that: justifiable homicide as per New York State law. I had done what I had to do to save my life and the life of my partner.

Over four decades later, long after I'd retired from the NYPD, a civilian, Eric Garner, died on Staten Island during the course of a lawful arrest. When the local DA declared the incident a homicide, the crowd took this to mean the arresting officer intentionally and without provocation killed Garner, and riots ensued. Mayor Bill de Blasio, in my opinion, kowtowed to the marauding bands, allowing mobs to take over the Brooklyn Bridge by letting them run wild while ordering the cops not to take any action. Cops and civilians were hurt.

To have effective policing, cops must feel that the mayor has their backs. This is not to say that renegade police officers should get a pass; it means that every incident gets fair treatment. Currently, as a result of what cops feel is biased treatment by City Hall, tension is palpable between the NYPD and the mayor, as evidenced by police officers turning their backs on the mayor during police funerals. When this happens, the civilian population suffers.

But in the South Bronx of the 1970s, the use of deadly force by police officers was much more common, the populace was less politically motivated, and the politicians backed cops who were correct in our actions.

There was also a grudging respect for the police by civilians when I was a police officer. A cop is never loved; we interact with citizens from a negative point of view. Most of the time, we are locking them up, giving them summonses, or just being the bearer of bad news. But it used to be that the respect was always there, albeit mostly grudgingly.

Would a mayor today drop what he was doing, commandeer a helicopter, and disrupt traffic just to tell a cop that he cared about him and his wounded partner? By Mayor Lindsay doing exactly that, he broadcasted to the NYPD that he backed us and viewed our actions as justified.

What we see currently is mostly a rush to judgment whenever a minority civilian is killed by a police officer. Rumors fly and politicians pander to the press for the minority vote at the expense of the police.

As of this writing (September 2016), not one inquiry by the FBI has ever led to an arrest, let alone a conviction, of a police officer in a civil-rights-violation investigation resulting from a police officer's use of deadly physical force during the numerous publicized incidents since 2014. Investigations are a good thing and not a tool to be used by a city administration to garner votes.

I often wonder if my killing Charles Williams in today's climate would have resulted in an attaboy from the mayor or an indictment. My heart goes out to police officers working in their current hostile environment. Might it be "just part of the job," and they're expected to soldier on? A civilian might change his mind if he's involved in a life-or-death situation and the responding officer hesitates to pull the trigger to avoid a line-of-duty death. Sometimes being a cop requires a split-second decision. Most of the time, it's the correct decision, and when it's not, the penal law recognizes that a police officer need only make a "reasonable" decision. If a cop reasonably believes someone is pointing a gun at him or is armed, whether he "sees" a gun or not, and then fires in self-defense but the gun turns out to be a replica weapon, incapable of firing a shot, the law allows for the police officer's decision to shoot.

The shooting of Williams was my second; the first one didn't result in death and will be recounted later. I would be involved in more shootings—many more—some with fatalities. How I would deal with them would be an evolving process. We all change. To survive the streets of New York, I had to remain in firm control of my emotions and deal with the ramifications of a life I chose and cherished.

What I wanted was to get back on the street. That's where I belonged. I liked the action, but I liked taking criminals off the street even more. The decent people of the Four-One and my later commands deserved someone who cared about them. I was that person.

1

July 10, 1967, 10:00 PM —
Connecting Highway, Astoria, Queens

I braked my '67 Mustang to a screeching halt under the first over-pass, engine rumbling. To my left was my opponent, behind the wheel of a '64 Mercury coupe. He looked to be about my age, with a head of greasy hair slicked back into a pompadour that seemed to defy gravity. He revved his engine, and I did likewise as we waited for the "go" handkerchief to signal the beginning of the race.

The road we were on was a straight quarter mile trench situated between twenty-foot walls, an overpass on each end. A crowd of at least a thousand onlookers looked down on us from both sides of the road, waving and screaming. How much money was being wagered on this race and the dozens like it that would take place on this sweltering summer night was anyone's guess.

Most of the drivers were racing for the glory; a few older guys with investments in their cars might be betting on their machines and their ability to win, but at eighteen I was lucky to have had enough money to buy my car to begin with. I had socked away cash from the several jobs I'd worked and bought the Mustang to race it at local tracks. I also raced at established tracks like National Speedway and West Hampton Raceway. My parents knew I had the car but had no idea about the racing, and I wasn't about to share.

The buildup to the race was almost as thrilling as the race itself. Our track was a length of well-paved highway that connected (hence the name "Connecting Highway") the eastbound lanes of the Grand Central Parkway (GCP) to the Brooklyn-Queens Expressway (BQE). You couldn't ask for a better road short of a professional speedway.

It took coordination to run these races. The road was heavily traveled around the clock, and this was a holiday weekend. People were going places. Race participants and fans would walk out onto the off-ramp of the GCP and stop traffic while the next two cars set to race would line up. It had to be done quickly to avoid pissing off the wrong driver.

The races would go on all night. Where were the cops? you might ask. They didn't have the manpower to control the hordes of racers, aggravated commuters, and thousands of fans who lined up on both sides of the trench to watch. The police would ride the road every so often, but as soon as they left the races would resume. Occasionally, the police would embarrass themselves by trying to chase a participant, getting left in the dust every time. Eventually, someone had the bright idea to call the fire department and have them hose down the highway, which stopped the races cold as soon as the drivers learned they could hydroplane their prized autos into the high concrete walls that braced the road. But it took years to come up with the hosing solution, and for many years, the Connecting Highway was the place for speed buffs to race cars on a weekend night.

The races went very quickly. But it was a bitch waiting to start, sitting in your car with the air-conditioning turned off to add off-the-starting-line thrust and with your windows rolled up to reduce the drag coefficient. July 10, 1967, was a scorcher. At 10 PM, the sun was down, but it still had to be in the mid-90s.

When we finally blasted off the starting line, I was sweating profusely, both from the heat and nervous energy. I fishtailed a bit and took the lead immediately, ramming through the gears in my custom Bang shifter automatic transmission in a blur, leaving my opponent in the midst of a burnt-rubber cloud. I won handily, my time fifteen seconds for the quarter mile, and basked in the glow of cheering spectators.

Anyone could race the Connecting Highway. While winning was about bragging rights, the thrill from throngs of spectators cheering you on was its own reward. Therefore, it wasn't odd to see the occasional six-cylinder heap going for the gold. Involvement was all about having fun and experiencing the adrenaline rush of competition and speed. If someone would've told me that night that I'd be policing the hellish world of the South Bronx in two years, I'd have thought him crazy.

We lived in the middle-class Fordham section of the Bronx on Kingsbridge Road, a mostly white, cohesive neighborhood of Italian, Jewish, and Irish families. My mom, Fay, was a stay-at-home mom, like most mothers I knew back then. My dad, David, managed the San Carlos Hotel in Manhattan. My brother, Stu, was four years younger than me, and we were very close. Because of the age difference, we had different friends, but I still looked out for him. That was my job as the older brother; it was my obligation under the unwritten rules of life on the street.

Boys get into the occasional fight, and we were no different, but if I felt Stu was getting unjustly persecuted, bullied, or outnumbered, because of his age and size, I came to the rescue. These incidents didn't happen often, but when they did I wasn't shy about kicking some ass. Such was life on the street in the Bronx. We learned from an early age that family is sacrosanct. Ambush my brother, and you'd be dealing with me. I was detained a few times by the local police for fighting but never arrested. Years later, I would work with two of those police officers.

It was a good neighborhood, and I couldn't imagine having better parents. My father was very involved in our lives, something I didn't see much of in some of my friends' families, where their fathers worked their asses off, came home, ate dinner, had a few cocktails, and went to sleep. I can't recall a day passing without my father asking questions at the dinner table about our day and involving himself in our lives every chance he got. Dinner was always a treat. The hotel where my father worked was connected to the Black Angus Restaurant, and so he was always bringing home the best cuts of meat.

I began seriously lifting weights in my early teens, and with the massive amounts of food I was consuming—I could put away an entire pie and quart of milk in one sitting, not to mention those rich, meaty dinners—my scrawny body was transforming into a powerhouse. I worked hard at it.

The Vietnam War was in full swing, and while most guys my age were smoking weed and drinking any cheap form of booze they could find, I never touched either. I viewed that crap as poison and abstained from it totally because I regarded my body as sacred. I don't drink alcohol, and getting high to me means standing on a chair.

My main concern—and that of my parents—was what I was going to do with the rest of my life. I'd had a fierce work ethic since I was twelve years old and had an after-school job delivering clothes for a neighborhood dry cleaner. There were times when I had two jobs, one in Manhattan delivering packages for a few hours and then back to the Bronx, where I'd finish off the day working for a butcher. After graduating high school, my dad got me a job as a furniture mover for the princely sum of $4.50 an hour, the minimum wage back then being $1.15 an hour. I saved my money and bought my first car, a 1959 Cadillac, which was as big as an aircraft carrier with Godzilla fins.

I wasn't lacking for drive; direction was another story.

I contemplated joining the army, but the three-year enlistment commitment didn't thrill me. When you're that age, three years doing anything seems like a lifetime. A few of my friends were joining, and most wound up in Vietnam.

Also, my father was vociferous in his objection to my enlisting. "You know there's a war going on, right?"

My father, a World War II–wounded army combat veteran, had a point, so I crossed the military off my list. But perhaps I'd have no choice: there was a lottery system back then based on birth dates, and, when the numbers were drawn, I was way down the list with little chance of being called up. Probably the only time in my life I'd ever win a lottery.

Time went by. I was eighteen and still pretty much aimless, but that was about to change. On a Friday night, I was hanging out with two friends when the subject of what we were going to do with the rest of the weekend came up. Rain was forecast; therefore, I didn't consider drag racing.

"Taking the police test," one guy said, which was quickly echoed by my other friend. "It's a walk-in, over at Clinton." I'd graduated from Clinton, an all-boys high school in the neighborhood.

I knew nothing about any police test. "What's a walk-in?" I asked.

They explained to me that in an effort to attract more applicants to the police department, the usual mountain of paperwork that accompanied an application to be a cop had been waived. This was 1967, when the Vietnam War was kicking into high gear and there was a general fuck-the-government sentiment in the country. Cops weren't popular, and the city's recruitment effort to fill the ranks that were rapidly depleting due to retirement and the draft was going nowhere. Eliminating some of the paperwork seemed like a good idea, and the test might attract people who didn't have anything better to do that day.

"What time's this test?" I asked. I was curious but not really interested.

"Nine."

I considered this. On the one hand, I'd been working all week and wanted to sleep in tomorrow morning; on the other hand, I was hauling other people's furniture for Neptune Movers for a living and there was nothing to look forward to in that line of work except a bad back.

I decided to give my future half a damn. "Tell you what . . . come by and ring my bell when you're on your way. If I'm up, I'll go with you."

Well, I *was* up, and I took the test along with thousands of applicants in other schools throughout the city.

I didn't know what to expect, but the test was made very easy to get the 3,500 cops the city needed. I was sure I scored high and expected to be called up when I turned twenty-one. The moment I completed the test, I began to get psyched about the job. The day before, I couldn't have cared less about the NYPD, but after the test I was envisioning what seemed to be a bright future.

I was half right: I scored in the top 5 percent, but instead of waiting to turn twenty-one before I went on the job, I was offered the position of trainee in the interim. A trainee is a civilian member of the NYPD who is basically in the civil service equivalent of purgatory. Too young to be a sworn officer, you languish in a non–law enforcement job until you hit the magic age. So on January 28, 1968, I was appointed an NYPD trainee.

Trainees wore gray uniforms and attended the police academy on East Twentieth Street in Manhattan. The uniforms, which displayed the NYPD shoulder patch, were also worn to and from the academy because the city wanted us to be visible and, as such, a deterrent to crime. I thought nothing about traveling the New York City subway with a uniform that clearly identified me as belonging to the NYPD. No gun, no shield, no nightstick, just a blissfully content trainee riding in the belly of the beast with no fear of being slaughtered by a cop hater. True, I wasn't a cop, but I was on my way to being one and was identified with the job by the uniform. Only when I think back on it now does it strike me as strange. Anyone with a score to settle or a political statement to make could've taken me out with no fuss. Those were different times, however, and while cops were unpopular—that never changes—they weren't being ambushed for no other reason than that they chose the wrong profession, like they are today.

Trainees were taught nonlethal skills, learning how the job worked on an administrative level. The NYPD, like any law enforcement agency, documents everything, and has a form to fit any police contingency. We learned them all, plus some technical expertise like how to fingerprint civilians who needed prints taken for a variety of city licenses and permits.

After training, I was assigned to the 44th Precinct, located near Yankee Stadium in the Bronx, pretty close to home. I was no longer required to wear the gray uniform and came to work dressed pretty much in anything I wanted. The cops were glad to have me; whatever I was assigned to do meant they didn't have to, which in this case was fingerprinting civilians.

Tedious and frustrating, fingerprinting people who weren't used to the process often screwed up the print cards by unnecessary movement or failure to listen to directions to remain relaxed and let me roll their fingers. Still, being around real cops every day made me even more anxious to get my shield and hit the street.

I wasn't comfortable working indoors, but I had little choice. The cops had a lot of freedom, did their jobs, and had leeway as to how they performed their duties. The job was proactive; the bosses wanted their troops to make arrests and stir up the pot. Cops were respected by their bosses, if not by the community, but it made little difference. Cops liked being cops; I could see it on their faces, their interaction with each other, and their respect for the sergeants who supervised them. The sergeants backed their cops, and cops wanted to please their sergeants. Morale is everything in police work.

I fully expected to spend my trainee time in the Four-Four, but after seven months was abruptly transferred to police headquarters at 240 Centre Street in Manhattan with the advent of the new 911 emergency system. New Yorkers could now dial three digits in the event of a police emergency instead of calling an operator, who would then direct the call to the appropriate precinct or dial seven numbers to a borough emergency line.

Initially, I took incoming phone calls from those needing police assistance. It was a bit of a learning curve—not for me, but for the good citizens of the city who didn't seem to know what an emergency was. I'd get calls for literally everything, from the proverbial lost cat to people who needed directions. I gained a respect for anyone who has to deal with the public, particularly over the phone.

Luckily, I got moved within the 911 system to the action desk, which is where ranking members of the job got informed regarding important or high-profile occurrences throughout the city. Details of violent crimes, multivictim accidents, fires, floods, etcetera got relayed to the people who made the decisions.

There were no personal computers back then; information was passed the old-fashioned way, by writing it on an index card, putting it on a conveyer belt, and sending it on its way. I did this for fourteen months until the day I turned twenty-one. This is a milestone in anyone's life, but for me it was like being reborn.

I was going to be a police officer—finally.

I was sworn in on February 2, 1970, and went back to the police academy, this time to learn the job of being a New York City cop.

I took to the training immediately, particularly the physical portion. I'd been weight training for years and was in top shape, still following my no-booze, no-cigarettes, no-drugs policy. My fellow recruits, especially those who smoked, had a difficult time keeping up with the daily runs. We ran inside the gym, circling it numerous times until we were ready to drop. These runs had been conducted outside at one time, with hour-long jogs through the neighborhood, until people who didn't like cops very much started to throw stuff from rooftops at the rookies.

As part of our physical training we also had to become CPR certified. While we were taught how to resuscitate someone, using the technique wasn't mandatory. Locking lips with an unconscious stranger while trying to breathe life into him can be hazardous to your own life. I know quite a few cops who contracted diseases, mostly hepatitis, doing just that. The unwritten rule adhered to by most of the rank and file was that we would use CPR only on someone we knew (read: family). Soon enough, I would come to discover how important CPR training would be, but for now it was just another skill we were adding to our résumé on a daily basis.

What the recruits most looked forward to was firearms training, which was conducted at the outdoor range at Rodman's Neck in the Bronx. The facility was under the command of Lieutenant Frank McGee, a former World War II submariner who ran the range like a military installation. Rodman's Neck was a self-contained operation with dining facilities, expansive firing ranges, and numerous Quonset-hut classrooms. The place was kept orderly by trusted prisoners from nearby Rikers Island, who roamed the sixty-acre facility with landscaping tools.

I initially questioned the wisdom of having convicts mingling with cops, but that apprehension proved to be unfounded when I became aware of the numerous incidents where the prisoners would turn in guns found in bathrooms, classrooms, and the mess hall, left there by negligent police officers. I guess that's why they called the cons "trusties."

We learned our sidearm, the .38 caliber pistol, through live-fire exercises and classroom tactical instruction. I'd never fired a gun before but became proficient quickly; however, I never became a "gun guy" like many other police officers.

Most cops, whether they had a predilection toward guns before they came on the job or not, naturally developed an interest in them because of the proliferation of firearms on the street. Most cops research firearms over the course of their careers and purchase them occasionally. By the end of a career, a cop could accumulate quite a collection, ten or more firearms being a modest number.

I remember when the Dirty Harry movies were popular that a lot of guys I worked with bought Harry's gun, a .44 caliber Smith & Wesson revolver, wielding thoughts of kicking ass and shooting bad guys like Clint Eastwood. The same thing happened with the James Bond movies, only in that case it was the .380 Walther PPK.

Both were strictly fantasies; the NYPD had a strict policy of what guns we could carry, and the two celebrity pistols weren't on the list. One of the firearms instructors at Rodman's Neck told us, "You can carry any gun you want, just as long as it's either a Smith & Wesson or Colt .38." That didn't leave us much room to comparison shop. I chose the Colt because it carried six rounds, an improvement on the Smith's five.

I considered the gun a tool and treated it with respect. I had no idea at the time that proficiency with my gun would save my life on numerous occasions. I've been retired for more years than I was on the job and I still carry my six-shot, snub-nosed Colt Detective Special revolver, while some other retirees opt for semiautomatics with large magazine capacities. I was good with my revolvers—I carried two while on duty—so why learn an entirely new weapon? Surviving a gunfight is about shot placement, not throwing numerous rounds at a target and hoping a few hit their mark. Training is the key, not necessarily large-capacity weapons.

The academic part of the training was tougher, especially if we had the gym in the morning and class in the afternoon. Staying awake after running countless miles, swimming, boxing, and eating a massive lunch was its own learning curve. The academy ran Monday through Friday, and the weekends were a much-needed respite. On Friday, March 13, my plans for a weekend away from studying were dashed by the blizzard that came to be known as the Great March Superstorm.

All days off were canceled when the snow began to fall. Accompanying the snow were winds of forty to sixty miles per hour that made those pretty flakes feel like darts when they struck your face. I was assigned to Midtown with six other rookies. We were told to "keep the peace," even though the city probably hadn't been this safe since the last super snowstorm. Nary a soul was on the street except for us rookies. Manhattan resembled a New York version of the movie *The Omega Man*, in which Charlton Heston is the lone survivor of the human race in a postapocalyptic Los Angeles.

As luck would have it, we were making New York safe from bad guys about half a mile from the San Carlos Hotel, the very same that my dad managed. After freezing our asses off for a few hours and not once seeing a sergeant (or any other cop, for that matter), we decided we needed a break. New York would have to fend for itself until we warmed up.

When we arrived at the hotel, we looked like survivors of an avalanche. Our uniforms were frozen solid and we had icicles hanging from our noses and eyebrows. Our hands were cold to the point of futility in the event we had to draw our weapons.

My father took one look at me and said, "Maybe you should've gone to Vietnam after all. At least it's warmer over there."

I grunted in agreement.

"You guys hungry?" he asked rhetorically.

Cops are always hungry.

Within minutes we were seated in the deserted adjoining Black Angus Restaurant. I knew prices in this place were steep, and I had a feeling we were about to get a free meal.

We were a group of rookies who'd been inundated with numerous lectures in the academy on how to avoid corruption, and here we were about to be fed a few hundred dollars' worth of prime beef. We exchanged glances, not knowing what to say when my father recognized our dilemma.

"Look, guys, the meal's on me," he said with a broad smile. "I'm paying."

We immediately began to protest, insisting on paying, but my dad persisted. "I run the hotel. I can do whatever I want. C'mon, eat; I'll take care of it." He looked at me. "A father can't buy his son and his friends a meal?"

We knew damn well that he was covering our asses and that the food was a freebee. We relented. Famished, the cook didn't even have to broil the steaks as far as we were concerned. All these years later, I still can taste that meal.

Out the window we could see the snow was accumulating at a rapid pace. There had to be at least ten inches, and now sleet was mixing in and the wind was roaring through Fiftieth Street like a freight train.

My dad called me aside during dessert. "Listen . . . roads are impassible, subways are frozen to their tracks. You and your buddies aren't going to be able to get home."

I wondered where this was going.

"So come back here when you're done. I've got rooms set aside. I'm staying here too. Your mother already knows we won't be home." At that, he patted me on the shoulder and walked away before I had a chance to protest.

I went back to the table and told the other rookies about the accommodations. No one bitched; they knew we had little choice other than walking home. They called their families. We were the guests of the San Carlos Hotel.

We went back out on the street for the remainder of our tour, mostly huddled in doorways to avoid the biting winds. At midnight we made it back to the hotel. My dad had already turned in.

Quite a guy, my father.

After a week of classes and more snow duty, I looked forward to kicking back, seeing friends, being with my family. On the evening of March 21, 1970, a Saturday, my dad and I had a talk about my new job. My father was always interested in what his sons were doing.

"So, you like it, Ralph . . . the police?"

"Yeah, I really do." I laughed. "Who knew I'd be doing this? I can see a future here, get promoted someday, maybe make detective or go to a motorcycle unit." Of course, I still had no idea what the job was going to be like once I got assigned to a command. What we were learning in the academy was The Book—the laws, rules, procedures—and we were whipping ourselves into great shape.

I'd talked to a veteran patrolman one day—we didn't get the unisex title of "police officer" until a few years later—outside the 13th Precinct, which shared the building with the academy. He told me two things: "You know all that stuff they crammed into your head in the academy? Well, forget it. It's not the real job; *that* you're going to learn when you hit the street." And the other pearl: "This is no job for an adult . . . you get your twenty years in, take your pension, and get the fuck out."

He was right about the first one, but I would never make it to the twenty-year milestone.

My father had said, "You're going to see a lot, Ralph. Don't let it get to you." He shrugged. "I can only relate to the army . . . the war, but I think both are similar in some ways."

My dad rarely spoke of his wartime experiences, like most combat veterans, and when he did he was vague. But I did know he was shot in the leg and that he'd dug out the bullet with a knife rather than be evacuated to a field hospital, where his chances of getting his leg amputated were high because of the lack of adequate medical care. He still had the knife after all these years, and the scar from his handiwork.

"What I'm saying," he said, "is be your own man. You lead a clean life and I'm proud of you. Don't be swayed by what others do. Think for yourself."

We talked a while longer, then I left to see my friends. My dad was still up when I got home after midnight, and we spoke some more before I went to bed. I think back on that night often and cherish the time we had spent together. It would be our last.

I awoke with a start when my brother burst into my room screaming. "Ralph, it's Dad!"

I heard my mother shouting my father's name in the living room.

I shook the sleep from my head and leapt to my feet. Racing to the living room, I saw my father prone on the floor wearing just shorts and a T-shirt. My mother was on her knees bending over him, crying.

I hit the floor next to my dad. He was very pale and was unresponsive when I called his name and grabbed his shoulder.

I was close to panic; my arms felt weak and I began shaking him, calling out "Dad!" numerous times.

No movement, no response.

All of us were crying, but tears weren't going help my father. I began CPR, which I'd learned just weeks before. Between breathing into my father's mouth and chest compressions, I told my mother to dial 911. She ran for the phone.

A team from the emergency services unit (ESU) was there in literally less than two minutes; they must've been driving past my building when they got the call. ESU cops are the elite of the NYPD. Highly trained, they respond to everything from potential suicide jumpers on bridges to hostage situations. They are also experts in stabilizing sick and injured people until medical personnel arrive.

They worked on my dad feverishly while my mom, brother, and I stood back and watched. I felt utterly helpless. As minutes passed with no signs of life, I came to the realization that my dad wasn't going to regain consciousness. He was dead. We were devastated.

My father had succumbed to a massive heart attack. As is Jewish custom, he was laid to rest before sunset the following day. I couldn't comprehend how swiftly he left us. He was literally here one day, buried the next. The void in my life, as well as my mom's and brother's, was incalculable.

The NYPD excused me from duty, not necessarily out of compassion, but to comply with a contractual stipulation allotting four days off for the death of an immediate family member. Despite my overwhelming grief, I was ready to go back to training. I needed to get my mind on something else, and relieving my sorrow on a daily four-mile run proved cathartic. Four decades later, not a day goes by that I don't think about my father.

Just before graduation from the police academy in April 1970, we rookies got to request our desired precinct. We prepared a form appropriately called a "dream sheet" because if you thought you were going to be sent to the precinct you requested, you were dreaming.

I didn't care where I went, just as long as it was a high-crime command. I wanted to go where the action was—the more crime, the better. Most cops want this because you get to learn the job quicker and make quality arrests. For those of us who entertained ideas of becoming detectives, high-crime precincts were the way to go. I hadn't thought about my career path; at this point I was open to anything.

Much to my surprise I got my wish; I was assigned to the 41st Precinct in the South Bronx, which would become known as Fort Apache given the untamed territory that it covered and the propensity for the station house to get attacked—and in more than one case, overrun—by rioters. The Four-One had the city's highest crime rate and arguably the worst working conditions of the city's seventy-seven precincts. It was with great anticipation that I set out on the Monday morning after graduating—uniforms and gear slung over my shoulder—to what would be my home for the next five years.

The precinct station house was located on Simpson Street, right in the belly of the beast. A lone oasis surrounded by urban squalor, the station house was opened in 1914 and hadn't been refurbished since.

I entered the three-story building amid mass confusion. It was a little after 3 PM and the place was a whirlwind of cops coming and going with handcuffed prisoners, EMS attendants assisting a patrolman with a bandage around his head into the back of an ambulance, and a drunk on the front steps of the building asking cops for money. Most of the cops ignored him but a few made disparaging remarks about his mother. At least he got some recognition. I got none.

Someone once told me that one of the most stressful days in anyone's life is when they get married. Apparently that person never experienced the first day in a precinct as a rookie cop. Cops walked past me as if I didn't exist. I'd been told by instructors in the academy to expect this sort of greeting, or lack thereof, but it's unnerving when you experience it firsthand. All newly assigned rookies are treated like nonentities until such time as they prove themselves to be capable police officers.

I presented myself at the desk, which in every station house looks like an elevated alter with a sergeant or lieutenant presiding behind it. The desk is the nerve center of the station house, the first stop for cops and civilians as they enter the building. The desk officer is in charge of . . . well, everything. He's responsible for the entire shift and for running the command in the absence of the precinct's commanding officer.

There is protocol when dealing with the desk officer, in this case a blustery old lieutenant who looked as if the station house had been built around him. As procedure dictated, all superior officers were to be saluted, the desk officer being no exception. I whipped a sharp salute and introduced myself.

"Probationary patrolman Ralph Friedman reporting for duty, sir."

The good lieutenant had just hung up the phone and it'd started ringing again. A patrolman standing next to him with a pile of paper in his hands was vying for his attention, but the lieutenant stopped what he was doing and stared down at me as if to say, "Whogivesafuck?"

"Well, isn't that nice. I'll alert the media. And what can I do for you, Officer Friedman?"

"I, uh . . . just got assigned here. From the academy."

He shuffled some papers looking for my name "Yeah, here you

are. You're in the Fifth Squad. Go upstairs and find a locker. Then report to the 124 room to fill out some paperwork."

Finding an empty locker was easier said than done. Every cop was supposed to be assigned one locker, the essential word here being "one." Cops in the Four-One must've never gotten the memo, because here every cop had at least two lockers, sometimes three. The spares were for civilian clothes and what other stuff they didn't want their wives to see. The occasional case of beer usually found its way into one of those lockers. I checked every locker on the floor; all were taken, and so they were to remain for the next four months. I worked out of my car until I grabbed a locker from a retiring cop. I stood over him while he removed his belongings from his three lockers and made sure another cop didn't grab them. I only claimed one, taking pity on the next rookie.

After I got settled I went to the clerical office, or the 124 room as it's known on the job (no one knew why it was called that, just part of a new language I needed to learn), and filled out a pile of forms. That completed, I reported back to the desk.

The lieutenant I'd spoken to before was on his meal hour, and I had to reintroduce myself to his replacement, a sergeant who was younger and less harried.

"Okay, Friedman," the sergeant said after he consulted the roll-call sheet, "you're on a foot post, post eight." He gave me the location and boundaries; two blocks of stacked tenements with a few mom-and-pop businesses located four blocks from the station house. "Stick around a few minutes, I'll get you a ride over." He looked around for a stray cop.

"Nah, that's okay, boss. I'll walk," I said. "It'll help me get the lay of the land."

He pondered that. "Well, okay." After what seemed to be an afterthought he added, "Take it easy out there; might be a little time before you get acclimated to what goes on around here. You think you got a potential problem or an arrest situation, get to a phone and call for backup. And be sure and sign out before you go home." He gestured to a table where the roll call would be. "Got to account for all you guys at the end of the tour. You wouldn't want to be lying in an alley somewhere with an ax buried in your head and us not aware, right?" He smiled.

I thought that had to be a rhetorical question, as he turned away from me before I thought of an answer.

I heard the crowd before I saw it: an uproar composed of a mix of laughter, cheers, and jeers. There were about thirty people clumped in a tight circle about a block away. I jogged to the scene and pushed my way through the mob.

They'd cleared an opening for a man gyrating and spewing gibberish. He was about forty years old and naked as the day he was born. It might've been April, but it was chilly; I was wearing my brand-new job-approved winter overcoat, a snappy-looking garment called a choker. It was high and tight around the neck and it did just what the name implied. Meanwhile, Naked Man was sweating. Probably high on something, I surmised.

The crowd was having a great time taunting him. When they saw me they stepped back, as if to say, "What're you gonna do about this guy, Dick Tracy?"

Good question. I must've missed the class at the academy regarding naked lunatics, but figured there had to be a law against this behavior. So I whipped out my shiny new handcuffs and pounced on the guy. He resisted, but not much. Some of the pack of onlookers jeered, some applauded, and some cursed me. Cops got injured often by unruly mobs, but this crowd didn't strike me as violent; they seemed more bent on having a good time.

We didn't have portable radios back then, and I couldn't see myself jammed into a phone booth (providing I could even find one with a functioning phone) with Naked Man, so I decided to march him to the station house. Aside from gawking pedestrians, my trip to the house was without incident. Naked Man had calmed down and was now downright docile, although mumbling incoherently. As I approached the station house, a group of cops good-naturedly broke my chops.

"Hey, you looking for the pool? It's on the roof." "Talk about a fuckin' holdup! They left this guy with nothing." "Taking strip searches a bit far, aren't you, rookie?"

I stood before the desk. The older lieutenant was back, but he had his head buried in the command blotter, a huge bound book that was used to record the events of the day and acted as an ongoing history of a precinct. It could also double as a doorstop. Or as a handy weapon if the situation called for it.

I waited.

He finally looked up from whatever he was writing. I expected a look of shock, dismay, inquisitiveness . . . something. What I got was a bored expression and a line I'd come to hear thousands of times in my career, "What've you got, kid?"

Almost everyone on the job under the age of fifty gets called "kid" from time to time; nothing derogatory about it, just cop talk.

During my short stroll back to the station house I thought about what I'd do with this guy. An arrest? I didn't think so. More likely just a nut case, better known on the job as a "psycho." Years later, the job changed the designation to "emotionally disturbed person," or EDP.

"Looks like a psycho, Lou," I said, using the accepted diminutive for his rank. I could do that now. Hey, I'd brought in my first miscreant—broken my cherry so to speak, my first day on the street.

He shuffled some paper and mumbled, "I see you didn't waste any time making the streets safe."

I didn't respond.

The lieutenant who had assigned me to the post had a cop call an ambulance for Naked Man, and I accompanied him to a hospital mental ward. I was informed my "nut case" would probably be cut loose the next day after he came down from whatever he'd ingested, if that was in fact his problem. He could've been just plain crazy. Bottom line was I discovered that no one really cared. After preparing a mountain of paperwork, I went back to the street.

As minor as this incident was, I hadn't waited to take a watchful, cautious approach, as I'd been advised. I felt confident I could handle anything the street had to throw at me. Looking back, I knew just a little more than I did the day before meeting Naked Man (when I knew nothing), but my raging testosterone told me differently: I felt that I was ready for anything. I was also certain that I'd found my calling.

During the next few weeks I tore through the streets of the command. I was a cop on a mission—the mission being to lock up everyone who needed arresting. There was no shortage of targets. Fort Apache was replete with drug dealers, robbers, burglars, and any other criminal you could think of.

On one of my first days on patrol, I glanced through the window of a bodega (a small mom-and-pop grocery store) and spotted a thirtysomething male taking money from an older male and giving him a small slip of paper in return. I took off my uniform hat so as not to draw attention and observed the scene for a few minutes. The procedure was repeated several times with men and women of varying ages. The guy taking the money glanced around every so often, but didn't seem overcautious.

I didn't know what was going on, but whatever it was screamed "illegal!"

I entered the store and came up behind the guy when he was alone. Before he could react, he was cuffed and read his rights. His only response was "You're fucking kidding me, right?" After that, he took his right to remain silent seriously.

I searched him on the spot and found numerous policy slips. I figured I'd collared a numbers runner, which is a rare catch for a uniformed member of the job. Gamblers were usually arrested by the plainclothes cops of the Public Morals Division, whose job it was to enforce vice laws. But this guy was mine, and I took him on the now-familiar stroll to the station house.

I found myself back in front of the desk before the same lieutenant I'd dealt with when I brought in Naked Man. Behind the desk with him was a deputy inspector who was signing the blotter when he saw me with my prisoner.

"You know what you've got there, Officer?" the deputy inspector asked. He was in his fifties and looked every inch a high-ranking NYPD boss—pressed uniform and rack of departmental medals.

I snapped to attention, deferring to his rank. "Yes, sir. A policy runner." I waved a fistful of policy slips. "I got him . . ."

"You've got more than a policy runner there, son," he interrupted. He said to the desk officer, "Lou, secure this prisoner while I speak to the young officer here." He came from behind the desk and pointed to the muster room, where the platoons turned out for each shift.

Where was this going?

It was between tours so the muster room was empty. The DI went directly to a glass-enclosed bulletin board that was secured to a wall. Concealing it was a dark-green shade, the kind you'd find on a window, with a pull string on the bottom. "You know what this is, Officer?"

I'd obviously seen the shrouded bulletin board every day but hadn't given it much thought. In those first few weeks, my only interest in the station house was getting out of it as soon as possible.

"No, sir. Just got here, actually."

He looked at me quizzically. "From where?"

"Police academy, sir."

He grunted. "What's your name?"

I told him.

"Well, Officer Friedman, you just locked up one of the precinct's KGs," at which point he ceremoniously pulled down slightly on the shade, then released it.

The shade shot up to reveal a hierarchical chart, with pictures of all the known gamblers (KGs) operating within the confines of the Four-One. There were about ten men on the chart. All were members of organized crime and, as such, were police enforcement targets. Very elusive targets I was to find out. My prisoner was near the top of the chart.

"You should be proud of yourself, Officer. You not only bagged one of the slipperiest KGs around, but you made the command and yourself look good. And you know what else?"

"What, sir?"

"You made me look good." Turned out this particular inspector had been looking to go to the Public Morals Division. One of his cops taking a KG off the street would help him get there.

He gave me a day off on the spot for a good arrest. Time off was a common reward for quality arrests, the job being very proactive back then. This system of rewards was abandoned in the 1980s when administrators decided a reactive police force was more desirable than a proactive one; rather than seek out good arrests, the police would now be reacting to crime. The rationale was that if cops less actively looked to make collars, there would be fewer potential problems (such as cops being too aggressive). As a result, the number of arrests diminished, as did job morale. Cops are just like any other worker in any other field: reward them for quality work and they'll produce. It isn't all about pay raises; it's about recognition for a job well done.

But this was the 1970s, when getting a day off and an "attaboy" from an inspector meant I was appreciated. The incident with the DI may well have given me the impetus to make me the cop and detective I was to become. As for the KG, he got time served—a day in the can before being arraigned—and a small fine. I was learning that the police had little if any impact on sentencing.

Within a few months I found myself in a radio car. Every rookie's goal was to get a "seat," a permanent assignment to a patrol sector in a marked radio car. The Four-One had nineteen sectors, a large amount for a command that was only 2.5 square miles. The first step in the process of getting the coveted seat was proving yourself on foot patrol. In my first few months in Fort Apache, I'd made enough good arrests to catch the attention of the precinct commanding officer, Captain Tom Walker, whom I remember as the best CO of my career. He was tough but fair and backed up his cops. In 1976 he wrote the definitive book about the precinct, appropriately entitled *Fort Apache*. He was also a Sherlock Holmes expert and won the Holmes category on television's *$64,000 Question*, a popular quiz show back then.

Traditionally, radio-car assignments begin on a fill-in basis and are not a daily occurrence. I'd be assigned a seat where one partner was on vacation, in court, or out sick. Every few days I'd get lucky and land in a sector, but I was still mostly walking foot posts. The downside of filling in sector cars was that I didn't have a steady partner; I'd bounce around from sector to sector wherever I was needed.

In police work, particularly in a high-crime command like the Four-One, having a steady partner was reassuring because you worked as a team and always knew how your partner would react in any given situation. Partners worked out strategies and tactics well before they were needed. A cop relied on his partner to save his life should the shit hit the fan. It's often said that a cop's partner knows more about him than his significant other. The street breeds intimacy, and there's no one you trust more than your partner. No one.

The upside of being the fill-in guy was that you got to ride with many cops, so when the time came to get a permanent seat, you might seek out someone you once rode with, who also might be looking for a new partner because of his current partner's retirement or transfer. Sometimes, however, filling in can lead to disaster.

One such time was when I was temporarily partnered with patrolman Gus Paulson, who had a steady sector. This was my first time working with Gus. He had five years on the job, a veteran by Four-One standards. His regular partner was on vacation and we were to ride together for a week. Gus was a decent guy and he seemed to know what he was doing, but otherwise I knew nothing about him.

After a brief handshake, Gus explained how things were going to work.

"You're new to a sector, so maybe you should be the recorder for the tour so you get the paperwork down."

Partners usually switched jobs halfway through the tour so each got a turn preparing reports as the "recorder" and driving as the "operator." But since we weren't really partners, and I was a rookie, perhaps Gus had the right idea: get a trial by fire by being bombarded with forms and learn how that part of the job worked. While I didn't relish writing for eight hours, I went along with it because I had little choice. Gus and I may have been the same rank, but as a rookie I had no juice when it came to anything procedural. Seniority rules. Welcome to the world of civil service.

It was July and the Four-One was jumping. Even though the sector was composed of only a few square blocks, those streets were crammed with tenements and the crime and calls for service that went along with too many people in close proximity.

We were constantly rolling from one job to the next: fights, shots-fired calls, burglaries and robberies in progress, and crimes of lesser consequence, but just as time-consuming.

One thing about Gus, though, he always found the time to stop cars.

Car stops are a cop's reservoir for arrests. Most good collars come from car stops. The law dictates that a police officer can stop a car only if he has reasonable cause to make the stop. A traffic infraction is reasonable cause. Once the car is stopped, it can be determined if the driver's been drinking or perhaps wanted on a warrant, if there's contraband in plain view, or any number of other violations that could land the driver in jail.

I was always looking to make an arrest so I was up for stopping cars. Since I was the recorder, my tactical position would be behind the stopped car and off to the right while Gus spoke to the driver. I could observe what was going on through the rear window and be ready to take action should the stop go sideways. We stopped around six cars per tour, a pretty high number considering all the 911 calls we were responding to.

On a day I'll never forget, Gus and I were on a tour when the radio dispatcher advised: "Four-One Sector Mike, ten-two the house forthwith."

We were in Sector Mike. A "forthwith" was just shy of "you should be here already." Someone wanted us in the station house immediately. My initial feeling was one of mild curiosity—why were we being summoned ASAP?—followed by one of dread. When I had more years on the job, I'd know that a "forthwith" to the command was usually a bad thing, but even then I knew this couldn't be good.

I looked to Gus for clarification. "What do you think this is about?"

Gus looked forlorn. "I think I'm about to be locked up."

"What? Arrested?" I couldn't have heard him correctly.

Gus reached into his pocket and pulled out some neatly folded bills. "Here," he said, dumping them on my lap. "Hold on to this money for me." We turned onto Southern Boulevard, a few blocks from the station house.

I was confused. "Why? What is this?" I scooped up the bills and gave them a fast count; sixty dollars in fives and tens.

He stared straight ahead, driving calmly. "Ralph," he said, almost inaudibly, "just hold on to the money . . . No questions, please."

The bills were folded in half separately, one bill on top of another. I put them in my wallet. There was no more conversation. As we parked in front of the station house, Gus handed me the car keys, gave me a wan smile, and we went inside.

Lined up in front of the desk was a gauntlet of bosses of varying ranks, all above the rank of lieutenant. They were staring at us, which brought us to a halt. A grim-looking inspector came forward.

"Which one of you is Paulson?" These were the days before name tags.

Gus stepped forward. "I am, sir." He had turned a sickly shade of pale.

The inspector extended an open palm. "Your gun and shield, Officer." His eyes were sad, almost fatherly with evident pity. The rest of the bosses looked uneasy; a few slid their hands over their holstered guns. Cops have been known to do strange things when arrested, and the bosses' movement to their revolvers was cautionary. Suicide was not unusual, shooting one's arresting officer rare, but being prepared for any outcome is just good tactics.

Gus was being arrested for shaking down motorists. I was to find out later that there had been complaints from motorists that Gus was shaking them down for cash after being stopped for traffic violations. He'd been doing this during our car stops and had been doing it for quite a while. The shakedowns were unobtrusive and deftly conducted. I had no idea what was going on from my position at the rear of the stopped cars. All I knew was that I had the proceeds of the crimes in my wallet. Was I about to be searched? Was any of the money marked? I felt my throat close; my palms began to sweat. The inspector turned to me.

"Resume patrol, Officer. You're excused."

I turned and made for the door on wobbly legs, hoping they would get me to the radio car. I wanted to get as far from the station house as possible.

I fell into the driver's seat, my head spinning, the tainted money burning hot in my wallet. As I started the motor, I realized that I had no partner; mine was on his way to jail. All the radio cars in the NYPD are manned by two cops, but the last thing I wanted to do was go back into the house and ask for a partner. I had visions of one of the bosses saying, "Hey, Friedman, while you're here empty your pockets." The neatly folded single bills were obviously the proceeds of the shakedowns, and while that couldn't be assumed in a court of law, this was the NYPD, where a cop is guilty until proven innocent. What's more, I was a probationary police officer and, as such, could get canned for any reason or no reason until my probationary year was over.

I considered stashing the money in the car—between the seat cushions seemed like a good place. Then paranoia kicked in. Was I being watched? I was parked directly in front of the house, after all. I saw my job slipping away and I'd done nothing wrong. Sure, I knew I should've handed over the bills, but the unofficial code of the job forbade turning on a fellow cop. To do so would brand me as a rat. I'd live in my own hell for the rest of my career, unable to work anywhere in the city without my unsavory reputation preceding me. Gus, a crooked cop, would have better standing than me. Nope, I was going to set a precedent; I was going to be the first cop in the hellhole that was the Four-One to go on patrol in a one-man car. Did I have a death wish? Perhaps, but death seemed a better alternative than returning to the house.

I handled calls alone the rest of the day, with everyone from street junkies to cops in other radio cars giving me funny looks. Nothing of consequence occurred and I had plenty of time to think.

It wasn't rare for cops in the NYPD to shake down motorists in the 1960s and before, but in the '70s the tide began to turn. An increase in blue-ribbon commissions investigating the matter had a lot to do with it, but mostly it was the caliber of new cops that changed the way the job was done. Many recruits were returning

Vietnam vets, who thirsted for action and had enough indoctrination in the military to care about their honor. In my case, if it ever crossed my mind to do such a thing, the incident with Gus swayed me forever. The humiliation that getting arrested would bring to me and my family would be incalculable, and I vowed that day to resist temptation, do my job, and sleep well at night. No amount of money, especially the paltry sum Gus lost his job and freedom over, was worth it. When I think back on that incident today, I realize that I'd learned a valuable lesson. I like money and I made my share working overtime, but a dirty dollar wasn't part of my future. I would look to get assigned to units that had reputations for incorruptibility because being associated with police officers who were less than honest depressed me.

If a cop is going to go bad, it usually occurs in increments: taking small amounts like Gus, then steadily increasing the scores. A cop might shake down motorists one day and graduate to extorting money from drug dealers down the line.

I sought Gus out at his new job at a construction site about six months later. He'd been given a pass on jail time and was just fired. Gus's arrest occurred during the Knapp Commission hearings, a board of inquiry convened to root out corruption in the NYPD. The last thing the job needed was to broadcast that it'd found yet another corrupt cop. He was lucky; you don't want to be a cop in prison. Survival is highly doubtful.

Most fired cops can't get a decent job. Not too many employers want to hire a terminated police officer, the reason they lost their job being inconsequential. A cop who didn't make it to retirement and left the job was viewed with a jaundiced eye by most employers. Most cops in this predicament gravitate toward construction work, where anyone with a strong back can get scooped right up (and laid off just as quickly when weather turns bad). It's a tough way to make a living.

I spotted Gus before he spotted me, and I decided to approach him and say hello. Besides, I still had a chore left undone . . .

He was leaning on a shovel by a fifty-five-gallon drum that was burning wood, embers flying in the mid-January wind. There were several other workers getting warm, and when Gus saw me, he gestured for me to follow him, which I did at a discreet distance.

He had aged: the not-so-great outdoors in the dead of winter and the physical labor not agreeing with him. He forced a grin and shook my hand.

"How're you doing, Gus?" I asked.

He shrugged. "I'm doing. You?"

"I'm okay," I said.

And so it went for a few minutes—small talk that trailed into minutiae. Finally, I said what I came to say. "You know, I still got that money you asked me to hold."

His eyebrows shot up. "Money?"

I removed the bills from my wallet. They were in the same configuration as when he'd passed them to me six months ago, stacked atop each other like business cards. He took a half step back and held up his hands. "Hey, I don't know nothing about any money." He was shaking his head, feigning bewilderment. "I never asked you to hold any money for me."

I realized Gus thought he was being set up—for what, I had no idea. His case had already been adjudicated; he was done with the criminal justice system, both as an employee and a temporary guest. He was paranoid. Most cops are, and we never lose it, but we choose to call it "healthy skepticism." Gus, however, was overestimating himself as a target. He was an ex-cop, a fired cop. No one gave a shit about him anymore.

I was going to explain to him that it was *me* he was talking to, not a rat. He wasn't being recorded, there were no Internal Affairs bogeymen hiding in dump trucks. I opened my mouth to speak and then reconsidered. I didn't need to defend myself. I didn't even know why I'd stopped to talk to him in the first place or why I'd held on to the money. Maybe I just felt sorry for him. In the coming years, I'd hear about other corrupt police officers. Most of them were excellent cops . . . some genuine heroes.

"Forget it, man," I mumbled, then I did an about-face and started back to my car. Before reaching it, I tossed the stacked bills into the burning drum, much to the astonishment of the huddled masses.

I picked up a steady seat with Rafael Torres, a bright cop but not the most active in the arrest department, which was fine with me. I would take all the collars he didn't want. Torres had a working wife and a platoon of kids. One parent had to be home with the kids while the other one worked, and arrests got in the way of their finely tuned schedule.

There were quite a few cops in the same situation. I believe my annual salary was around $9,600 back then, and I had a hard time just supporting myself. I couldn't imagine trying to take care of a family on that kind of money. A lot of cops also had second jobs, and it was a hassle to go to court, so they would seek out a partner who would take the arrests.

I could depend on Rafael, and that's all I cared about. His family came first, and that's the way it should be. I learned a lesson from him and other cops in a similar financial squeeze: I intended to stay single for as long as possible. I liked my creature comforts, my Harley, my leisure time at the gym, and dating up a storm. Many women gravitated toward cops because they assumed we weren't serial killers, and I was taking full advantage of my single status.

We were cruising up Southern Boulevard late into a day tour with Rafael driving when he elbowed my arm. "Holy shit, Ralph, get a load of that fucking guy!"

He was pointing to a big man—had to be at least six foot four—pistol-whipping a girl half his size. He was wailing on her face and body, rapidly pounding at her with the gun. Blood was spewing everywhere, and she was trying to protect her head. A few passersby glanced at the mayhem but kept on walking. This was New York, and, to take it down a notch, the South Bronx.

Our sector car was in middle of the street, stuck at a red light. I jumped out, yelling to Rafael to pull around as I ran toward the one-sided battle.

The thug saw me racing toward him and screaming for him to stop. I had my gun drawn. Apparently, he didn't give a shit who I was because he kept brutalizing the woman.

I kicked him in his rib cage with everything I had, and he toppled off his victim. His gun went flying, and I holstered mine. He let out a stream of curses, jumped to his feet, and came for me. He had a good five inches and fifty pounds on me, but he was heavy and out of shape. I pummeled his face with roundhouse punches and kneed him in the balls, which brought him down.

He was done but still gurgling and made an attempt to get up. By now, I had a cheering section; there must've been fifty people urging me on. Rafael tried to jump in, but I waved him off. "Look after the girl!" I told him and went back to subduing the guy. I broke his right arm; he would be hospitalized for a week. His victim was also admitted but released before he was.

When his yellow sheet (criminal record) came back, I discovered he was a Mafia associate, a street scumbag who thought his intimidating size gave him carte blanche to do whatever the hell he wanted. The incident was a boyfriend-girlfriend "dispute" that could've turned into a homicide had we not happened by.

We recovered a .45 semiautomatic pistol, an expensive piece and a rarity in those days. Guns seized back then were usually of the Saturday-night-special variety, cheap stamped metal pieces of garbage that shot inaccurately, were manufactured mostly in the South, and were sold on the street for fifty bucks.

This was my first incident where I used excessive force, but it certainly wasn't going to be my last. The NYPD of the 1970s didn't frown on force, excessive or otherwise. Bringing a prisoner in dead wasn't advised, but anything just short of it was usually overlooked and considered good police work. The job has changed, and most police officers today aren't apt to exert the amount of force we did, whether because of more training or the proliferation of smartphones with cameras. For us cops it was a fight for survival in a borough gone rogue: if a cop showed fear or went easy on thugs, he was viewed as weak. If that happened, your career, at least in the shithole of high-crime precincts, was over. I wanted to be respected and feared.

I wanted to be the last man standing.

A battle-weary Fort Apache cop, a survivor of many street encounters, once told me, "We use violence to implement justice." In the Four-One, these were words to live (and survive) by.

Not every incident, however, ended with victory.

A few weeks later, my partner was on vacation and someone was filling in. I don't recall who I was riding with, but a routine car stop we made will be forever etched in my memory.

We were working a four-to-midnight tour. A few hours in, we observed two males in a brand-new Lincoln cruising casually through a section of the precinct known for street drug sales. Even by Four-One standards, this was a reckless area.

We decided to pull them over strictly on gut feelings. These guys hadn't done anything illegal, but that indefinable sense cops get when they know something's wrong was nagging at us. Profiling? It wasn't the fact that the men in the car were black—the precinct is predominantly black and Hispanic—it was the new expensive car, which was rare for the area, plus, after following them for a while, they didn't seem to have a destination. Our judgment told us they were trolling for a drug dealer.

The car pulled over as soon as we gave it a short blast on the siren and momentarily flipped on the roof lights. We got out of the car and approached the Lincoln from two sides, which was tactically correct. We did, however, forget something that would have us fighting for our lives shortly: we left our nightsticks in the radio car, a big tactical error.

This is how cops get hurt. The constant repetition of stopping cars made us sloppy; it was just another car stop that might result in an arrest, or a few issued summonses. If there was cause to arrest and they resisted, we thought we could control the situation—people who resist arrest always lose the battle. Cops come out on top, right? Not this time.

Both men were large. Later we would find out they were hired muscle for labor organizations and had no fear of cops.

The driver was sullen but handed over his paperwork. The car and license were legit, but we decided to search the vehicle anyway. Both driver and passenger objected and got out of the car. This was a bad sign; exiting a car during a police stop is forbidden, and we told them so. They didn't give a shit, and before we knew it the battle was on.

They pounced immediately, the driver on me, the passenger on my partner. They had caught us unaware and unprepared. These guys were professional enforcers and knew if they were going to win this battle with the police, their attack had to be overwhelming and brutal . . . and it was.

Both of us were putting up a good fight, but we were outclassed; their fists and feet pummeled us with lightning speed. If I can be thankful for anything, it's that neither of them had any weapons.

Speaking of weapons . . .

I reached for my nightstick—oops! That's when I realized our error. The nightstick could've evened the odds. Known as a "baton" on the job (sounds more user-friendly than "nightstick"), it's made of cocobolo wood, which is very dense, heavy, and durable. Cocobolo makes for a devastating weapon, but of course you have to have it to swing it.

To make matters worse, our nearest radio was the hardwired one in the car. I was on the ground trying to remain conscious and knew that the radio was our only chance to get out of this mess alive. I was being kicked like a football as I started crawling toward the car. It was twenty feet away, which might as well have been twenty miles. I prayed I could reach it before being beaten into a coma or shot with my own gun.

I finally reached the car and called in a 10-13 (officer needs assistance) while still getting the shit kicked out of me. Almost immediately, I heard sirens. A signal 10-13 is the most urgent call a police officer can broadcast. It is not overused but saved for desperate, life-threatening situations. If the position my partner and I were in didn't fit that definition, I don't know what did. Cops drop what they're doing and respond, and not necessarily from the parent command; they come from *everywhere*.

The sound of that familiar siren whine helped me hang on; it was the sweetest music I'd ever heard.

Cops were there in less than a minute—lots of them. And as hard as it is to believe, the two guys who had been beating us didn't take off; they continued to beat us until the responding cops arrived and then they took on the reinforcements! These guys weren't even winded.

Cops met them head-on, nightsticks swinging. You have to give those two guys credit; they stood their ground and fought against overpowering odds. The word "tough" didn't begin to describe them, but within seconds they were down and cuffed. While I would have loved to take part in the victory, I was too exhausted and injured to do much except breathe, and doing that made me wince.

I was the arresting officer; don't ask me how I did the paperwork, because to say that I was hurting was a gross underestimation. My two prisoners were transported to the Four-One station house and placed in a holding cell until they were to be driven to court the next morning.

When someone assaults a police officer, retribution is swift and severe. While the two prisoners got their bruises on the street, it was nothing compared with what was about to happen.

Every cop working that night got a "forthwith" to the station house. You remember what that means? Drop what you're doing and get to the house yesterday.

Every team got five minutes alone in the cell with these two tough guys. There were probably at least twenty cops on duty that night. Those guys took a hell of a pounding. Sure, they fought back but not even those two could put up with the hammering they received. Within an hour, they were beaten so bloody their own mothers wouldn't have recognized them.

My two prisoners hobbled into court the next day. When asked by the judge what happened to them, they just shrugged. They had played the game, hurt some cops, and got their asses kicked as a result. To them it was the way the system worked, and they weren't about to complain. And on top of that they each got a year in jail.

About five years later, I got a call from an FBI agent regarding the two enforcers we'd collared that night. The mere mention of the incident made my ribs hurt. The agent was conducting an investigation into organizations promoting employment of blacks in the construction industry in New York.

"It's a scam," the agent said. "The group demonstrates at construction sites calling for jobs for black men who they say are underrepresented in the trade. They block deliveries, start fights, and wind up shutting down the site until they get positions for their members. Your guys—the two assholes you locked up—assault construction workers and bust up equipment. So when the construction companies relent and say, okay, they'll hire a few black guys, they find out it's for no-show jobs. None of these guys want a job. It's a shakedown."

None of this surprised me. "What do you need from me?"

"No one's willing to complain so we're trying to pin something on them. What can you tell me about the guys that attacked you?"

"The driver had a helluva right hook, and I'd say a size thirteen shoe. Other than that, the last I saw of them was when they were being led away to do their time, nothing since then." I wished the agent luck. "If I never see those two mopes again, it'll be too soon."

I got my first tattoo when I was twenty years old and still a police trainee. It was of an eagle and located on my right bicep. I never thought about getting any more ink, but over the years my body became a tapestry of my life and career. I memorialized or commemorated all that was important to me. As of this writing I have well over a hundred tattoos.

I frequented Big Joe's Tattoo Parlor in Mount Vernon, New York, right over the Bronx line. Back then it was the Mecca for quality work and I became one of Big Joe's best customers. Members of the New York chapter of the Hell's Angels were also regulars at Big Joe's. There, I met the president of the chapter, Chuck Zito, and we became friends; we're still in touch today. Chuck was tough and very smart. He'd later become an actor and was featured in dozens of TV shows and movies.

The Angels and law enforcement weren't exactly buddies. After all, they were about as antiestablishment as you could get. But I got along well with Chuck. His crew varied with their acceptance of me, but for the most part we were cool. I rode a Harley, so that helped. I also treated them with respect, and they reciprocated, some of them being Vietnam veterans who commiserated with cops because they knew what it was like to be a target.

I was filling in a sector on a day tour when we got a radio run of an assault in progress inside a building. The building housed a social club on the ground floor, and, while not an Angel hangout, that day there were about five bikers from the New York chapter present. Chuck Zito wasn't among them.

Some drunk had wandered in from the street wanting to shoot pool. The Angels had both pool tables occupied and told the interloper to wait his turn. The drunk, not knowing with whom he was about to tangle, began to get belligerent and said something that pissed off the bikers. He was roughed up and tossed out. It was the drunk who had called in the radio run; he was the victim.

The club was dim with a cloud of cigarette smoke hovering over the tables. I spotted the complainant right away; he was the bloody guy. The Angels acted like me and my partner weren't there at first, and to me that wasn't a good sign. I mentally mapped out escape routes, fields of fire, and methods of cover should things go bad.

The drunk started acting like an asshole as soon as he saw us—cursing, waving his arms, threatening to sue everybody. He figured he could spout his bullshit with relative impunity since two cops were there to protect him. I guess he *still* hadn't learned whom he was pissing off, because the Angels would just as soon beat the shit out of cops as revisit the complainant with another beating. These guys weren't afraid.

I looked for a familiar face from Big Joe's, but with the dim lighting and most Angels looking similar anyway, I couldn't spot anyone. While my partner was containing the drunk, I started over to talk to the bikers.

As I neared them, a mountain of a man said, "Hey, ain't you that cop from Big Joe's? Chuck's friend?"

The situation was defused in a few seconds. The biker, known as Tiny (he would be killed in a motorcycle wreck a few years later and have a spectacular funeral procession on the Lower East Side of Manhattan) introduced me to the other Angels. My partner and I talked the drunk out of pressing charges, and everyone was happy.

With a mixture of regret and relief, I can't help imagining the situation if someone had a smartphone back then. It would have been nice to preserve such a sweet moment, but then again a video of me with five outlaw bikers might have wound up on YouTube.

I was making numerous arrests for drugs, illegal possession of guns, assaults, robberies, burglaries, rapes—you name it. As a result, precinct supervisors were recommending me for departmental recognition—medals—for the best collars. I took a few of the most violent criminals into custody in walking condition, unusual for the times. Normally prisoners were transported directly to the station house for processing. Most of mine went to Lincoln Hospital.

I was getting a reputation as someone who didn't take shit from the street. If criminals cooperated during the arrest, they were fine; if they raised their hands to me, I raised mine to them. My goal was twofold: make it home in one piece and get the word out on the street that if you fucked with any cop, particularly with Ralph Friedman, you were going to pay for it.

The rules of the job, as dictated by the NYPD *Rules and Procedures*—a mammoth guidebook that would increase in size every time a cop did something that wasn't covered in the previous edition—said that a police officer could use only the amount of force that was necessary to control a situation. Any more could lead to charges, both departmental and criminal. The problem was defining what was "enough" and what was "too much" force. How should a police officer stop to evaluate in the middle of subduing a felon who is putting up a fight?

Did I use just enough force to stop him? Does he pose a threat or is he down for the count? Or is he faking, and is he about to rebound and kill me?

Questions, questions.

I always wanted to err on the side of caution when it came to my safety and that of my partner.

It's my belief that many cops today are inactive (forget proactive or reactive) for fear of being disgraced or losing their jobs on account of what the public deems excessive force. I'm in touch with many police officers through social media and Internet police forums, and the general feeling currently is that there are not too many cops who are going to put their careers and lives in jeopardy because some elected official wants to make a political football out of Monday-morning quarterbacking a cop's arrest.

The use of the chokehold is a good example. The press, politicians, and others consistently use the term "illegal chokehold" when describing this perfectly legal takedown method. The chokehold is against NYPD policy, but it's not illegal. This is why police officers who use this method of subduing a prisoner don't get arrested for it—departmental charges may result, but no one's going to jail for applying it. Unless, of course, it's used to excess and results in a fatality, which is a whole different deal.

As of this writing, a bill has been introduced in New York to make the chokehold illegal, meaning possible jail time for a police officer who uses it. Picture a police officer in a life-or-death struggle on the street with a criminal, during which the cop uses a chokehold to subdue the guy. If this bill passes into law, that cop is going to be arrested, whether he was making a good arrest or not. I'm wondering if a better law would require lawmakers to ride along with patrol officers for a week and then make an educated judgment about what should be against the law.

There isn't a cop out there who wouldn't use a chokehold if his physical safety depended on it, rules or no rules. A cop will take the fine or loss of vacation days, but he'll be *alive*.

I was constantly on the prowl to make quality arrests, the important word being *quality*. I doubt there's a police officer in New York who couldn't lock someone up thirty minutes into a shift.

There's always someone doing something wrong, but most infractions are trifling, and police officers are given discretion when deciding whether to make arrests for minor transgressions. These include simple assaults (particularly when the offender and complainant are friends), personal marijuana use, and misdemeanor criminal mischief when the offender is willing to make restitution. The NYPD allows discretion.

I was after felons. They don't get the luxury of discretion, and, even if they did, they wouldn't get it from me. This meant both on duty *and* off.

I remember one off-duty arrest vividly. It was a blisteringly hot August day and I was with a date at Orchard Beach, otherwise known as the Bronx Riviera. While the Bronx had quite a few beaches abutting Long Island Sound, Orchard Beach was the only one where you could enter the water and come out pretty confident you didn't contract typhoid. It was crowded, noisy, and not the cleanest beach in America, but it belonged to us denizens of the Bronx and I went there often.

I was never off duty, as the term is defined. Constantly looking for bad guys, I didn't care whether I was on a date, as I was that day, or in a gym, or on my motorcycle; I was always looking for something out of place. When I watch boxing on television, I'm looking more at the spectators than I am at the fighters. Same goes for everywhere else people congregate: movies, subways, funerals—you name it.

Station houses have wanted posters in a big-ring binder behind the desk. I didn't know many cops who perused these posters. I did, although I was beginning to view this as an exercise in futility, because after months of sifting through them, the pictures and names were beginning to blur and I doubted I'd ever apprehend a wanted felon based on a wanted poster. There are literally thousands of wanted criminals in New York City; what are the odds that I'd ever remember a specific poster?

On that hot summer day at the beach, I was walking with my date on the boardwalk when I spotted a guy wanted for a burglary in Brooklyn. I'd seen a poster the previous week, and the picture displayed looked exactly like the man I'd almost bumped into, who was walking in the opposite direction.

I was going to go up against this guy without a weapon or handcuffs and no way to call for backup, so my normal policy of "don't hurt me, I won't hurt you" was on the back burner. If I were armed, my approach would have been to draw my weapon, identify myself, get him on the ground, and cuff him before he had a chance to run or retaliate.

I whirled and got up behind him. "Yo, bro," I said, and tapped him on the shoulder. I didn't recall his name from the poster. He turned with a pleasant expression on his face, which was quickly erased when I punched him in the jaw with everything I had. He hit the ground like a load of wet laundry.

People began screaming, running, falling over each other. The woman I was with stood wide-eyed. Someone yelled for the police. There was a summer police detail at Orchard Beach, and it didn't take long before two cops came running over. I identified myself and explained what I had. They called for an ambulance for my still-comatose prisoner.

One cop, an old-timer, looked at me skeptically. "You recognized this guy from a wanted poster? You sure it's him?"

Doubt engulfed me. What if this guy wasn't who I thought he was? Had I seriously injured a look-alike? The bad guy's twin brother?

There is a happy ending to this story: he was the guy on the wanted poster and the arrest earned yet another medal recommendation to be added to the several I already had pending. And in an unpredictable twist of fate, it turned out to be a happy ending for the perp, too.

About five years later, a man approached me as I was leaving the station house and asked me if I was Officer Friedman. I was immediately wary, as any cop would've been, particularly because I wasn't in uniform and I had no idea who this guy was. How did he know me? I casually turned sideways to avoid that unpleasant kick to the testicles. My hand rested on my gun. "Yeah, that's me. I know you?" This man could've been someone I'd arrested, now out of prison and looking for revenge.

I was half right. I had locked him up, and he was fresh out of the joint, but he didn't have revenge on his mind.

He introduced himself and extended a hand for me to shake. I was still leery, but I shifted my weight and shook his hand. I had leverage if I needed to defend myself, though my gut told me I wasn't going to have a problem.

"You don't remember me, do you?" he said.

I had no idea who he was and told him so.

Now he broke into a wide grin. "I'm the guy you knocked out at Orchard Beach. I was wanted on the burglary beef in Brooklyn, remember? I just wanted to thank you. I needed to get that shit behind me, but most of all I needed a real lot of dental work, and I got it for free in prison." He smiled again, flashing a nice set of choppers.

We bullshitted awhile; he said he went straight, had a great job in construction. We parted with another handshake.

And people ask me why I love police work.

I was spending an inordinate amount of time in court because I was making arrests in record numbers, the arrest process being long and frustrating. It isn't rare to spend an entire tour in criminal court preparing paperwork and being interviewed by an assistant district attorney.

A few other active cops and I came up with a streamlined system that would get us in and out of court in under an hour. We would type up the ADA's criminal complaints in the station house, using court forms. This saved us hours since the ADA interview process was the chokepoint in the system. Sometimes ADAs would be backed up for hours with a line of very antsy cops waiting their turns to get their criminal complaints prepared. We'd just present the prepared complaint to the ADA without the wait. Initially, the ADAs balked: we never went to law school, what the hell did we know about legalese and the accepted formatting of a criminal complaint? Turns out we knew plenty from our numerous arrests and could write these things in our sleep. The overwhelmed ADA's original skepticism morphed into gratitude; we were doing their work for them, and they knew it. After a while, they just skimmed through and signed them.

With the accepted system of processing arrests, cops were only permitted one arrest at a time. With our new take on speeding up the process, we could now take multiple arrests through the system because all the paperwork was prepared before getting to court. All we did was plop the paper in front of an ADA, and we were good to go. I would later make three separate gun collars in one night, and I was back out on the street in as little time as it took to walk one arrest through the system.

If the *Guinness World Records* book had a category for quickest prep time for a criminal case in the Bronx, we would've won. Our goal was to get back on the street as quickly as possible, and we accomplished that. So what if we broke some administrative rules? It gave the term "revolving-door justice" a whole new meaning;

we were the ones out on the street in record time rather than the bad guys.

It may seem odd to anyone who's not a cop, but I was having the time of my life. I was doing a good job and being recognized for it. I loved going to work every day. In retrospect, I was living in a cocoon, because I hadn't yet felt loss or very much stress. I felt as if I could handle anything, but I would soon emerge from my reverie when two tragedies woke me up to the realities of police work and how uncertain life really is.

2

Police work isn't all one big mind-blowing rush. Mostly it's hours of tedium, interrupted by a few minutes of adrenaline-pumping, heart-pounding, gut-wrenching excitement. Even in high-crime commands like Fort Apache, there's plenty of boredom.

One post where nothing much happens is station-house security. A uniformed police officer is assigned to the front of a precinct station house around the clock. The cop's job is to direct civilians who have business in the house, as well as to apprehend the occasional anarchist looking to blow up the building.

There have been incidents throughout the city in the past where mentally disturbed individuals, criminals, and domestic terrorists have attempted to breach precinct security and kill cops. The most famous incident occurred in the 1970s when snipers positioned themselves across the Harlem River in Manhattan from the 44th Precinct station house in the Bronx, waiting to pick off the outgoing platoon as they left to start their tour. A sharp cop spotted light reflecting off telescopic sights and the plot was thwarted. So the post is not without its hazards, but for the most part it's an exercise in tedium.

I was assigned to station-house security on a midnight-to-8 AM tour once and took my post pretty much expecting to be counting the hours until dawn. What could possibly go wrong?

An hour in, I was going crazy. I must've answered twenty inane questions and been harassed by the usual assortment of eccentrics who are attracted to cops. One nut asked me for directions to Texas. I told him to go to Chicago and turn left.

Cops and detectives came and went, most with prisoners. I envied these guys out doing real police work. I never imagined it would occur *behind* me.

Four and a half hours into the tour (it felt like ten), two gunshots, followed by a fusillade of many more, echoed from inside the station house. I froze for a second, trying to process, then ran inside. The first thing I noticed was the fresh odor of cordite (residue from fired bullets). The shots had come from the precinct detective unit, which was located on the second floor. I was the first cop racing up the stairs, followed by a herd of other cops. A sickening sensation overwhelmed me. I dreaded the moment I would reach the top of the stairs.

A gunpowder cloud hung over the detective squad room. On the floor in front of the fingerprinting station lay the body of Detective Joe Picciano. He was on his back, blood pooling around his torso. No question, he was dead. A few feet away from him lay a Hispanic man who looked to be in his thirties, also very dead, numerous gunshot wounds to his side and chest. A lone snub-nosed revolver was on the ground between both bodies. I halted in the doorway, other cops piling up behind me. This was a crime scene, and we knew we couldn't go any farther.

Detectives were openly weeping. A frazzled boss—I think he was a lieutenant—was on the phone calling for an ambulance, even though it could do no good. He was adhering to department procedure; only a doctor can pronounce someone dead.

Detective Picciano had been fingerprinting a prisoner who was under arrest for abducting a thirteen-year-old boy. A struggle ensued over the detective's holstered revolver, and the bad guy wrestled it away and shot Picciano twice, and in a bid for freedom bolted for the door. He must've been very desperate because there were five other detectives present, plus an entire building of armed cops, not to mention that he would have to navigate the stairs and make it through the front door. If he had made it that far, he would've run right into me on my security post, or perhaps caught me coming inside in response to the shots fired. Either way, I wouldn't have expected him and maybe I'd be that night's second cop killed.

Detective Picciano was married and had three kids. I knew him from turning over prisoners from the arrests I'd made, and he was a good cop. There were no rules for securing your personal weapon while fingerprinting a prisoner until this incident. Detective Picciano's death lead to a rule mandating that all members of the department lock up their guns prior to fingerprinting anyone. We all want to leave a lasting legacy on the job once we're gone, but nobody wants to be remembered as the guy who died creating a new rule.

Detective Picciano's murder was the first line-of-duty death I'd experienced firsthand, and because it occurred right in our "home," it was especially devastating. For the first time in my short career I realized that I was vulnerable and that literally *any* police officer might not make it through his tour. Blazing gun battles notwithstanding, to die while performing the mundane task of fingerprinting someone seems ironic; inside the station house, surrounded by other armed cops, the last thing you're concerned about is your safety.

Detective Picciano's funeral was gut-wrenching. Thousands of police officers attended, their shields banded with black mourning tape, dressed right and covered down in military formation, standing ramrod straight and silent. It was my first experience of an officer being murdered, but it wouldn't be my last.

I stopped counting at thirty-two.

Every line-of-duty death is tragic, but it's also a fact of the job. We're shocked by it, go through the grieving process, and then get back to work. Every ensuing death gives us a heightened sense of our own mortality and makes us sharper, more aware. The police officer who dies sacrifices his life for his job, but his death may save the lives of the officers who survive him and who are reminded with every funeral how cautious they must be. We can deal with it; we must because we have no other choice.

But when a cop takes his own life, the logic and learning process isn't part of the equation.

Nicky Costa and I were good friends. We grew up together, went to the same schools, hung out, doubled-dated. Toward our later teenage years, we talked about our plans for the future, which were uncertain. Oddly enough, we both became cops; Nicky was in the academy class after mine, but we both worked in the Bronx. We stayed in touch but didn't get together as much as we used to when we were kids. Both of us were active cops and single, but we traveled in different social circles.

Nicky committed suicide in his parents' home. He shot himself in the head with his service gun. He didn't leave a note—I never heard of a cop who killed himself who did. I was devastated, confused, and had a sense of foreboding. I had just over a year on the job, and Nicky's suicide was the latest addition to an already-long list of cops who had taken their own lives. He was a happy guy, well adjusted and popular. His suicide came out of nowhere; his funeral was attended by many friends and family, all with the same dumbfounded look on their faces, as if to say, "What the hell just happened here?"

I think that when most cops hear of a fellow officer's suicide, an icy finger of dread runs down their spine. If these other cops killed themselves, what's to stop me from doing the same? Dwelling on this is terrifying. But the thought always remains: will I ever reach the point where I eat my own gun?

Nicky was the first cop I knew personally who killed himself. He seemed so goddamn *normal*. Something came over him that was so overwhelming he could imagine no alternative. I remember him often.

Without getting into the psychology of why cops kill themselves, which I am not qualified to discuss, I have my own theory about what pushes people in my profession to take their own lives: the availability of the gun. In a moment of despair, sometimes fueled by alcohol, a self-destructive police officer will go to the most expedient means to an end: his gun, which is always nearby, if not on his hip. A cop might reach for it in a sudden and fatal moment of decision making. Too late to take it back once the trigger is pulled. I believe most cop suicides are spur-of-the-moment decisions, which could be why suicide notes are rarely written.

In a short period of time I came to grasp the realities of the job. The deaths of two cops who were my friends forever changed me, adding a layer of stress that would increase over the years.

A police officer, much like a member of the military, is struck by an uncomfortable feeling of relief when someone close to them is killed. We try to push back the feeling that haunts us, and the unfathomable mantra forces itself into our minds, "I'm relieved it was him and not me." We fight the thought, but it visits all of us. We're torn by our grief as well as our reprieve from the death sentence that took our brother in arms.

So we're hammered by guilt; for some of us, it can be devastating. There are many factors that can put a police officer on a self-destructive path to alcoholism, domestic problems . . . and suicide. Stress is the universal cause, and it transcends an occupation. But cops get assaulted by it on a daily basis. Lives lost, a public that doesn't care unless they need us, abused children, victimized women and the elderly—it all comes home to roost.

Staying away from alcohol and concentrating on being in top shape certainly helped me, but stress is a train wreck that leaves no one immune. It's just a matter of time before most police officers burn out and turn to self-destructive behavior. I'd fight it over the years, but it would take its toll on me too. Police officers should never let down their guard, even while performing the most trivial tasks. I became hypervigilant that day and remained so for the rest of my career, but I would eventually find that being aware of one's surroundings *constantly* causes stress. And stress can be its own death sentence. Not many people talked about PTSD back then, but they did talk about heart disease. The NYPD recognizes heart disease as job-related, and thus allows a cop with heart issues to retire on a disability, tax-free pension. Stress has been known to exacerbate the onset of heart disease, and the NYPD is a stress magnet.

I had two years on the job and thought it was time for me to choose a career path. I could stay on patrol, which I loved, or move on to something else. The NYPD offers a broad range of assignments, too numerous to list here. Any cop has the opportunity to request a transfer to an assignment of their choice. But while the opportunity is there, most positions in plum units are highly sought after. As in private industry, the best jobs go to the people who are most qualified. There were many superb cops working in uniform in the command who chose to stay on patrol; they loved it. This was good for them, but I wanted to see what else the job had to offer.

I was thinking of two details, the Motorcycle Unit or the Detective Division. I loved riding motorcycles, and the thought of riding a bike for the job was alluring. The Motorcycle Unit was a specialized outfit that worked security for dignitaries, parades, and other special assignments, in addition to patrolling the city's highways. Conversely, to be a member of the Detective Division would make me part of a legendary elite organization of the best investigators on the planet.

I mulled over my choices and decided that, while the Motorcycle Unit might be exhilarating, I came on the job for more than thrills. I wanted excitement, sure, but mostly I was motivated by locking up bad—very bad—people. I'd have to be satisfied riding my Harley on my own time. I set my sights on being a detective.

My arrest record would give me an entrée, I hoped, into the 41st Precinct's Anti-Crime (A/C) Unit, a good prerequisite for the coveted gold shield of an NYPD detective. There were other pathways; I could apply for Narcotics, Vice (Public Morals Division), or the Organized Crime Control Bureau, but I didn't know anyone in those units, and the last time I'd worked with a stranger— Gus Paulson—he wound up getting arrested. I cast no aspersion on those units or the personnel in them; it was just the natural discomfort of venturing into the unknown.

I knew the guys in Four-One A/C. All were honest, dedicated

cops who shared the same vision as me: lock up every criminal who was preying on the decent people of the South Bronx. The unit consisted of around twenty cops—the number varied because of transfers, promotions, and retirements—and two bosses, Sergeants William "Wild Bill" Taylor and John Battaglia. Both had over fifteen years on the job and were excellent street supervisors. A/C operated from an office on the second floor of the command and was largely autonomous. While the precinct commanding officer technically oversaw every cop in the command, he left A/C pretty much alone to do what they wanted. Why? Because they produced an astonishing number of arrests.

I sent a U.F. 49 (a letter written on an unadorned blank piece of paper—everything has a designation in the NYPD) to A/C for an interview. I didn't have to wait very long. The interview process was very informal. A/C was a precinct unit, and everyone knows everyone in a precinct, similar to a small town. Cops were assigned to A/C because their arrest activity was not only high in numbers but outstanding in quality. In addition, disciplinary problems had to be nonexistent, their history of sick time should be minimal, and semiannual job performance evaluations needed to far exceed expectations. Me in a nutshell.

The interview with Sergeant Battaglia was relaxed and friendly. He'd seen me numerous times during the arrest procedure when his men and I were processing our individual collars. He told me I'd be good for the unit and I'd be assigned as soon as there was an opening. Within a month, I was in.

A/C is like any other assignment on the job when it came to being bounced around between various temporary partners until you make a good fit. All these guys were professionals; top cops in a command top-heavy with excellent cops. Picking one to partner up with didn't have me looking for the best of the best, which would be near impossible because they were all the best. I was looking for that magic that cops detect right away when they find their perfect match. There's no checklist of attributes. Mostly it's about personality. Partners watch each other's back and pull their own weight. But that's not all. What makes a good partnership is the ability to work together for extended hours and get along. You may ride with someone day after day and feel perfectly secure with his policing skills, but if his personality rubs you the wrong way, you'll dread going to work.

A month or so of bouncing from cop to cop was part of the scrutinizing process. I hit it off the best with Kenny Mahon, who had been assigned to A/C about a month before I was. Kenny was big, a solid guy who was also gentle—he never pushed his weight around. At six foot one and 220 pounds, he could've done that to great effect, but it wasn't his style. There are many cops on the job who become bitter and cynical. Kenny had a positive attitude despite a combat tour with the army in Vietnam. He was tough when he had to be, always stoic, and focused. The term "the strong, silent type" described Kenny perfectly. Quiet and reserved, he exuded confidence. His size made him seem indestructible.

Funny thing was that if you saw him in civilian clothes, you'd never make him for a cop. He had an all-American look. With dark, short-clipped hair, he looked more like a football coach than a police officer. That haunted thousand-mile stare many cops develop after they've seen enough misery to last several lifetimes was absent in Kenny. Life may have been cheap in the Fort Apache battlefield, but you'd never know it to look at Kenny.

He was 100 percent cop while working, but when his tour ended he went straight home to his wife, Linda, and daughter, Melinda, in Queens. He was the ultimate family man. Just to be clear, going straight home after work was not the norm for many police officers, particularly after a tour from 4 PM to midnight. While most New Yorkers were in their jammies tucked away in bed, cops were wound tight and generally stopped for "just one drink" to unwind. The one drink usually morphed into several, and the "unwinding" only ceased when the bars reached their mandatory closing time of 4 AM. This was known on the job as a 4-to-4 tour.

While we didn't socialize much off-duty given our disparate lifestyles—I was single, after all—we were thick as thieves when we worked together. Kenny had my back more times than I can count. He was one helluva cop.

And so it was that Kenny Mahon and Ralph Friedman took it upon themselves to rid the Four-One of crime. A lofty goal, but we gave it a good shot.

Kenny and I liked to work the roofs of tenements. We'd sneak up to a roof and scan the street with binoculars for anything illegal, drug sales being one of our main targets. Low-level dealers thought they were pretty slick by not carrying the drugs on them; they'd take a junkie's money and direct him (or her) to where the stash was hidden, usually about twenty feet away. We'd watch the transaction, then go down to the street and make the arrest.

One day Kenny and I were out with one of the bosses, Sergeant Taylor, looking for arrests. A/C bosses were on the street with us; they were hands-on supervisors, unlike uniformed sergeants, who mostly supervised their platoon from a radio car driven by a chauffeur. Since we were a smaller unit, the boss could go out with us. The sergeants were always welcome; we were that kind of unit. Everyone worked together.

On this particular night we spotted a suspicious individual walk into a building. What made him suspicious? A cop's antenna gets a signal mostly from street experience. You have a feeling. You notice things: a furtive glance, a tug on the pants (which might indicate the weight of a gun), anything out of the ordinary. Sometimes it's just a hunch. In this case we observed a bulge under the man's coat. It might've been a gun (or maybe not). Bottom line is, some people just look bad, like they're about to do something illegal.

We followed him into the building. He was waiting for us—he swung his fist at me as soon as I cleared the door. Kenny blocked the blow, and a subsequent search yielded a .22 revolver. He fought us, but we prevailed quickly. After running his fingerprints, we found he was wanted for a murder in which the victim was shot six times while asleep in his bed. We couldn't have known any of that. Like I said: a hunch.

On another occasion we spotted a guy loading a gun outside in broad daylight. We identified ourselves, and the thug fired a shot at us. We fired back, but the gunman made good his escape through an empty lot. Another time we got into a fight with patrons of an unlicensed social club when we attempted to arrest a man with a gun. It was the two of us against at least seven attackers. Before it all ended, it was their pool cues against our batons, and we had to call for reinforcements. The Tactical Patrol Force (TPF) responded as well as troops from our command. It was a brawl of epic proportions. The good guys prevailed. Kenny whacked a guy so hard with his gun that the pistol grip broke.

In the early 1970s, the Black Liberation Army (BLA) made its presence known. The BLA was a small group of radical criminals who decided to overthrow the government by exacerbating racial strife. Their plan included killing as many black-and-white cop teams as they could, thereby igniting a race war. It made little sense to me.

The BLA was already on the NYPD's radar because it had attempted a robbery at a Fanny Farmer candy store next to Manhattan's Grand Central Terminal. Members of the NYPD Stakeout Unit, which was created in 1968 to stem the tide of violent armed robberies, were stationed inside the store because it had been victimized by armed robbers a dozen times before. The Stakeout Unit's sole job was to thwart robberies, and they were good at it, perhaps too good. Once the holdup men announced a robbery, heavily armed members of the Stakeout Unit would emerge from their cover and engage the robbers. There was usually gunfire. The cops always won. Robbery stats went *way* down, much to the delight of almost everyone except politicians, who deemed the unit "too violent." The Stakeout Unit was disbanded in 1974.

On the evening of January 26, 1972, two armed men entered the store and announced a stickup. Three Stakeout Unit police officers emerged from a back room and identified themselves as cops. When both robbers whirled to face them with pointed weapons, all three police officers unloaded rounds from two shotguns and a handgun into the bad guys, who were both mortally wounded. Before he expired, one robber muttered something about the BLA, the same group that had murdered two teams of black and white cops from the NYPD a year before. On another occasion, two cops sitting in their radio car as part of a security detail in front of Manhattan DA Frank Hogan's home were machine-gunned by BLA members. They survived with devastating injuries. The NYPD thought the Fanny Farmer robbery was an attempt to raise money for the BLA (surprisingly, three weeks later another armed robbery occurred at the *same store,* leaving one bad guy dead and one critically wounded at the hands of the Stakeout Unit).

The NYPD had gone on a war footing the previous year when four police officers had been ambushed, but now the rank-and-file cops decided to take their protection to a higher level.

I'd made it my mission to catch these cop killers, and to that end I didn't go anywhere without pictures of eight members of the BLA thought to be in the New York area. I also had pictures of them in my apartment, spread out in an array, right by my bed. Their faces were the last thing I'd see at night and the first thing I'd see in the morning. I had copies of the same pictures affixed to the dashboard of my personal car. I wanted these guys bad. The odds of running into them were small, but the best you can do is be prepared.

The murdered and wounded cops were all ambushed, taken completely by surprise without the chance to draw their weapons. Throughout the city, heavily armed off-duty cops took it upon themselves to protect on-duty cops while they patrolled in radio cars.

The NYPD only authorized its police officers to carry .38 caliber revolvers—woefully inadequate when going up against adversaries armed with automatics. We disregarded the rules and scrounged up heavy weaponry to protect our brothers. Off-duty cops commandeered their fathers' World War trophies: Browning automatic rifles, Thompson submachine guns, and the cheaply made but effective fully automatic grease gun. Some Vietnam vets showed up with automatic rifles, the parts of which were smuggled back to the States piecemeal in packages sent to their families from the jungles and reassembled when they got home. Cops without access to that kind of firepower carried shotguns and sporting rifles. It wasn't odd to see civilian cars with four off-duty cops each, barrels partly protruding from open windows, following sector cars around as they answered calls for service.

While there was never any confrontation between the off-duty cops and the BLA, the members of the radical group gradually were either killed in gun battles with the police or wound up serving long prison sentences. The only member of the group to escape justice was Joanne Chesimard, who escaped from police custody after murdering a New Jersey State Trooper. She managed to get to Cuba, where she was afforded political asylum by Fidel Castro. Chesimard was convicted in absentia, and I'm hoping she'll finally face justice after the recent normalization of relations between the United States and Cuba.

Those were troubling, tumultuous times, and the city's first encounter with domestic terrorism, but we would see more.

"Hey, Ralph," Rafael Fernandez said, almost whispering into the phone's receiver. "We gotta meet." I was in the Anti-Crime office catching up on paperwork before the tour. Fernandez was my most valued confidential informant (CI).

CIs are the lifeblood of any cop's skill set. Without reliable information from someone who lives on the streets, where the ebb and flow of crime is nonstop, many cases would go unsolved. As one seasoned detective once told me, "There aren't too many Charlie Chans on this job. We need our snitches to help clear cases."

In the world of CIs, Rafael Fernandez was one of the best; he was certainly *my* best. An informant is only as good as the information he provides. As in any other line of work, some people are better at what they do than others. Fernandez was always on the money; everything he gave me proved to be accurate. If I requested a search warrant based on information he'd supplied, a judge was likely to sign off on the warrant because of Fernandez's track record of reliability. So when Fernandez talked, I listened.

Most CIs don't become informants out of a sense of civic responsibility; they provide information on a quid pro quo basis. They give a cop some useful information, and they expect something in return. Usually it's a few bucks; sometimes it's a get-out-of-jail-free favor. In the 1950s and '60s, before the NYPD began registering informants—making them part of the system by assigning them confidential numbers and keeping performance records—cops paid off their CIs with drugs, which were usually withheld from drug arrests. This practice was illegal and corrupts both the system as a whole and the police officer. Registering informants keeps them on the record and makes the police officer accountable for interactions with their CIs.

Fernandez entered my stable of informants when he volunteered to be my CI. This meant that somewhere down the road, I'd either overlook minor infractions of the law or pay him a stipend for the information he provided regarding a crime or just street gossip that might prove useful. The money was usually provided by a fund earmarked for that purpose. Sometimes, if the cash payment was minor, I skipped the paperwork hassle and paid Fernandez and my other informants out of my own pocket. Other cops did the same.

It also meant that if Fernandez was detained by another police officer, he could drop my name and he *might* be cut loose, but that was up to the individual officer. If that happened, I'd owe that cop a favor. If I released other cops' informants, those cops would owe me. We have our own quid pro quo system too. This is how things get done and crimes get solved in big-city police departments. Cops protectively guard their relationships with their CIs. It's considered a breach of protocol for one cop to poach another cop's CI.

"What do you have?" I asked.

"Not on the phone, man."

We agreed on an isolated place to meet outside the precinct. Needless to say, the life expectancy of a CI is limited if care isn't taken to ensure his anonymity. Security is paramount, and I protected Fernandez as if he were family.

Our meeting was in the 44th Precinct on a frigid day in a deserted stretch of road not too far from Yankee Stadium, flanked by burned-out tenements and garbage-strewn lots. I was alone in my personal auto—I rarely brought another cop to a CI meeting because it tended to spook the informant—and I was early. It's always a good habit to arrive early for a meeting with anyone other than your family or Mother Teresa. You never know what awaits you, the recent past with BLA ambushes fresh in my mind.

Fernandez slipped silently into my car while blowing into his cupped hands. He was thirty years old, skinny, with slicked-back black hair. He had a wispy goatee and was definitely underdressed in a skimpy leather jacket and jeans so old they looked to be paper-thin. "Friggin' cold, man."

We didn't shake hands; we never did. No particular reason, it was just something that wasn't done with CIs unless they wanted to. They usually didn't. Maybe they had their own protocol.

I got right down to it. "Whaddya got?"

He looked around, eyes darting, looking for danger. There wasn't a soul on the street. Junkies and criminals aren't morning people. Besides, it was February and freezing.

"You know the Frances Bar thing?" He asked.

I was at a loss, had no idea what he was talking about. Then it hit me. "You mean *Fraunces* Tavern in Manhattan? The bombing?" His eyes lit up. "Yeah, yeah, that's it! I know who did that, man." Now he had my interest. About a month earlier, the landmark Fraunces Tavern in lower Manhattan had been bombed by the Puerto Rican separatist group Fuerzas Armadas de Liberación Nacional Puertorriqueña (FALN). Four people were killed and fifty injured. The tavern had been around since the Revolutionary War. George Washington was known to have tipped a few there.

The attack was in retaliation for what the FALN called a CIA-ordered bombing that killed three and injured eleven in a restaurant in Puerto Rico. FALN, a Marxist-Leninist paramilitary organization, was mostly interested in obtaining total Puerto Rican independence from the United States. They would come to be credited with 120 bombings on U.S. targets between 1974 and 1983. How blowing things up is meant to swing popular opinion your way is beyond me.

Fernandez had been in a crowded bar in the Bronx two weeks after the Fraunces Tavern bombing. A group of Hispanic men were close by drinking heavily and appeared to be celebrating. Others soon joined the group, and some of them began bragging that they'd taken part in the terrorist attack. Seeing a way to curry favor with me, he entered into the conversation and soon found himself meeting up with the self-confessed terrorists at bars and clubs throughout the borough.

"Did you get names, Rafael?"

"I got street names, man. No one goes by real names anymore, especially these guys."

"So what do you think? These guys on the level or bullshit artists?"

Fernandez was an intelligent, streetwise person. I valued his judgment.

"The real deal, man. These guys did it."

His steady eye contact and convincing voice swayed me. He believed what he was saying. If he was wrong, this would be the first time.

I pumped him for the street names, descriptions, hangouts, and names or descriptions of their friends, who might not be involved in the bombing but could be sworn as witnesses.

This was big. I wanted to get right on it, but I wasn't so full of myself that I thought I could accompany Fernandez to one of these bomber get-togethers and lock up everyone by waving around handcuffs and a six-shot revolver. I needed to talk to someone.

Back at the command, I repeated Fernandez's story to Captain Walker, who sat transfixed. When I finished, he nodded his head imperceptively for a few seconds, apparently digesting what I'd just told him. The bombing was a major case with a lot of political pressure to make quick arrests. Captain Walker never asked me if I thought Fernandez was believable. I was in his office; I wouldn't have gone that far if I had thought differently.

"I'm calling Arson/Explosion," the captain said.

The Arson/Explosion Unit was in charge of the Fraunces Tavern bombing case. Captain Walker related the story to Sergeant Joe Coffey, who was running the investigation. After a five-minute back-and-forth, the captain hung up, sighed, and said to me, "Okay, Coffey's very interested. Truth be told, they have nothing so far." He shook his head. "A month into it and squat to show."

It would be ascertained later that the FALN worked in small cells. There were quite a few cells in the organization, but no one cell knew what any other cell was doing or its membership. This system made it difficult for law enforcement to infiltrate the group, and, if an arrest was made, no information could be garnered from the prisoner other than what he knew about his own cell.

The captain continued. "You'll be working exclusively with Arson/ Explosion, nothing with Anti-Crime. I'll tell your bosses you're doing something for me for a while." It wasn't that Captain Walker didn't trust other cops, just that the fewer people who knew what I was doing, the better. An inadvertent slip somewhere could wind up in tomorrow's *Daily News* and the suspects would scatter. "Don't tell anyone . . . no one . . . That includes your partner. Get hold of your CI . . . what's his name?"

"Rafael Fernandez."

"Fernandez. You think he'll talk to Arson/Explosion?"

"He'll talk some, but I don't think he'll trust anyone to be on the street with him but me."

Captain Walker pondered this. "Sounds reasonable. I'll talk to Coffey about him." He gave me a look as if to say that we were both on the same page when it came to Coffey's reputation.

Joe Coffey was a great cop; there wasn't anyone on the job who knew him that didn't think so. But he had a reputation for being a headline grabber and liked to micromanage his cases. A flashy guy who was always well turned out in tailored suits, the press loved him. The brass respected him too because he got results. I didn't see a problem working with Coffey—but I was soon to find out that my confidence was premature.

I met with the Arson/Explosion Unit detectives the following day in their office in 1 Police Plaza in Manhattan. The team working on the bombing case was made up of seasoned professionals, each detective with many years on the job. It was a specialized outfit consisting of detectives who had paid their dues in borough detective squads before being bumped to the more specialized unit. These guys were the best at what they did and they were under pressure to get the case solved ASAP.

Coffey, who was wearing a tie that probably cost more than my car, introduced me around and then we got down to it. I was to continue meeting with Fernandez, stick with him, and pick his brain every day. When we knew for sure where the bombing suspects were, I was going to get wired with a recording device and show up with Fernandez to do a little socializing and tip off Coffey's guys when everyone had arrived. Fernandez wouldn't have to meet the detectives until the day the arrests were going down. Coffey was smart enough to realize that I was in the CI's comfort zone and they weren't. The upside of this plan was that they trusted me to do the right thing with the CI and make their case. The downside was that if the plan went bad, I'd get blamed for it. *"That fucking Friedman screwed up the whole thing."* This would be the NYPD's plausible deniability.

I would pretty much fit right in for a meeting with the bad guys. I'd always been a jeans-and-boots kind of guy, tattooed, bearded, and looking nothing like a cop. We were into March, and if we got a halfway-decent day, I even planned to roll up on my Harley. What could possibly go wrong?

Over the next month, I met with Fernandez ten times while he searched the Bronx for the bombers. He talked to people and asked subtle questions trying to pin the suspects down. In the meantime, Sergeant Coffey was getting edgy. I'd check in with him daily, and with each call he was getting more and more impatient.

"Time's not standing still, Ralph. What the fuck is your boy doing?"

I knew whatever I said wouldn't placate him; he was under pressure from his bosses to make some collars. "He's doing his best, Sarge," I said. "I can't rush this guy. I don't think he wants the next bomb shoved up his ass, which is what'll happen if they make him."

Another week went by, and then Fernandez got something. He called me at home.

"These guys, Ralph, they're gonna be at the Eastchester Manor for a wedding on Saturday. One of their own is getting married. Gonna be eighty guys and whoever they're bringing, like dates."

Eastchester Manor was a well-known Bronx catering hall on Eastchester Avenue in the 47th Precinct. "What's the guest list like?"

"I was told FALN, some supporters, some neighborhood guys," he said breathlessly. "And me. I'm a neighborhood guy, I suppose."

"Neighborhood guys" meant assorted stickup men, burglars, and dope dealers. I was sure most would be armed. Wonderful.

I called Coffey.

I got wired for sound in an unmarked, blacked-out Arson/Explosion Unit van. Coffey originally wanted Fernandez to wear the wire, but he would hear none of it.

"No fucking way, man. You think I'm James fucking Bond?" Fernandez was a nervous wreck, and I couldn't blame him; he was going with me into a den of killers. The detectives treated him with respect—he could probably count on the fingers of one hand how many times he'd been referred to as Mr. Fernandez before that day—and he soaked in all the instructions without asking too many questions. These detectives didn't want to do anything to give Fernandez a reason to walk away from what some people might call a suicide mission.

What would happen if we were searched? We were, after all, strangers in a crowd where everyone knew each other. I was wearing a tape recorder called a Nagra. It was state of the art for its time, about as small as a pack of cigarettes (king-size) but still big enough not to be overlooked in a pat-down.

Joe Coffey went over the dos and don'ts for Fernandez. Basically, "Don't fuck up."

And he said to me, "Don't touch the recorder. Stay away from a live radio, or you may start broadcasting music out of your crotch." Everyone except me got a big laugh out of that.

"And don't get it wet," Coffey continued. "It may short out . . . catch fire."

Great, in addition to risking my life, I had to be concerned about self-immolating.

Coffey gave a dismissal wave. "Don't sweat anything—you'll be fine. We can hear everything that is said in real time."

The plan was to arrive on time so we could mingle with other guests. We departed for the hall in my car with an unmarked department auto following at a discreet distance. A vanload of armed-to-the-teeth cops from the Emergency Services Unit was right behind them. After Fernandez fingered the suspects, the cops would burst in and lock them up. Fernandez and I would stick around, at least for a while. If the cops decided to take every male in the joint, we'd go along with the program. What the hell? We were guests.

It was cold, not a Harley day. I was wound tight but tried to exude control and calmness. Fernandez was fidgeting like a junkie after a two-day heroin drought.

"Be cool, Rafael," I said. "No one will suspect a thing. You're invited and you're bringing a friend like they said it was okay to do. Nothing can go wrong." I wished I believed my own words.

"Yeah, well, just in case I got this." He reached into the bag he was carrying and extracted a .38 Smith & Wesson snub-nosed re-volver. "Nice fucking gun," he added. Not only was this numb nuts carrying a weapon (which I was sure was stolen), but, because the transmitter strapped to my body was live, he'd just admitted as much *to a carload of detectives.*

"Holy shit!" I bellowed, but didn't get anything else out before we got a short yelp on the siren from the unmarked car behind us. I turned around to see a frantic Coffey with his arm out the win-dow pointing to the curb signaling us to pull over. I complied.

Coffey ran to the passenger side of the car. He grabbed Fernan-dez by the collar and dragged him to the street. He was pissed.

"You've got a fucking gun, asshole?" It was a rhetorical ques-tion. He confiscated the revolver from the floor mat. To me he said, "You knew about this?"

"First I'm seeing it, Sarge." I tried to remain calm, but Coffey's tirade didn't make it easy.

"If I find out you bought him this gun, you're gonna wish you never met me." He had one of his detectives cuff Fernandez, who was shoved into the backseat of the unmarked car. He would be booked for criminal possession of a firearm, a felony. Coffey looked at me. "Follow me to the Four-Seven."

My mind was spinning in a thousand different directions. Cof-fey actually thought I gave the gun to Fernandez. By the time we got to the detective squad room at the Four-Seven station house, Coffey was livid. For five hours he kept accusing me of supplying the gun. The more I denied it, the more pissed off he got. I was getting nowhere with him, and I had no advocate to back me up. I was in that gray area between interrogation and getting placed under arrest, or at the very least suspended from the job. I needed help fast, and my first thought was of Captain Walker. I called him.

The captain was there within fifteen minutes. He and Coffey

went into an empty office and shut the door behind them. Within ten minutes Captain Walker came out, made a beeline for me parked in a chair, and said, "Grab your coat, Ralph. We're getting out of here." He had talked some sense into Coffey, citing my record and lack of any disciplinary problems.

And that was that. Everything seemed to shut down after the gun incident. I never heard another word from Coffey and the investigation into the bombing went nowhere. I tried to go to bat for Fernandez on the gun rap with the Bronx DA but got no cooperation. Sure, Fernandez screwed up, but I had to try to help him. For one thing, if I didn't, word would've gotten out on the street that I didn't take care of my CIs and I'd have been hard-pressed to get cooperation from my other informants or anyone even thinking about cooperating with me.

I heard later that some detectives returned to Fernandez to try to get him back into the fold on the bombing case, but he told them to go fuck themselves. I couldn't really blame him.

The Fraunces Tavern bombing was never solved.

3

hings were heating up.

I was working a tour from 10 PM to 6 AM with Detective
Eddie Fennell and police officers Bobby DeMatas and Nathan Mc-
Cain. It was around one in the morning, and the streets were quiet,
or as quiet as they get in Fort Apache, when we heard a radio run
of an armed robbery in progress at a bar on Longwood Avenue.
Uniforms had been assigned to the job, but we arrived first.

As we spilled out of the unmarked auto, we encountered gunfire from the occupants of a parked car. McCain returned fire, and
the car sped off. At that point we saw a man in front of the bar
leveling a sawed-off 16-gauge pump-action shotgun at us. Eddie
Fennell fired at him, and the guy dropped the weapon and ran
away on foot. Eddie and I took off after him.

Meanwhile, DeMatas and McCain raced back to our auto to
pursue the getaway car. More cops spilled into the area in marked
cars and cornered the fleeing auto. There were four occupants and
two handguns in the car, as well as the robbery spoils—jewelry
and cash.

Eddie and I overtook the fleeing suspect after a three-block chase. He fought us with everything he had, which of course wasn't enough—another fool who thought he could beat up two cops. We searched him once he was subdued, finding a quantity of cocaine.

We arrested a total of five holdup men from this one incident. We prepared our paperwork for the rest of the night, then slid through the court process as we had been doing.

Juggling court cases at a slower rate than I was making arrests had created a logistical nightmare for me. I was piling up the overtime—that was a good thing—but I needed to take more shortcuts to cut down on administrative work. Streamlining the court intake process had been a time saver, for sure, but there was still evidence to be logged and stored. Seized guns had to be analyzed at the Ballistics Unit located at the police academy. Balistics could catalog it and ascertain if the gun had been stolen or used in another crime. The evidence had to be delivered to Ballistics on the officer's next tour of duty after the arrest was made, which meant driving from my home in Yonkers to the precinct, picking up the gun, then driving to Manhattan.

Most active cops sped up the process by taking the evidence home with them and driving straight to Ballistics the next day, cutting out the trip to the command. While certainly efficient, this was a blatant violation of NYPD rules, and legally the case could get tossed due to the broken chain of evidence, which had to be signed in and out every step of the way. No matter, many cops did it; the bosses knew it and turned a blind eye. The faster we got through the lab process, the quicker we were back out on the street. Of course, if something out of the ordinary happened to bring this detour around protocol to the attention of the courts—or, worse, the press—the bosses would feign ignorance, and the cop would be left swinging. I ended up taking this shortcut countless times and expected that things would always go well. I was never concerned that it would go wrong, but on one occasion this system did set me up for quite a bit of anxiety.

I had made a gun collar and took the firearm home with me, which by then was nothing out of the ordinary for me. Only this time, since it was Sunday and my day off, I decided to take a girl I had been seeing with me on the road trip to Manhattan the next day. Why did I do this? Good question, but it was a combination of her not being busy that day, having lunch at a restaurant whose name wasn't preceded by the word "El," and having some decent conversation.

It was raining when we reached Ballistics in Manhattan. While I dropped off the gun, the techs showed off for my lady friend by firing a machine gun into a drum of water. Afterward, we decided to head uptown to find a place to stop for lunch, avoiding the FDR, which was now flooded.

We'd stopped for a red light at 105th Street and 1st Avenue when all hell broke loose. Two men in a knife-and-gun fight came out of nowhere and flopped onto the hood of my car. The guy with the knife, who had been shot at least once, was slashing away at his opponent with one hand and trying to keep his victim from shooting him again with the other.

My friend let out a yelp. I thought quickly—my first thought was for her safety. To that end I told her to get on the floor, then I got out of the car, locked her in, drew my gun, and identified myself as a police officer. The two combatants kept on fighting, but in a second or two they registered the "police officer" part of my announcement. The guy with the knife tried to run, but I grabbed him and cold cocked him with the butt of my gun. The other guy was cut badly and surrendered meekly. He would die soon after in the hospital.

I heard sirens in the distance: the cavalry to the rescue. My adrenaline was flowing like a raging river while I tried to gather my thoughts. What I was a bit concerned about was the woman I'd been with, because she wasn't my steady girlfriend. Numerous witnesses and a platoon of cops saw her; if the story hit the press, I'd have plenty of explaining to do to the woman I'd been seeing on a steady basis. Fortunately, that never happened. I was off-duty and in my own car, so there was no apparent violation of department rules involved in the incident except that I'd taken the gun home with me, which the department never addressed.

A few months later I had a male friend who wanted to do a "ride-along." This is when a civilian asks for official permission from the NYPD to accompany a team out on patrol. Usually civilians must supply a reason other than *cops are cool*. For example, writers or actors are normally given authorization to conduct research. My friend wasn't either; he just thought he'd enjoy the experience. He didn't have permission, but I had known the guy a long time, trusted him. Still, I set a few ground rules. There were going to be two other Anti-Crime cops in the car, and they needed to be protected; this was my idea, and I shouldered the blame for anything that went wrong.

"Okay, first: if we tell you to get out of the car, don't question it, just do it. This'll happen if we're going on a possibly hazardous job."

My friend said, "No problem."

"Second: if we're approached by a civilian, don't say anything. Not a goddamn thing."

He agreed.

"Last: if *you* want to get out of the car, say so. We're trained for this shit, you're not."

"Sure, got it."

And off we went, three cops and my buddy. Almost immediately we spotted a car with four males inside cruising down Southern Boulevard. The car was going at a snail's pace, which is what attracted our attention. When I pulled alongside it none of the passengers glanced at us. To me this was a sure sign that they made the unmarked car we were in, were up to no good, and wanted to avoid eye contact.

I pulled back, gave them a blast on the siren, and they pulled over. We had them up against the car and spread-eagled in seconds and searched. All four were armed with guns. They surrendered meekly and were quickly cuffed. We got an "attaboy" from our bosses for good collars. I took the arrests with my two partners assisting. This, of course, *after* we dropped off my civilian buddy by his car and told him to forget what he saw—in fact, to forget everything that occurred after he got out of bed that morning.

Eventually, I had to go to court for a preliminary hearing, and as the arresting officer I was called to the stand to testify as to the circumstances surrounding the arrest of the four defendants. The assistant district attorney (ADA) who was prosecuting the case ran me through particulars, which were pretty cut and dried; nothing I hadn't done hundreds of times before. After going through the standard who, what, when, where, and how scenario with the ADA, defense counsel had its turn.

The lawyer was a young guy who was sharply dressed and looked prepared. I didn't know what he could possibly ask that would exonerate his clients, but that was his job. This is standard operating procedure when the police have the defendants dead to rights and I was prepared for that line of questioning. I wasn't, however, prepared for his first question.

"Officer Friedman," the lawyer said, waving a piece of paper. "I've got your arrest report here, and it doesn't make mention of the fourth police officer in the car at the time of the arrests. Why is that?"

That "fourth officer" was my buddy. I had a problem, but I decided to try and bullshit my way out of it. "That's because there wasn't any fourth officer, counselor." I made sure I worded my answer so I wasn't perjuring myself; there wasn't a fourth officer. My friend was there, but he wasn't a cop.

"Well, then, we have bit of a conundrum," the lawyer said drily. "I'm prepared to put my private investigator on the stand, who will testify that a fourth officer was in fact in the car. He has a signed statement from an independent witness to corroborate that fact."

"Your PI is mistaken, sir," I said. "There was no fourth officer with us when the arrests were made, just me and the two other officers I listed on the arrest report."

I was still telling the truth, and I was hoping the attorney wasn't sharp enough to question my choice of words. He could call his PI to the stand and even the witness, but it was the word of three police officers against a civilian. The only way my friend would get exposed as the fourth passenger was if my two partners or I confessed, and that wasn't going to happen. If through some fluke my friend was tracked down by the lawyer's private investigator, he'd deny everything. I figured the lawyer's badgering would go nowhere, but I knew the attorney wouldn't give up easily. If he could prove I'd lied on the arrest report, he could get all four of his clients off the hook.

We went back and forth for a while as to other aspects of the arrest, and he did his best to confuse the facts and trip me up.

A week after the court hearing, everything was quiet. I began to think the attorney knew he was going to get nowhere trying to establish the existence of the phantom "fourth officer." My relief was short-lived: I got a "forthwith" to the Internal Affairs Division (IAD).

My last "forthwith" was when Gus Paulson got locked up for shaking down motorists. I was hoping that my time hadn't come and that I wasn't going to leave the IAD interrogation in handcuffs.

No trip to IAD is a pleasant experience. The Internal Affairs Division was housed in a foreboding-looking building on Poplar Street in downtown Brooklyn, nowhere near any other police department facility. There was a logical reason for this: IAD was supposed to be a completely autonomous unit, devoid of any political or police interference. This, of course, was bullshit. There is no such thing anywhere in this country as a police department unit that isn't influenced by politics or headquarters' brass. It's the American way. I think the unspoken reason for IAD's remote location was that they didn't want to be located in maximum effective firing range of police-issue .38 caliber revolvers. IAD wasn't very popular with the rank and file.

I was placed in a bare-bones interrogation room consisting of one table, two chairs, and the obligatory two-way mirror. Since I was the subject of an investigation and not a witness, I was read what boiled down to my rights and told to sit tight; an investigator would be in to talk to me "shortly." I waited three hours, which was not unusual, and I was mentally prepared for it because I used the same tactics on prisoners I'd arrested. The excess waiting time was used to "soften up" the subject, the theory being that after all that time staring at the walls, I'd be ready to confess to killing JFK just to get the hell out of there. They did other petty things like depriving you of food and water and lying to you about the evidence they had and what was going to happen to you. *"You're gonna lose your job and your pension. THEN we're gonna hand you over to the DA for prosecution for perjury."* At least waterboarding hadn't been invented yet.

I was asked the same questions over and over by a not-so-sharp detective. I stuck to my story. What fourth cop? Prior to my trip to Poplar Street, I'd gotten together with the two cops that had been with me on that day, and we agreed on the same story, with some minor deviations so as not to make it sound rehearsed. We persevered; the investigation went nowhere.

I learned two things after my IAD visit: One, I was *never* going to put another civilian in a department auto without proper authorization. Two, if I didn't go out and have a few drinks after the investigation was completed, I knew I'd never have a drink in my lifetime. Thoughts of booze dissipated, however, when I got back to the Bronx, but the smile on my face stayed for a few days.

Kal Unger and I were working together while Kenny Mahon was on vacation. A few weeks before Kal got shot in that darkened apartment and almost died, he and I arrested a robbery suspect. It was a standard arrest, no heroics, no gunplay, and the prisoner submitted peacefully. What was unique was what happened on the way to the station house to process the arrest.

A young Hispanic man ran up to our car, breathless. He spewed out a story of getting robbed by a group of gang members while walking down the street with his girlfriend. He knew they were gangbangers by their "colors." A gang member could be identified by what he wore—God help you if you weren't in the gang and were wearing their colors while passing through their turf.

"They took my girlfriend!" He was near tears.

We were familiar with the gang and knew where their clubhouse was located. "Get in the car," Kal said to the victim. "We're gonna take a ride."

Kal and I both had the same unspoken thought: the kidnapped girl was going to get gang-raped at the club, then disposed of, probably by strangulation, and dumped somewhere.

We got another unit to transport our prisoner to the command.

I called for backup, but we were the first to arrive at the gang's headquarters, the basement of a dilapidated tenement on the northern end of the precinct. Kal and I heard the sirens of the sector cars approaching but vetoed waiting for them to arrive. We had no idea what was being done to the kidnapped girl. When seconds count, the police are minutes away. We decided to go in.

We hit the door simultaneously; it literally flew off the hinges. It took less than a second for our eyes to acclimate to the semi-darkness and what we saw enraged us.

A naked young woman was spread-eagle on her back on the floor, whimpering. A gangbanger with his pants around his knees was mounting her as we made our entrance, with a group of about fifteen guys standing around the victim masturbating on her. She was covered in semen. A few others were milling around the table and cheering. We assumed they'd already taken their turn at the victim.

The good news was that the rapists had discarded any weapons they normally carry; guns would have gotten in their way when it was their turn at their prey.

Kal and I waded into them, swinging away with our batons, no specific target in mind. Our goal was to put as many of these shitheads out of commission as possible. To that end, parting their hair with nightsticks was the order of the day. Most were on the floor in seconds; the guy on top of the victim was the last to go. Everyone left standing made for the door and was met by the responding sectors. They were also beaten bloody.

Many things piss off cops, but victimizing women and children top the list. All our prisoners arrived at the local hospital emergency room in a horizontal position. No one said anything. Doctors and nurses got along well with cops, and we owe our lives to their skill. All we heard from them was "good work" or a variation of that. The bosses who responded praised us for a doing a good job, and the press who covered the story never mentioned the condition of the prisoners when they reported their stories. Instant justice was sometimes called for, and the noncriminal element in the city silently agreed.

I still think about that poor girl. What's her life like forty years later? Does she have nightmares about the attack, or has time dulled her wounds and mental scars? I doubt it.

A week later Kenny came back from vacation, and he was riding with me and Kal.

"How was your vacation?" I asked.

"Vacations are overrated," Kenny said. "Loved being home with my family, but I needed to come back." He smiled. "What can I say? I like fighting crime, beats working for a living."

The next few days were busy. The three of us arrested two brothers who held up a supermarket. They attempted a getaway in their car, and we leapt on the vehicle as it pulled away. I was hanging on for dear life with my arm hooked inside the open driver's window while Kenny and Kal held the post between the front and backseat on the passenger side. No amount of screaming for the driver to stop worked, and, as the car gained speed, my adrenaline started pumping. If the car sideswiped something on either side, we'd be hurt or killed. I began beating the driver about his head with my gun, steady blows that must've hurt. Finally, he stopped the car and we dragged the robbers onto the street.

I was livid, my heart pounding like a jackhammer. We could've been killed, and now it was *their* turn to get tossed around. Kenny, Kal, and I used everything we had: nightsticks, gun butts, feet, elbows, fists. When we let up, it wasn't because we felt merciful but because we were just worn out. It wasn't the first time since I'd come on the job that I was close to getting seriously injured or killed, and it wouldn't be the last, but any such experience is always memorable.

Both stickup men were convicted in court. They never used the police-brutality card. Back then it was rare that a criminal complained or sued about his treatment at the hands of the police. The times dictated that such complaints would go nowhere, and if any of those thugs did make an official complaint, the deposition would usually be disposed of as "unfounded" after an internal department investigation. Criminals also realized that they were going back onto the street eventually to commit more mayhem, and that being recognized as brutality complainants just might mean another trip to the ER. The police were vastly outnumbered, particularly in Fort Apache, and we needed to be in control to survive and keep the area as safe as possible for the law-abiding residents of the command.

The following day, Kenny and I made two more robbery arrests in separate incidents. Since working together we'd taken sixty guns off the street.

I was tired and feeling jumpy. The word "stress" wasn't a word heard much in police work in the 1970s. The macho aspect of the job dictated that cops keep their feelings bottled up, never admitting to the weariness and fear that comes naturally with police work.

Currently the NYPD offers assistance through mental health professionals who are available around the clock to assist an officer who has trouble coping with the realities of the job. Back then options didn't exist; guidelines weren't established. If a cop was feeling depressed and was having problems functioning, he could call in sick and see a department doctor. Most cops didn't do this, discouraged by the machismo that permeates any police department—an ailing cop didn't want to appear weak—and by the perceived detriment that showing weakness might have on one's career.

Only when the suicide rate among police officers began to creep up to an alarming rate did NYPD policy shift. Officers with personal problems were urged to avail themselves of newly expanded services created exclusively for such issues. The department emphasized that seeking help would have zero negative effect on a career. Alcoholism, which often triggers depression, common in police work, was treated as a disease, not a career-stifling addiction. Slowly, the revised policies took hold. Even the most skeptical of cops realized that a depressed cop with a gun is a dangerous thing and that the department genuinely wanted to help. Knowing that compassionate help was but a phone call away was reassuring, but I hoped I never needed it.

The day after Kal Unger got shot I awoke in a fog on a couch in the hospital waiting room where I and numerous other cops had spent the night. The reality of how close I came to being where Kal was now was palpable. Kal wouldn't come off the critical list for another six days, and I'd spend quite a few days in the hospital waiting for his condition to improve.

I sat among my brother officers, most of us in silent contemplation.

I knew I needed a break from policing but fell into the cage that most active cops inhabit: I loved my job and looked forward to going to work every day. Police work *was* my break from a humdrum life. But the incident with Kal made me reevaluate my thinking.

My off-duty time was spent at the gym and seeing whomever I was dating a few times a week. Most women couldn't take the hours I worked, and real relationships never got off the ground. I spent much of the time riding my Harley Sportster. To me, getting on that bike was like flying. I was living in Yonkers, and a portion of the ride home after a tour in the Four-One was on the Bronx River Parkway, where I could get up some speed, particularly after a tour ending at midnight, when the roadway was sparsely utilized. Opening up the Harley and hearing its unique rumbling exhaust reminded me of riding through an impending storm with the boom of thunder and howling wind. I could lose myself in the fantasy of traveling the winding roads somewhere out west and forget where I really was.

What I needed was a long respite—longer than the ride home— to give my body and psyche time to rejuvenate. Trouble was, not much else interested me. Sports? I loved playing ball before I became a cop, but my schedule wouldn't allow me to commit to any organized team. Spectator sports? I never liked watching sports . . . odd for a cop. Most police officers live and breathe football, basketball, or baseball, mostly all three. Watching sports puts me to sleep; if I wasn't participating, I'd get bored very quickly. And people who characterized sports figures as "heroes" really pissed me off. I worked with real heroes every day, and a guy who throws a football didn't qualify. Bottom line: I'm not a couch potato.

Then there was golf . . . the unofficial sport of cops. Most police social events revolve around golf: golf outings, golf fund-raisers, golf "rackets" (a euphemism for any party that gets you out of the house). Hitting a little ball into a hole with a stick never held much allure for me—besides, most golf events revolve around drinking, which also wasn't one of my pastimes.

How about a real vacation? An A/C cop once told me that if I went to the Caribbean for a few weeks, I'd lock up tourists for taking too much sun.

Then I met Lisa. She was the daughter of a former cop who had left the job under less than ideal circumstances, but she knew cops and understood the culture. Her mother also knew cops, having been married to one, and didn't have a very high opinion of me. She called me a "whore master" even though she knew next to nothing about me. I think she was channeling her husband and thought all cops were like him. Personally, I liked Lisa's dad. He always treated me with respect; her mom and I avoided each other whenever possible. Lisa moved in with me, but she would be gone in three years, the relationship a victim of my crazy hours and lack of a normal social life. I guess it's one thing to have a father who was on the job, but having a romantic relationship with a cop was something else altogether. Also, while I liked her friends, we had nothing in common. Vacations? We went places, took trips, but I was always itching to get back to the job. How much of this can any woman take?

My younger brother, Stu, joined the Transit Police Department, those police officers responsible for keeping the peace and enforcing the law in subways. Stu had wanted to be a member of the NYPD, but back in the 1970s you could be assigned to any of New York City's three law enforcement agencies upon graduation from the police academy. Stu got Transit, which was better than being chosen for the Housing Police Department, responsible for enforcing the law in the city's public housing—a nightmare job by all accounts. Trying to stem the flow of crime in the low-income projects was a thankless job. The Transit PD wasn't the NYPD, but it was close enough. In 1995, under Police Commissioner William Bratton—who left in 1996 only to return in 2014 and make an abrupt exit in September 2016 as I write this—all three departments would combine into one department and come under the umbrella of the NYPD.

Stu and I had been very close since we were kids. He was four years my junior, so our social lives didn't mesh when we were younger, but we often hung out together, just the two of us. Before Stu became a police officer the opportunity to get together wasn't always that easy. Now that he was on the job, we had similar schedules and socializing became more frequent.

On one double date, Stu and I spotted three young men acting suspiciously outside a candy store. We were in a car; Stu was driving, and my date and I were in the back. We pulled over and watched the three men, who seemed to be casing the store and furtively glancing about like they were looking for cops.

Stu parked the car a safe distance away from the store to avoid involving our dates in what we were sure was going to happen.

Stu and I cautiously approached the men, using buildings and parked cars for concealment. As they were about to enter the candy store, one pulled a sawed-off rifle and the two others drew knives. Stu and I identified ourselves, and the trio took off on foot.

We caught up to them easily, but they put up a hell of a fight when we tried to handcuff them. It took a few minutes to get the robbers under control; then we escorted them to the nearest precinct, the charges being attempted robbery and weapons possesion. I was beginning to realize that some of these lowlifes don't want to go quietly no matter how professionally they're treated. Moral: Don't fight the police; you're almost sure to lose. Even if you're arrested and consider the arrest to be unwarranted, it's still against the law to resist arrest. Whatever beef you have with the police can be sorted out later. This is what courts and lawyers are for. I'd been in similar situations before, but never with my brother. Now, with my brother in the mix, a different concern was evident. The bad guys I'd protected him from back on the block when we were kids were now armed with more than just their big mouths.

This time my brother's life had been at stake. Part of my focus had been on Stu, which is natural while working with any partner. But when it's your brother, things shift slightly. I was unconcerned for my well-being, other than that I needed to survive to make sure he did.

Our first off-duty collar together went well. There would be a few more, and we worked together like we'd been doing it for years. This incident subsequently turned into an episode of the nationally syndicated CBS television show *Top Cops*. Stu and I appeared on camera as narrators, with actors portraying us in the dramatization.

I recall one incident that I was involved in that I think would've been viewed differently if the same set of circumstances were repeated in today's climate.

I was working in an unmarked car with one of the best cops in A/C, Stanley Gamb. Stan was a supercop among supercops, and he was already a legend when I'd first arrived at the Four-One as a rookie. About six years older than me, Stan had made more good arrests than probably anyone else in the command, and his rack of medals was impressive. He was very aggressive: bad guys in the South Bronx were afraid of Stan. I learned a lot from him and truly believe that watching and emulating him made me a better cop. Certainly, he was instrumental in my becoming the cop I became.

We were stopped at a red light when a frantic young Hispanic man ran up to our car claiming that he'd been robbed at gunpoint.

"How long ago?" Stan asked.

"Maybe ten minutes, man," he said breathlessly.

We were about to do a canvass of the neighborhood with the victim in the car when the victim said, "I know who the guy is and I know where he lives. His name's George Carter." He described how he was dressed.

That changed everything, and we tried for more information, such as how he knew the robber's name and where he lived. The complainant was vague: "Seen him around the neighborhood."

"That might give you his name, but how do you know where he lives?" Stan asked.

"I dunno," the victim said. "Someone musta told me."

The more information you had regarding a criminal and his relationship to the victim, the better. While this incident could be exactly what the complainant was reporting, it could also be an ambush; lure two cops into a building and murder them. It had happened before.

Our gut feeling, however, was that the victim was telling the truth, but it seemed as if he wasn't being forthcoming with all he knew about the guy who had stuck him up.

We put the complainant in the car and drove to the perp's apartment building. By the time we got there, we had a very good physical description of the robber.

I said to the victim, "I don't suppose you have an apartment number?"

I got a quick response: "Third floor, rear."

This seemed too good to be true. Now, if George Carter surrendered and handed over his gun and the victim's wallet, I'd be sure that there was indeed a God.

We left the complaint in the car and made it up to the third floor of the five-story dilapidated walk-up. A young black woman in her twenties answered the door. We displayed our shields and asked for George Carter.

"George isn't home. I'm his wife," the woman said. She closed the door around her, not allowing us to look into the apartment. "What's this about?"

"Routine investigation," I said. "You know when he'll be back?" Stan was craning his neck trying to look past the wife.

The wife was nervous, but most people are when they talk to cops. "No . . . I don't know. Maybe not until tomorrow. If you want . . ."

I heard a window open in the apartment and glanced at Stan. He heard it too. We pushed past the wife, who yelled, "Run, George!" I think George already figured that out for himself.

As we charged into a bedroom, we saw two legs slipping through a window. I reached the window first—in time to see our suspect, dressed as described by the robbery victim, land on the roof of the building adjacent. It was about a ten-foot drop. While we wanted to catch the guy, we didn't want to break our legs doing it. We climbed down a nearby fire escape and were on the roof in time to see our suspect go over the ledge in an attempt to reach the street. We were on what was known as a taxpayer building, a two-story building that housed a retail store on the ground level, usually of the mom-and-pop variety. Our bad guy had taken the leap from the roof in an effort to escape.

By the time we got to the edge of the building, our bad guy was twenty feet below us on the street staring up at us. He was holding a revolver. As soon as he saw us look over the ledge, he fired at least one round at us. There were a handful of people on the street. No one ran; shooting at cops in the South Bronx is a spectator sport.

Stan and I fired back in unison, one round each, and the perp clutched his chest and crumpled to the ground.

We weren't about to exit the roof the same way as our perp; jumping two stories to a concrete sidewalk could prove hazardous, and besides it didn't look like the robber was going anywhere. We took the stairs three at a time and were beside the prone robber in less than a minute. The spectators who'd witnessed the exchange of gunfire were now gone.

Our bad guy was very dead; a bullet struck him square in the center of the chest. One of our rounds had found its mark, but we'd never find out which one of us fired the fatal shot. The round had been completely disfigured and useless for ballistic comparison.

This incident is what the department would call a good shooting, except for one problem . . . no gun. The revolver Stan and I had last seen in the late George Carter's hand was missing.

While the lack of a gun was cause for concern, Stan and I weren't that worried. In the South Bronx dropped guns and drugs don't usually even have time to hit the street before someone snatched them up. Besides, we were two good cops with exemplary records;

our bosses would stand behind us, and we'd either find the gun or prove with best evidence that he'd had one.

The Emergency Services Unit (ESU) responded to search the area for the missing gun. Over the course of the next few hours, they would find ten guns in sewers, garbage cans, vacant buildings, and empty lots. None of the firearms, however, would prove to be the right gun.

While ESU was doing their thing, Stan and I, with the help of numerous cops, searched the dead guy's apartment. One of the uniforms found loose handgun ammunition. This helped our case, but we needed more. After the devoted Mrs. Carter had been removed to the station house, Stan and I searched every inch of the apartment.

While rummaging around a closet, I came upon a photo album. In this album were hundreds of pictures of the late Mr. Carter and numerous others. Near the middle of the album was a picture of Carter holding a revolver posed in a threatening manner. Bingo!

Such a picture might not seem like an oddity these days, when jerkoff criminals pose with all manner of firearms and post pictures on social media. Back then, to take a picture of yourself committing a felony was unheard of. Nowadays I've seen bank robbers display fans of money on Facebook after a holdup. The stupidity of criminals always baffles me.

The discovery of the ammo and the picture of the shooter holding the same type of weapon he used to fire on us, and a cooperative complainant, was enough to clear us of any wrongdoing. Of course, there's the chance that Stan and I could've been indicted for murder, our excellent records notwithstanding. But the NYPD of that era considered a cop's past history extremely important when evaluating a police incident and would give the officers the benefit of the doubt in cases where the involved cops had unblemished records. In our case a gun was never found, but a reasonable analysis would come to the conclusion that Stan and I had been shot at by the late Mr. Carter and that our return fire was in accordance with departmental guidelines.

We were still nagged by the victim's knowledge of who stuck him up. He wasn't vague in his ID of George Carter and knew much more than the average victim would've known. Being the budding detectives that we were, we asked around.

It turned out that the victim and the deceased Mr. Carter had been involved in a homosexual relationship. Our best guess was that they'd had an argument, probably over money or drugs, and Carter decided to take what he had considered rightfully his. But did it really go down that way? We'll never know, because investigating the incident would've exposed Carter's and his "victim's" alternative lifestyle, something not done in the macho South Bronx of the '70s.

The Four-One continued to go downhill. In addition to the overwhelming incidence of violent crimes against individuals, we began seeing more of a mob mentality. Riots, once a rarity, began to proliferate. The almost daily media coverage of peace demonstrations (which were usually anything but peaceful) protesting the Vietnam War might've given cop haters an idea that there was strength in numbers when it came to harming the police. The Four-One was earning its nickname of Fort Apache.

Licensed cabdrivers wouldn't enter the South Bronx on a bet. Holdups and murders of cabdrivers were epidemic in the city in the 1970s, and the odds of a cabbie not surviving a cruise through the confines of the Four-One were high.

Enter the gypsy cab, an unlicensed, uninsured private vehicle for hire. Gypsy-cab drivers would go anywhere, anytime, and were stuck up often, many times not surviving the encounter. The city had gotten a lot of heat from legitimate drivers who had paid hundreds of thousands of dollars for their cab medallions and were watching their livelihood infringed upon by gypsies, who meanwhile were expanding to other parts of the city. The Hack Bureau, which enforced taxi regulations, was unleashed to put the outlaws out of business. They swooped into the South Bronx and elsewhere, summons books in hand, and began to make the lives of the renegade drivers miserable.

These drivers considered the treatment they were getting by the Hack Bureau unfair and decided to stage a series of "peaceful demonstrations" to vocalize their point. One of the first demonstrations was held in front of the 41st Precinct station house by hundreds of alleged gypsy drivers (most of the demonstrators were neighborhood troublemakers who decided to make the police targets of their rage). The demonstration developed into a full-blown riot in minutes.

Any object that wasn't nailed down was hurled at police officers assigned to protect the station house and keep the peace. An order came down from somewhere that the cops on the scene were not to get involved with the rioters. We were supposed to stand there and dodge debris.

We arrived at the station house to see rioters trying to breech the building and the overwhelmed cops doing their best to push them back. It was during an earlier riot that the desk officer, Lieutenant Lloyd Gittens, uttered the words that would forever be remembered in department lore when he pleaded with the borough command to send reinforcements: "Send help; we're being overrun like Fort Apache!" From that day forward the Four-One was known as Fort Apache.

On another day with the same group I came as close to getting killed as I'd ever get—six shots fired directly at me, and not by a street punk . . . the shots were fired by a cop.

The Tactical Patrol Force (TPF) was a unit of nomad cops who traveled from command to command whenever the need arose, usually to address a specific crime problem . . . or a riot.

TPF was dispatched to help quell the riot and waded into the crowd, batons swinging. It was at about this time that my A/C team and I arrived on the scene, unaware that we weren't supposed to be there because we didn't have a radio—plus, we were in plainclothes with guns drawn. With a beard, numerous tattoos, and street clothes, I looked nothing like a police officer. While cops assigned to the Four-One knew everyone in Anti-Crime, many of the TPF cops clearly didn't.

I knew I had a problem when I saw a uniformed TPF cop aim at me with his revolver. I didn't have time to say anything that could be heard above the din, so I took off running. He emptied his weapon in my direction. The TPF officer missed with all six shots. Thank God he was a poor shot and that I could run fast. No one else was hit either.

I could take a hint. Retreating to a roof across the street, I found a cache of over a hundred Molotov cocktails, vicious little gasoline bombs in soda bottles that someone planned to lob onto the cops down below. Either I'd scared that someone away or he just hadn't arrived yet. It wasn't odd for neighborhood assholes to preload roofs with projectiles. The riot ended with casualties on both sides and many arrests.

My close brush with death hit me later in the day after the riot was suppressed. Every day was a new experience on the job. The reality that I may be killed had dawned on me long before, but I never expected my street persona to be so spot-on that other cops would take me for a bad guy. It shook me up. I was still wrapped up in my ability to survive, however. Call it the perceived invincibility of youth.

Not too long afterward I was back in the maelstrom when yet another riot threatened to overwhelm the station house. There was no reason for this "demonstration." The main goal was to hurt as many cops and cause as much property damage as possible. Initially, a captain had ordered all the cops inside the house, the plan being to defend the building if the mob broke through the front door. As we waited for what we considered the inevitable, a thought ran through my mind that Fort Apache was about to become the Alamo.

The captain glanced outside to assess the enemy when he spotted a guy setting a marked radio car on fire with a burning torch. The captain had enough of curbing police response; all prior orders advising restraint went out the window, and the enraged boss yelled, "Get the sonuvabitch!" Sticks and stones may break my bones, but fuck with department property and it's *your* bones that're going to pay the price.

Cops poured from the station house like marauding barbarians and waded into the crowd, batons finding targets. Bodies dropped like bowling pins, but the guy who had torched the radio car took off sprinting up Simpson Street with me and my partner that day, Lester Rudnick, in hot pursuit.

He turned a corner and thought he was slick by dashing into a building. When we entered after him, the bad guy was already past the second floor. I figured he was headed toward the roof; if that happened, he'd run across the connected rooftops and down the stairs of another building. We had no choice but to continue the chase, hoping he'd run out of steam. We were right behind him when he ran headlong into the roof door—which by law is supposed to remain unlocked in case of a fire, but in this case wasn't. Apparently, the superintendent had locked the door to keep burglars out of the building.

Our arsonist turned to face us, eyes wide, horror spreading across his face. He knew he'd run out of options. He uttered just two words—"Oh, shit"—and proceeded to take his beating.

The mission was accomplished; we'd nailed the arsonist, but back at the command things were still going full tilt. Fed up with self-control, the precinct cops were exacting payback. Rioters began to scatter, and cops were taking them down quickly. Within ten minutes the street was covered with moaning prisoners.

After that experience, people with a desire to take down Fort Apache had a change of heart. We had some mini riots in the future, usually by small groups of individuals protesting an arrest, but none like the battle we had engaged in that day.

With practically no time to catch our breath, Kenny Mahon and I got involved in a pursuit of a stolen car that spanned fifty miles and several upstate counties.

We had run the license plate of a suspicious auto that initially caught our attention when the driver kept eyeballing us in his rearview mirror. Since we were in an unmarked car, we figured the driver was savvy enough to make the car and us as police officers. Individuals that sharp are generally up to no good. I gave the driver a short blast on the siren to get his attention and gestured to the curb for him to pull over. He responded by flooring the vehicle, a late model Chevy, just as Central got back to us over the radio to say that the car was stolen.

The driver took us on a wild chase through side streets before getting on the Cross Bronx Expressway, where he really let loose. Within seconds we were up to 80 miles per hour, careening in and out of traffic. Kenny broadcast the chase over the radio, and sectors from several precincts joined the pursuit as we passed through their commands. By the time the Chevy turned northbound on the Bronx River Parkway, there was a caravan of at least twenty radio cars behind him.

Within minutes we were leaving New York City and entering Westchester County. Marked and unmarked cars from numerous county departments were now joining the chase; we were up to about thirty police cars pursuing the stolen car at speeds up to 100 miles per hour.

Some of the pursuit vehicles began overheating or otherwise breaking down during the chase. Most cop cars, primarily those assigned to precinct patrol, are in bad shape and poorly maintained. They are meant for cruising side streets at low speeds; high-speed car chases are not their specialty.

Some cars in A/C were better than others. I always tried to get the cars in good shape, but I had to be quick to beat out the other guys who also wanted reliable vehicles. Fortunately, on this day I'd gotten the best car in the bunch, a new Ford Crown Victoria with less than ten thousand miles on the clock and a good-size V-8 engine.

We were keeping up with the Chevy as we entered Westchester County, now thirty-five minutes into the pursuit. The New York State Police were notified of the chase with a delay because they weren't on the NYPD's radio frequency. Several trooper cars joined in as we passed an entrance ramp. There were now over forty-five law enforcement vehicles in the queue.

State troopers are assigned cars with beefy engines because

most of their patrol is done on highways and pursuits are pretty common. I was doing a steady 90–100 miles per hour when a trooper's car roared past me like I was out for a leisurely Sunday drive. He rammed the Chevy, sending it into a spin. It finally came to a halt after crashing into a road divider.

Numerous cops from more departments than I knew existed dragged the driver from the Chevy. He was fine and putting up a struggle. Cops, adrenaline pumping like a broken water main and highly agitated from risking their lives in a prolonged pursuit, spilled from their vehicles and pounced on the car thief.

Days went on, routine resumed.

But in Fort Apache nothing is ever truly routine. What was about to transpire would be the second time I'd killed a criminal for sure—the third if it indeed was my bullet that pierced George Carter—and it wouldn't be my last. I'd never get used to it.

My partner now was Bobby DeMatas, an active cop about three years older than me. We were in a yellow cab, one of the under-cover vehicles assigned to the unit. I was driving.

At about 9 PM, three hours into our tour, we observed several teenage boys walking along Southern Boulevard stopping pass-ersby and asking for money. Some complied, offering up change, sometimes a bill, while others just kept walking. Then they walked up to a Hispanic man who looked to be in his late thirties. We later found out the conversation went as follows:

"Hey, man," one of the teenagers asked, "you got some money?"

"Fuck you," the man said. "Take a walk."

The kid got his macho up, machismo being the cause of more homicides in the South Bronx than I can count. "Fuck me?" the kid replied, and shoved the man, knocking him back a few paces.

The man's response was to produce a revolver from his waistband and fire a round into the kid's chest. The kid went down; it happened in the blink of an eye, before Bobby or I had a chance to react.

I drove right up to the shooter, drew my gun, jumped out of the cab and yelled, "Police—don't move!"

The guy with the gun whirled and took off, but not before he and I exchanged gunfire. I was right behind him while Bobby pursued from across the street, running parallel to the shooter.

Within half a block, the shooter took cover behind a parked car as pedestrians scattered, including most of the kids who had been asking for money. The kid who got shot remained motionless on the ground.

Bobby ducked behind a car directly across the street from the gunman, while I sought cover in a stairway leading to the basement of a tenement. My partner and I had the shooter triangulated.

The gunman and I continued to trade shots. Bobby didn't have a clear view from where he was and so far hadn't fired at the guy, but this didn't stop the shooter from firing at Bobby. The gunman was methodical; he'd fire a shot at each of us in turn.

I was incredulous. How could I have missed at this range? The shooter began to reload with loose rounds (not only was this guy carrying a good weapon, but he had extra ammo—something that was rare for the times), and I took the opportunity to draw my backup gun and aim three more rounds at his torso. Still nothing. It only seemed to piss him off, because he emptied his gun at me and Bobby and began to reload again! I had to have hit him. What was keeping this son of a bitch up?

I was behind the shooter, who was about thirty-five feet from me, a clear and easy shot. I aimed carefully and let two shots go. The shooter didn't budge; instead, he fired another round at me, while Bobby, who didn't have much visibility, fired at the shooter, striking him in the shoulder.

The shooter grabbed his shoulder, dropped to his knees, and then rolled over on his back.

I shouted, "He's down!" I had two rounds left and ran up to the gunman. I was a few feet away when he propped himself up and leveled his gun at me. I fired one round, getting him in the forehead, watching the back of his skull blow off. He was down for the count now, no doubt.

Bobby came running over. Passersby began coming out of their homes. Cars stopped. Radio cars were responding.

The rest was pretty much a blur. The wounded kid, who turned out to be fifteen, was rushed to the hospital; he would survive. I'd hit the gunman *eight times,* the last shot obviously fatal. My first seven rounds were grouped tightly, and all had hit his torso— exactly what we were trained to aim for. The results of the autopsy would show a combination of booze and drugs in his system, which I figured kept him impervious to the bullet strikes.

Bobby DeMatas and I were awarded the coveted Combat Cross, the department's second-highest honor after the Medal of Honor, during the NYPD's annual Medal Day ceremony.

While I was grateful to be recognized for the incident, I'd prefer if it had never occurred. Taking a life hits me when the shooting is over, when I sit in the quiet of my apartment and reflect. I'd wonder what was in the mind of these guys and how they thought they could take on two cops and hope to survive. Similar thoughts came to me when cops killed themselves: What the hell were they thinking to bring them to a point where they had to know that they were going to die that day, and they could have prevented it.

This was my third shootout to end in a fatality, but they don't come any easier with numbers. This engagement was prolonged; in comparison, when Kal Unger got shot, it lasted seconds. I was physically and mentally exhausted. I only had a few years on the job, and I'd seen and done what most cops never experience in their entire careers. What would be next for me?

There were numerous federal agencies working within the confines of the Four-One precinct, all investigating crimes that came under their jurisdiction. The FBI; Drug Enforcement Agency (DEA); Alcohol, Tobacco, and Firearms (ATF), and other alphabet agencies too numerous to count wandered in and out of the station house on occasion. We worked in different worlds and rarely interacted.

The Anti-Crime Unit was enlisted to help the FBI, however, when one of their agents operating in the Four-One was robbed of his gun and thousands of dollars in marked bills during a fairly classic drug rip-off. During the sting operation, the bad guys were supposed to get busted but, instead, mugged the FBI agent.

One thing I'd learned about the FBI was that they really disliked being embarrassed, and having one of their agents lose his gun *and* "buy" money was a major faux pas.

I was with Bobby DeMatas in Captain Walker's office as he explained the game plan. The captain was currently embroiled in a legal battle over the movie *Fort Apache* starring Paul Newman. It was Captain Walker's contention that the film was ripped off from his book of the same name, and he was spending a lot of time with lawyers. This, however, didn't stop him from being the exemplary boss he was; he was always focused on his cops and his job with the department.

"Special request from the head of the New York office of the FBI," Captain Walker said, outlining the current problem. "You guys are good. Go out there and *do whatever you have to do* to get the stuff back."

Bobby and I looked at each other. We got the message. We were given free rein, which included the use of force.

Captain Walker gave us the location where the agent was robbed and a description of the two guys who robbed him. "Any questions?"

I was going to ask if we could wear ski masks, but the captain didn't look like he was in the mood for wise-guy humor. "Nope," we both said in unison, and waited to be dismissed.

The captain said, "Why are you guys still here?"

The people we were looking for were obviously not law-abiding citizens; therefore, the individuals we'd be talking to were cut from the same cloth. To catch a scumbag, talk to a scumbag. Gentleness and understanding were not part of the interrogation plan.

We began hitting known criminal hangouts, mostly bars and social clubs, hammering these places with enough muscle so the creeps inside knew we meant business.

Most doors were locked, but we didn't knock, opting to break the doors down for effect. Such an entrance is usually met with everyone initially freezing. If we were bad guys looking for trouble, guns would be drawn, and the standard mayhem would ensue. But Bobby and I were well known in the area, so all we got were looks of amazement.

We made a general announcement as to the particulars of the rip-off, asking if anyone knew who did it. Blank stares were forthcoming, but everyone got searched and we were coming up with numerous guns and drugs. We couldn't make arrests because of our mission, so we called for sectors to follow us around to take the collars. We gave away over twenty arrests that night.

Little by little we gathered intelligence, which led us to a tenement in another Bronx precinct where one of the guys who ripped off the agent was said to live. The apartment door was made of heavy metal, and the jambs were solid too. It would take too many kicks to breech such a door, so we knocked and announced a water leak on the floor above. A male began to open the door, and that's when I kicked it in, sending him sprawling backward on the floor. He fit the description of one of the robbers and was alone in the apartment.

Initially denying he had anything to do with the crime, within minutes he gave himself and his partner up. The money was under his bed, but the robber swore he didn't know where the gun was and that when he last saw it, his partner had it. We had him call his buddy to come over. It took his partner in crime a half hour to arrive. In the interim, we tore through the apartment like Walmart shoppers on Black Friday, looking for any other contraband he might have hidden. The place was clean. His partner, completely oblivious to the trap, looked like a deer caught in headlights when we dragged him into the apartment and deposited him on the couch next to his buddy.

We read them their rights. When Bobby began waving around a blackjack, they invoked their right to talk; frantically telling us that the gun was on the roof, hidden at the top of the elevator shaft.

Elapsed time from inception of assignment to recovery of the items in question: three hours. When you absolutely, positively need something done quickly, call Anti-Crime.

Accolades came from our boss, and the FBI sent us a very complimentary letter, heaping praise on us. Basking in the gratitude of your boss is a good feeling. In my case, however, the feeling was fleeting. Within a week I got another dreaded forthwith to the station house. The captain wanted to see Kenny Mahon and me. I had a bad feeling about this.

4

The forthwith we'd gotten to the station house had to do with an incident that had occurred a month before.

Kenny and I were patrolling with another team in an unmarked auto when an alert came over the radio instructing all units to be on the lookout for a car wanted in connection with a drug transaction. The description of the car was vague, but there was a license plate number. Kenny wrote down the number, and we continued on patrol.

About an hour later, the four of us were bullshitting about nothing in particular when I spotted a car that fit the description.

"Kenny, you got that plate number?" I asked.

He checked his notes. It was a match.

There were four males in the car. We pulled alongside the vehicle, identified ourselves as police officers, and signaled for the driver to pull over, at which point we saw one of the males in the backseat pull a gun. Then the driver floored the car and took off.

We drew our guns and announced a pursuit over the radio. The chase was on.

We were shooting at the fleeing auto, but there was no return fire. Sector cars were converging from all over the command, but within minutes we had lost the car. We looked for it for the better part of the next hour.

When we understood the car was gone, we had a decision to make: whether or not to report that shots were fired at the car. A department directive had come down a few months prior prohibiting a member of the NYPD to fire shots at a fleeing auto unless deadly physical force had been used (or would imminently be used) against the pursuing officers.

We'd seen one of the car's occupants holding a gun, but we couldn't effectively demonstrate the imminent use of deadly physical force against us. Did we really want to be the poster boys for enforcement of the new department regulation against firing at fleeing autos? I think not. The paperwork alone would bury us. No one was hurt and the car and passengers were gone, so we decided to omit the fired shots from our official version of what went down.

We also came to discover that we were chasing the wrong car. When Central broadcast the alarm and plate number, they neglected to mention that it was a *New Jersey* license plate. What are the odds?

Weeks passed without fallout, and we forgot about the incident. Then, out of nowhere, about two weeks before the forthwith, a civilian got a flat tire, the result of a slow air leak. He thought he'd picked up a nail and went to a mechanic to get the tire fixed. The mechanic didn't find a nail . . . he found a bullet.

The mechanic called the police, and the bullet went to Ballistics. In the meantime, it was determined that the car with the flat tire matched the car we had been chasing. The investigation began. Kenny and I, plus the other team, were interrogated by a captain. Had any of us fired any rounds at the car in violation of department policy? We had agreed to stick to our story and enthusiastically denied that any of us fired at the car. The captain told us that the recovered bullet was in pristine condition and we could have our guns tested to see which of us had fired the shot. He said he'd give us an out.

"You tell me who fired at the car now, and we'll only hold the shooter responsible. The other three will take a verbal reprimand and that'll be it. If no one fesses up and we have to test all your guns to find the one that fired the shots, all of you will suffer the penalty."

The captain's gesture was reasonable. However, we had anticipated the ploy and figured out a way to turn him down without punishment for anyone.

After the bullet had been recovered from the tire, all four of us went to a junkyard in another precinct and fired rounds into car tires using our service revolvers. An experiment. We fired quite a few, and all the rounds were disfigured to the point that a ballistics comparison would be impossible. The various tires had decimated all our bullets. The captain was bluffing.

We didn't think the captain had a magic bullet, so we turned down the offer. Frustrated, the captain knew he wasn't going to get anywhere, and the investigation was dropped.

We had the charges beat for sure, but knowing the NYPD as we did, we figured they would get us back for outsmarting them. And this is where the story began: with the forthwith.

Every command has an integrity control officer (ICO), usually a lieutenant. It's the ICO's job to investigate and punish violations of department rules on a command level (violations of the law were investigated by the Internal Affairs Division). The NYPD's internal judicial system views cops suspected of wrongdoing as guilty until proven innocent. In this case, the job assumed we were lying about firing a shot and we weren't going to get away with it.

The ICO recommended to the commanding officer that our partnerships be broken up. Kenny and I would be split, as well as the other team. The CO went along with the recommendation.

This was a devastating blow. Truthfully, I'd rather have taken a loss of vacation days or a monetary fine (or both!) than lose Kenny Mahon as a partner. We'd been working together for a couple of years, and Kenny had been more than a partner. He was a good friend. I mourned the loss, and I'm sure the other team went through the same.

It was too late to change our testimony—to do so was to admit we lied, and an entirely new investigation would be opened. We had won the battle but lost the war.

I was in my apartment working out and listening to music, some much needed alone time away from the craziness of Fort Apache, when the phone rang.

It was my current girlfriend, and she was in a panic. "Ralph, you gotta help! Me and my mom, we're at Gunhill Road and Jerome Avenue . . . There're two guys here threatening us. Could you come here? We're scared!"

The panic and fear in her voice was palpable. "I'm on my way . . . ten minutes." I was out of my apartment and in my car in a flash. Her location was less than two miles away, and I broke numerous traffic laws getting there in record time.

My girlfriend and her mom had gotten into a verbal dispute with two white males over a parking spot. By the time I got there, both guys were brandishing tire irons. I screeched to a halt, exiting the car at a run, gun drawn. I had my shield out and visible, and I identified myself as a police officer.

I was double-teamed almost immediately. One guy circled behind me while the other remained in front of me. Both of them attacked at the same time, tire irons swinging. The women began screaming. The first blow struck my right hand—my gun hand—breaking it, but I didn't drop my gun. The guy behind me got me square in the head with his tire iron, fracturing my skull. My knees buckled and my vision began to darken. I knew I had to take these guys out or they'd wind up beating me to death while I was unconscious. I heard radio car sirens close by as I raised my weapon and fired a shot. The last thing I remembered was seeing my target go down. He was hit in the neck, the round exiting, traveling into his shoulder, and exiting once again; four bullet holes from one bullet. The guy behind me was about to strike me in the head again when a responding uniformed cop grabbed the pipe on the downswing. He probably saved my life.

Another close call.

My afternoon workout at home turned out to be something entirely different. I was hospitalized overnight because of the skull fracture and was on sick leave from work for two months while I healed. My head mended fairly quickly; the hand took months to get back to normal.

I understood that police work was hazardous and that, no matter how tough I was, there was always the chance that I'd be hurt bad. I now had one bad injury under my belt and knew there would probably be more in the future. I'd always mentally prepared for that future; I welcomed the challenge but now understood that the outcome might not always be favorable.

———

I was three days back on full duty and in my apartment with my girlfriend—the same one I'd rescued from the tire-iron-wielding thugs—when I glanced out the living room window to see four men breaking into parked cars.

I sighed and said to her, "You're not gonna believe this," then I grabbed my gun and told her to dial 911 and report an off-duty cop making an arrest. She didn't look happy. "And tell them what I'm wearing." Last thing I needed was to be shot by responding officers thinking that the bearded, tattooed guy with a gun was a bad guy.

By the time I got downstairs, the car boosters were working on a Volkswagen. After hollering "Police, don't move!" as loud as I could (it disarms bad guys when they think you're a bit crazy), I placed them all under arrest. Turns out the VW belonged to a New York City cop who lived down the block. I didn't know the guy, but this is New York; I didn't know who lived next door to me either.

I spent the better part of the day processing the arrest and at arraignment. When I got home, my girlfriend was gone. No surprise there.

Most cops think that most of the training that rookies get at the police academy is a colossal waste of time. That attitude generally comes from the indoctrination rookies get as soon as they graduate from the academy and get assigned to a permanent command. They start believing everything they hear from seasoned cops.

"Forget all that bullshit you learned in the academy, kid. You'll learn how to do the real job on the street."

While some of the training is designed to teach rookies the

substance of law rather than the enforcement of the law using discretion, which is what's done in the real world of policing, it's a dangerous overstatement to say that *everything* taught in the academy is useless. If I had disregarded all I learned at the academy, I probably wouldn't be around to tell my story.

A good example of how academy training can be useful occurred one overcast, drizzly night when I was working with Bobby De-Matas and Eddie Fennell and we saw three suspicious-looking guys hanging out on a deserted street corner. We decided to talk to them. As soon as we got out of the unmarked car, the suspects made us as cops and took off running. While it was nice to know we were right about their being up to no good, having to chase three young guys who were fast as cheetahs wasn't amusing. To make matters worse, they knew enough to split up after a block; two of them peeled off going west on Kelly Street, while the third kept going straight on Fox Street.

DeMatas and Fennell took off after the two while I stuck with the lone runner.

The guy ran into a deserted building, which was boarded up and dark. It took a few seconds for my eyes to adjust, and I was glad I'd remembered to bring a flashlight because I was certainly going to need it.

I stood stock-still and listened for noise, senses alert, flashlight at the ready but not turned on. I heard something to my left, a shuffling sound. It could've been the world's biggest rat, my guy, or some junkie who was taking refuge from the weather. I needed to have trigger discipline and the correct target in front of me. I was taking shallow breaths, almost able to hear my pulse pounding.

I recalled something I'd learned in the academy regarding the use of flashlights in a gunfight in a darkened area. The natural response was to hold the flashlight straight out in front to illuminate your path. Tactically, this was a mistake because holding the light outstretched in front of you could make you an easy target for your adversary. He'd shoot at the light; shame on you if you were standing behind it.

I extended the flashlight out to my left before turning it on. This move, getting the light as far away from my body as possible, saved my life. As soon as I activated the light, the shooter opened fire on it.

I fired one round in the direction of the shooter's muzzle flash, and I heard a scream and the sound of a gun hitting the floor. I advanced carefully looking for the gunman, but he wasn't to be found. When the Emergency Services Unit responded, it lit up the interior of the building with powerful lights. It appeared the shooter had discovered a way to exit without going past me. We found his gun and a trail of blood leading to the rear yard.

An alarm was broadcast to hospitals citywide, but no one matching the description showed up with a gunshot wound. My partners had better luck: they captured their two guys. Both were wanted on outstanding warrants.

I never forgot the tactical side of my training. While some procedures needed tweaking depending on the circumstances, the instruction had been spot-on.

My off-duty time was becoming more important to me. Despite the acknowledged danger of police work, I loved what I did. My swing—a cop's version of a weekend, no matter what days it fell on—was time I could slow down. Unfortunately, my instinct for recognizing trouble never took time off.

Most cops go through their careers without making any off-duty arrests. This isn't to say most cops avoid doing their job when they're not on duty; it sometimes comes down to situational awareness, how observant they are. Everyone is different and just because someone is a cop doesn't necessarily mean they're streetwise and aware of what's going on around them.

I was always in a state of hypervigilance. I didn't believe this was intentional, just a by-product of where I worked.

My sanctuary was the gym. I loved working out, and the gym was a place I could unwind and lose myself in a strenuous session with weights. The gym was also the last place I'd expect to become involved in a situation that would lead to an arrest. The eyes give most of us away. There's the "thousand-mile stare," plus the constant looking around to continuously evaluate our surroundings. Most cops—active or retired—survey a room before entering it; it's a subtle scan of the environment, not noticeable except to other cops. Show me an ex-cop who doesn't sit with their back to a wall in a public place with a clear view of the entrance and comings and goings, and I'll show you one who had a desk job or rarely worked the street.

My gym was located on the Grand Concourse in the Bronx. I was in the locker room, and there was a guy about ten lockers down from me that I'd caught in my peripheral vision. He was hanging up his clothes, much the same thing I was doing, when I thought I saw a glimpse of what might be a gun. It was a fleeting moment, and I couldn't be sure.

I gave the guy a closer look. He looked too young to be a police officer, but that didn't mean he wasn't armed legally . . . if what I saw was in fact a gun.

I waited until he left the locker room. Then I summoned the attendant, who had a passkey to all the lockers. I identified myself as a police officer and had the attendant open the guy's locker.

Sure enough, there was a gun. It was cheap semiauto—definitely not a cop's gun.

I waited for the guy to return to the locker room, change, and leave the facility before stopping him outside. He wasn't a police officer and didn't have a license for the gun. Busted! Under arrest.

The case was eventually tossed because of my illegal search of the man's locker. Constitutionally, my arrestee had a reasonable expectation of privacy in a secured locker and I'd violated his rights by not securing a search warrant before gaining access to the locker. But at the time, I had a decision to make: with no time to get the required warrant, I either had to make the arrest or let the guy go on his merry way. I knew exactly what I was doing when I locked him up. My object was to get an illegal gun off the street, a gun that might kill me, another cop, or a civilian. I stand by my choice.

I made a similar arrest in a different gym with comparable results. Win or lose, right or wrong, it was another gun off the street.

I was in another gym months later when someone I knew pointed to a guy working out.

"You know that guy, Ralph? He's on your job."

My grandmother looked more like a cop. He was out of shape, pasty-faced, and looked oblivious to the world. If he was a cop, he never saw the street or the light of day. Cops know other cops. I decided to make sure.

Small talk in gyms is common; people bullshit with each other while waiting for equipment to free up or just to pass time between sets.

I made an inane comment about the weather, and within two minutes the inevitable question arose.

"What do you do?" I asked.

"I'm a cop," Dough Boy replied, an air of superiority entering the conversation.

"Oh, yeah? My brother's a cop. When'd you come on?" I responded.

He gave me a date.

"How about that?" I said. "My brother did too. What's your tax number?"

Police officers are given six-digit tax numbers when they're sworn in, and they're numbers you don't forget. Most cops can tell exactly when someone came on the job by their tax number.

When he gave me a four-digit tax number, I knew I had him. I placed him under arrest and searched his belongings. He had a gun in his locker and a fake badge in his wallet. To an unsuspecting civilian it could've passed for a police shield. He was eventually convicted of carrying a concealed weapon and impersonating a police officer, both of which are felonies.

Phony cops, like phony military personnel, are quite common, but a fake soldier can't do nearly the harm that someone impersonating a police officer can. Fake cops often carry illegal guns, and even a phony or duplicate shield can cause considerable damage. People who impersonate cops (and soldiers for that matter) are wannabes who, often, tried out for the job and were found to be unqualified. So they enter a fantasy world where they'd become what they couldn't be in real life. Some take the fantasy to a higher level and commit crimes under the guise of being a police officer. Sick people.

Off-duty arrests seemed to be taking up my leisure time. Over the course of my fourteen-year career, I'd make just over a hundred of them.

Once, off duty, I was in a police-equipment supply store buying a holster when I noticed a guy in civilian clothes. He hadn't talked to a salesperson; he was just wandering around the store.

He stopped at a display case where a number of sample shields ("badges" to everyone other than police officers) were on top of a glass display case. The shields seemed to hold his interest. I couldn't see what he was doing because he had his back to me, and he was also out of view of store employees.

He departed the store several minutes later, me right behind him. I challenged him on the sidewalk, identified myself, and searched him. He had stolen a dozen shields. Plus, he had a phony police ID and a loaded gun. I assumed he was going to turn the shields into NYPD shields and sell them on the street.

He eventually pleaded guilty to two felonies.

I had other off-duty situations that might surprise you, since I was a cop.

My brother, Stu, and I took dates to a boxing match at a local school one Friday night. The gym was packed with neighborhood fans cheering local boxers. Smoke hung heavy, and raucous laughter filled the air. A nonthreatening crowd if there ever was one.

As we were taking seats, one of two guys walking past us bumped Stu with more force than seemed accidental. I shoved the guy back a step or two, and his friend immediately got into my face and shoved me.

The fight was on. We were battling it out toe to toe within a few seconds. What we didn't know was that the two guys had come to the fight with friends—about twenty of them—who were seated right behind us. They jumped in, and Stu and I were quickly overcome.

The school gym was set up with hundreds of folding chairs, which made excellent weapons. Excellent for them, anyway. Things were definitely not going well for the Brothers Friedman.

Spectators were screaming and running for the doors. Our dates disappeared to wait patiently in my car. The fight spilled into the ring and back onto the floor. I was buried under a mountain of folding chairs getting my ass handed to me. Stu wasn't doing much better. Then, in the distance, we heard the sirens; the cops were on the way.

Several sectors arrived and pulled everyone apart. Once I was free of the fight and not tripping over chairs, I realized that the gun I kept tucked into my waistband was missing. My backup gun, also a .38 revolver, was secure in an ankle holster. My belt holster had evidently dislodged during the melee.

Only another police officer can imagine what went through my mind when I went to touch my gun to make sure it was in place and found nothing there. Losing a gun is devastating to a cop. If someone found it, the murder it might commit was in part your fault.

Two things happened simultaneously: my blood pressure shot up to stratospheric levels, and my heart dropped to my stomach. In addition to the embarrassment of losing a gun, the mistake was going to take at least five days' pay from me, and the blemish on my record certainly wouldn't help me get into the Detective Bureau. What's more, the conditions under which I'd lost the gun didn't exactly cover me; I lost it in a brawl, not in a life-or-death struggle with a bank robber. I envisioned my career circling the drain. By the next day, I could be walking a foot post in a cemetery.

As these doomsday scenarios were going through my mind, I felt a tap on my shoulder.

A uniformed sergeant was dangling my gun on his finger through the trigger guard. "This belong to you? Found it under a chair."

Relief swept over me instantly, and I thanked the sergeant, who elected to forget he ever found a gun. "Failure to safeguard" a gun is another department violation. Our night, however, was by no means over. We spent the next four hours in the hospital getting patched up. Stu got some stitches. No one wanted to make a beef, us especially. All we wanted was to get our dates and get the hell out of there. The four of us wound up going to my apartment and watching porn movies, too beat up to do much of anything else.

I figured it would be a good thing to get away from the Bronx every now and then. A night in Manhattan seemed like a good break, so I jumped on my Harley and took off for Chinatown in lower Manhattan, scooping up Maria, a woman I knew, along the way. We planned on strolling around and sampling some of the food the area had to offer: a nice, quiet, romantic evening.

We had a great time. After a few hours of gorging ourselves, I checked my answering machine. My brother called wanting to know if we'd like to join him and his date at the car races on the Connecting Highway in Queens, where I used to race before I became a police officer. I bounced the idea off Maria, who thought it sounded fun. We got on the FDR and headed north in light traffic.

I realized we'd arrive in Queens way too early. Stu wasn't getting there for at least another hour, so I pulled off the FDR into an emergency vehicle cutout to hang out by the East River for a while. We found a bench facing the water, where we sat for a while doing what couples do to pass the time.

About a hundred feet to our left was a footbridge that crossed over the FDR. I observed three young guys coming down the ramp from the footbridge and walking in our direction, studying us as they got closer. I told Maria, "If anything happens, hit the ground." Her eyes went wide, but she nodded. I drew my gun from my waistband and held it under my forearm with my arms crossed.

I was dressed in jeans, a T-shirt, and boots and had numerous tattoos and a beard. As a reminder: I looked nothing like a cop. But perhaps I didn't look like a victim either, because the three guys passed us without saying anything and then strolled back toward the footbridge.

The story doesn't end there; I kept watching them. They exchanged words with two guys and a girl at the foot of the ramp and with a couple in the middle of the footbridge. I didn't know what they said, but I decided to find out.

I identified myself to the three people at the bottom of the ramp.

In a barrage of words (and some tears) they said they'd been robbed at gunpoint. I told them to stay put and ran up to the couple in the middle of the ramp. Same thing, robbed at gunpoint.

I ran toward the stickup men, who were still on the bridge. When I got close, I identified myself as a police officer. The three took off, but not before they fired several shots at me. I returned fire, not hitting anyone, and chased them off the bridge onto Seventy-Eighth Street, where they jumped into a blue Ford. The assholes had a getaway car, driver at the wheel. There were numerous pedestrians on the street, who scattered like cockroaches.

The Ford left rubber fleeing the scene but got stuck in a queue of cars at a red light. I knew if I tried to reach it on foot, the car would be long gone by the time I got there. I was left standing there, feeling useless. Then I spotted a cab cruising for a fare.

I leapt into the backseat and hollered, "I'm a cop, follow that car!"

The driver, a young black man, saw my gun and thought I was sticking him up. He reached into a cigar box stuffed with cash and began throwing bills at me in the backseat. The cab was still stopped as I saw the light turn green and the Ford fade off into the distance.

I slammed my shield against the Plexiglas divider and repeated that I was a cop. The money kept on coming.

"Please don't kill me, man," the driver pleaded. "Take the fucking money!"

It took me another thirty seconds to convince the driver I was indeed a police officer, but by that time it was too late.

Frustrated and pissed off, I knew I still had to report the incident because shots had been fired. I directed the driver back to the FDR, where I got my bike and Maria, told her what had happened, and explained to her that we needed to go to the 19th Precinct station house (the precinct of occurrence) to make a police report. I looked around for the five robbery victims.

"You see where the five people that were held up went?" I asked her.

"Last I saw they were walking south on the service road."

The station house was in that direction, so naturally I assumed the victims went there to report the robberies.

At the station house I explained to the desk officer, a lieutenant, who I was and what had happened. He looked at me skeptically.

"And where are the victims of this crime spree, Officer?" he asked sarcastically.

That took me by surprise. "You mean they're not here?"

The lieutenant shook his head. I could tell he didn't want any part of what I was telling him. The 19th Precinct encompasses the Upper East Side, some of the priciest real estate in the country and not considered a high-crime area—far from it. Here was a story that defied credulity. All this desk officer saw was a mountain of paperwork and numerous official notifications on account of some shots fired by a cop who looked like a thug. I don't think he believed anything I told him.

"Tell you what, Officer, go in that office over there." He pointed. "That's the CO. He's gonna want to hear your story." He emphasized the word "story" like it should have begun with "Once upon a time." The lieutenant wanted to get rid of me, and what better person to sort all this out than the precinct commanding officer?

The CO was about fifty, with salt-and-pepper hair that I figured would turn white when I related my tale. I ran through the facts with him nodding as I spoke.

When I was finished he said, "So . . . what you're telling me is you had this running shootout with three robbery perps, commandeered a cab when they jumped into a getaway car, and lost them because the cabby thought you were holding him up?"

"Yes sir," I said. "That's it."

"Uh, huh. And where are the vics?"

I shrugged. "Don't know. I thought they'd be coming here to report the stickups."

He smiled. "Well, they didn't. Tell me, Officer Friedman, this your first shooting?"

I shook my head. "No, sir, not even close. I've been in ten shootings," I said, then thought about it. "Make that eleven."

The captain sat bolt upright. "You've been in eleven shootings?"

"Right," I said, considering this number not out of the ordinary for the Four-One. Then I realized where I was. If there's one police-involved shooting a year in the 19th, that's a lot. "We, uh, have a crime problem in the Four-One . . . sir."

I don't know what was swimming around in his head, but I knew he wanted nothing to do with me. He reached for the phone. "Ya know, Officer, I'll get the borough duty captain down here. You can relate your . . . *story* to him." Again with the "story."

Everything I told this captain was unsubstantiated. Maria didn't see the shooting or know what the victims told me, and they had vanished. The cabdriver was just following orders. I was being viewed as a lunatic and could see a world of shit coming down on me. Cue the department shrink: *"So tell me, Officer Friedman, have you been involved in any other shootings where there are no witnesses or victims?"*

Wonderful.

I excused myself to bring Maria, who was waiting outside, up to date. As I left the CO's office, I saw five people standing in front of the desk talking animatedly to the desk officer. My victims! I don't know what took them so long to arrive, but at least they made it.

Within minutes I went from crazy cop to hero. While the bad guys had gotten away, at least I was vindicated. I'd taken proper police action and that would have to do. The CO and desk officer were looking at me now with expressions that combined wonderment and a please-get-back-to-the-fucking-Bronx look of fear that I might stick around the Upper East Side long enough to shoot one of its wealthy inhabitants.

I was on Anti-Crime patrol when two cops in a sector car responded to a radio run of a man with a gun on Intervale Avenue. Gun runs were common, and while many were unfounded or the bad guy got away before officers arrived, this one proved to be the real thing. The incident would escalate into a massive response involving cops from three precincts—the entire division—when things began to go sideways.

The responding cops pulled up and observed a black male, well over six feet tall and around 250 pounds, brandishing a large revolver later determined to be a .357 magnum. That's a big deal in the world of guns. He spotted the cops and retreated into a building with the two radio car officers in hot pursuit.

The gunman was fleeing up the stairs when the cops entered the building. Ordered to stop, the man turned and fired several shots. Both officers returned fire, and a running gun battle ensued as the cops chased the shooter up the stairs toward the roof.

The shooter, out of ammo, drew a second gun, a 9mm Browning semiautomatic, and unleashed a withering barrage of shots from a seventeen-round magazine.

The shooter busted through the door to the roof, and it slammed behind him. The pursuing cops knew that the gunman could be waiting for them on the other side of the door and used caution by not continuing the chase.

The cops had already called in a 10-13—officer needs assistance *now*—amid the sounds of escalating gunfire. Throughout the command, normal police operations ceased as cars sped to the scene.

The frantic call for help spread to the 43rd and 45th Precincts, both part of the division, which encompassed most of the South Bronx. A division-wide 10-13, a rarity, and every available cop from those commands raced to help their brother officers.

Bobby DeMatas, Eddie Fennell, Sergeant Vincent Barone, and Detective Rocco Tortorello, and I were on our way in two unmarked cars. We arrived in front of the Intervale Avenue address to pandemonium. Cops were everywhere: at least fifty uniforms, detectives, and sergeants. While everyone wanted a piece of the shooter, no one had a plan. And without a cohesive strategy, the perp had a good chance of escaping in the confusion.

Enter the Four-One commanding officer, Captain Tom Walker.

The captain and his driver screeched to a halt in an unmarked radio car among what can best be described as a cluster fuck of well-intentioned police officers. He immediately began shouting commands and gathering the sergeants to have them establish a perimeter around the block. Within minutes the street was sealed off by a ring of blue. The bad guy was trapped somewhere within that perimeter.

"Now we search," he said, as he assigned different groups of cops to different tasks. Captain Walker was what every captain should be: a superb field commander.

We were directed to an alley adjacent to Intervale Avenue, one building away from the crime scene. Tenements on the street were connected. It wasn't a stretch to assume that the shooter, in an attempt to escape, had made his way to another building and would try to flee that way.

As the Anti-Crime cops and I entered the alley, we ran straight into the gunman, who had done exactly what we thought he'd do: jump a building divider to the adjoining building and climb down the fire escape. He had already reached the ground but hadn't noticed us yet.

"Big" doesn't begin to describe him. And in addition to his size, he had a gun in each hand.

The same thought occurred to all five of us: we would disarm him without a shootout. After all, we had the element of surprise. There were five of us and one of him.

We pounced on the giant, blackjacks flailing. He put up a passionate resistance: we definitely had a fight on our hands. We pummeled him, careful not to brain each other with the blackjacks. The battle lasted three minutes; we were still mostly standing after it was over.

Turned out the perp was a card-carrying member of the Black

Panther Party, which explained his intense dislike for cops and extensive arrest record. He would have plenty of time in prison to think about his political leanings.

Those are a handful of stories from a rough few months. But tougher times were coming; I was about to experience a life-altering catastrophe, memories of which I will carry with me for the rest of my life.

5

Police Officer Kenneth Mahon
11/30/45–12/28/74 End of Tour

"He died as he lived . . . a hero."
—Assistant Chief Anthony Bouza,
Bronx Area Commander

I was at home working out and listening to music on the radio when the hourly news came on. A plainclothes police officer was reported shot and killed in the area encompassing the Four-One. That caught my attention. I became still as I stopped what I was doing and waited for more information, but there were no specifics forthcoming.

I've learned in my time that initial reports of any tragedy, be it police-involved or otherwise, are generally not strong on accuracy. There were many police officers working in plainclothes in the area: not only Four-One Anti-Crime but also City-Wide Anti-Crime, and the Tactical Patrol Force had some of its cops working out of uniform. As my heart raced and I reached for the phone to call the office, I rationalized how the media could confuse all sorts of characters with a "plainclothes police officer"—the list was endless. I would prefer no law enforcement officer were killed, but I said a silent prayer: let him not be a cop from my unit . . . please.

Sergeant Battaglia, one of my bosses, picked up. He confirmed that the victim was a cop from Four-One Anti-Crime. But not just any cop . . .

"It was Kenny, Ralph," Sergeant Battaglia said quietly. "He's gone."

Kenny Mahon was dead? I couldn't believe it. My head felt as if it took a direct hit from a brick. My mind went totally blank. I couldn't think, and I felt faint. Battaglia was still talking.

". . . perp still on the loose . . . Get here as fast as you can."

Regaining my composure, I told him I was on my way. I grabbed my two .38s, a shotgun, and my bulletproof vest. I was in my car in less than a minute.

The next thing I remember is driving like a madman to the Four-One. The roads were deserted given the early hour. I think I made the usual twenty-minute trip in ten, but it could've been less.

There were dozens of marked and unmarked cars blocking the street leading to the station house. A cop's murder is the time to circle the wagons—all available officers of every rank converge on the command of occurrence. Off-duty, on-duty, retired, in all manners of attire, police from all over the city and beyond answer the unspoken call to arms.

I left my car in the middle of Simpson Street, dodged TV reporters in front of the station house, and took the stairs three at a time to the Anti-Crime office.

The scene was surreal: cops were crying; others appeared cried out and were looking blankly around the room as if trying to figure out what to do. Every available phone was being used. I saw uniforms I didn't recognize—those of officers from other departments who had heard what happened and had reached out to help.

My first impulse was to break down. Kenny and I were close, and I was having a tough time wrapping my head around his being gone. But falling apart wouldn't help anything; I needed facts. If the killers or *a* killer was still being sought, I wanted to be the one to get him. I had revenge in my heart.

Sergeant Battaglia came out of his office, saw me, and waved me over. He looked like he'd aged ten years since yesterday. He was the strength of the Anti-Crime unit, the rock-solid boss, someone who would always have your back and have an answer to whatever problem might arise. For the first time since I met him, he actually looked helpless.

Sergeant Battaglia grabbed my arm, waking me from my reverie. "We just got a tip that the missing suspect in a rape/robbery of a young woman may have shot Kenny, who went looking for him . . . a guy named Vasquez . . . Daniel Vasquez is either on his way to JFK or there already looking to board a plane to PR. Grab someone and get to the airport *now* and see if that rat fuck is there. If he's on a plane, yank him off—fuck a warrant." He handed me an old booking picture. "This is him; he's got an extensive sheet." He stared at me. "Go! What are you waiting for?"

I teamed up with Billy Rath, Richie McLes, and another officer whose name I've forgotten; scooped up a set of keys to an unmarked auto; and ran for the car. Within minutes we were at the Triborough Bridge coming up on a tollbooth without any cars. At this hour of the morning, the toll taker was probably working on autopilot. He was standing in the booth ready to collect the next two-dollar toll when we shot past him doing eighty-five. I thought for sure the vacuum created by the wind blast was going to suck him out of the booth. I was relieved he didn't have his arm extended to grab my toll money, or it may have wound up splattered across the windshield.

I amped up the speed to over one hundred when we came off the slope leading from the bridge to the Grand Central Parkway, which was nearly deserted. We were at the Van Wyck Expressway within three minutes, and I slowed down for the first time since I left the station house to make the sharp turn onto the roadway. The Van Wyck is a straight three-lane road leading directly into JFK airport. Normally a ten-minute drive, we made the perimeter of the airport in four minutes. In two more minutes we were screeching to a halt in front of the international arrivals building on the upper departure level. We'd made a trip that should have taken forty-five minutes (with no traffic) from the Four-One to JFK Airport in fourteen minutes.

We ran into the building and found a Port Authority cop who told us a direct Eastern Airlines flight to San Juan, Puerto Rico, was loading passengers as we spoke. He gave us the gate number, and we took off running as fast as our legs would carry us. There were no security checkpoints back then to delay us.

The plane was fully loaded when we arrived. Breathless, we identified ourselves and babbled our mission to the flight attendant at the gate. I grabbed the passenger manifest . . . there was no Daniel Vasquez listed. Passengers didn't need passports to go to Puerto Rico, and realistically they didn't even have to give their actual name to buy a ticket, so we decided to see for ourselves if our man was here.

The Jetway was still attached to the plane, so we were no longer in a rush; if Vasquez was on board, he wasn't going anywhere. We slowed down, boarding the plane like we were passengers, dividing up and walking the two aisles. We asked the Port Authority cop, who was in uniform, to stay behind on the Jetway and out of sight. The plan was to pounce on the son of a bitch before he had a chance to react and possibly endanger other passengers.

1971. Gearing up for patrol during Black Liberation Army years.

1971. Ready for patrol.

1973. Front of 41st Precinct station house, Simpson Street.

1974. Employing stop and frisk of gang members while on patrol.

April 28, 1975. Being promoted to detective.

Promotion picture taken at Big Joe's Tattoo Parlor. *Photo by Big Joe*

May 19, 1975. Mayor Abe Beam awarding me the Combat Cross for actions taken on November 19, 1974.

1979. Me with my German Shepherd, Timba.

Upstate with friends, shooting my .30-caliber carbine M-1 Enforcer that was also taken on patrol on many occasions.

1981. On my
1980 Harley
that was used
many times
on patrol.

1970. In the gym
on the Grand
Concourse in the
Bronx.

August 31, 1982. With Timmy Kennedy and evidence taken from arrest of Jamaican gang members.

July 1983. Grace and me on a bike trip to Virginia Beach on my 1983 Harley.

August 1, 1983. NYPD radio car that collided with my unmarked car, ending my career.

1984. With my 1975 Corvette.

2016. Me and my Lab, Chase.

June 2016. In my office, still in fighting shape at 68 years old.

This story doesn't end heroically. Vasquez wasn't on the plane. There were no other planes leaving for Puerto Rico anytime soon. The Port Authority cop assured us he would put out the word and be on the lookout. I didn't hold out much hope.

Often, after a particularly heinous crime is committed, rumors fly because solid information is lacking, and sometimes it takes days to sort out exactly what happened. Since Kenny and Emile DeFoe were looking for Vasquez for the rape/robbery, it was assumed that he had been stopped and shot Kenny, but it could've been anyone with a gun who hated cops.

When Kenny and Emile entered the building where Vasquez was known to live, they encountered a man who identified himself as David. When asked for his identification, he told the two cops that he didn't have it on him but lived upstairs and would get it. He began to walk down the hallway; Kenny must have sensed something was wrong because he started to tell him to stop. But at that moment a second man appeared in a doorway, temporarily distracting Kenny and Emile.

When they regained their focus, they started down the hallway after David, Kenny leading. Kenny shouted "Halt," whereupon their subject whirled and fired two deafening .357 magnum rounds from a large revolver, both hitting Kenny, who went down, gravely wounded. Emile returned fire unsuccessfully while using his finger to plug up a badly bleeding bullet hole in Kenny's side. When he ran out of ammo, Emile seized his partner's unfired revolver and continued firing at the shooter. The gunman ducked into a stairwell, then reappeared, firing yet another round into Kenny. Emile fired back, missing again, and then the gunman took off up the stairs.

Kenny Mahon had been hit in the left hip, the left knee, and once in the chest. Emile dragged him outside, intending to get to the street and nearer to the ambulance that was surely on its way. He got as far as the courtyard when he began taking fire from the roof. Emile shielded Kenny's body with his own and returned fire in the direction of the muzzle flashes. He continued to keep his finger in Kenny's most severely bleeding wound.

Kenny would be rushed to Lincoln Hospital, where died on the operating table.

Meanwhile, Kenny's wife, Linda, was awoken by Detective Frank Macchio, who'd been dispatched to the Mahon home in College Point, Queens, to get her to the hospital as quickly as possible. Across the city, cops would know what had happened before Mrs. Mahon even got into Detective Macchio's department vehicle. They were all instructed to maintain radio silence regarding Kenny's shooting, lest Linda Mahon hear what happened through the radio chatter.

For hours after Kenny died, a small army of cops searched the building and immediate neighborhood for the shooter, witnesses, or clues. Most of the cops had Vasquez's picture and showed it to anyone who would stay still long enough to look at it. There was much confusion over whether the shooter, who'd identified himself as David, was actually Daniel Vasquez, lying about his real identity. Vasquez was, after all, wanted in connection with a rape/robbery.

Several hours after the gunman had shot Kenny, most of the officers were relieved from the scene and told to go home. Three cops from the 40th Precinct were assigned to remain (the shooting occurred in the 40th, one block outside the boundary of the Four-One). One of those cops, Kevin Henry, went to the roof; the other two, to the courtyard. A fresh set of officers would be assigned to continue the search at sunup.

At approximately 5 AM (after the JFK search came up empty for Vasquez), Henry heard a sound behind him on the dark roof. He turned to see a Hispanic man. After challenging the man with his gun drawn, the man shouted, "Don't shoot!" Henry ordered him to freeze and shoved him to the ground. Next to the prone man the officer saw a large gun—a .357 revolver, apparently dropped by the suspect, the same caliber that had killed Kenny.

Henry called for assistance, and the two cops in the courtyard came running, arriving in less than a minute. As Henry moved in to cuff his prisoner, the man lashed out and elbowed Officer Henry in the ribs. That's all the three cops had to see; they were sure they had the thug who murdered Kenny, and now the asshole couldn't resist hurting another cop. They beat the suspect, subsequently identified as David Navedo, bloody, pulverizing his face so badly that Emile DeFoe, the only witness to the shooting, couldn't identify him. It mattered little. It was Navedo, not Vasquez, who had killed Kenny; he was in possession of the murder weapon, had recently fired a gun (ascertained through a paraffin test of his hands), and was hiding at the scene of the crime. It was thought that he had waited a few hours for things to calm down and was going to make his escape across the rooftops when Officer Henry spotted him. Navedo had a record of five arrests for burglary, larceny, and other offenses, but this would be the crime to end it all.

He confessed, pleading guilty to manslaughter (he claimed he didn't know the two Anti-Crime officers were cops and thought they were going to rob him), and was sentenced to twenty years to life in prison. He had copped to a lesser charge, but he would never see the light of day. David Navedo died in prison in 2003 of natural causes after being repeatedly turned down for parole.

Kenny Mahon's funeral was held at Saint Gabriel's Roman Catholic Church in Jackson Heights, Queens, on December 31, 1974. It was a raw, bitterly cold day, but that didn't stop thousands of police officers, some from departments across the United States, from attending.

The church itself could only hold a few hundred people, so only family members, the usual assemblage of politicians, high-ranking brass, and pretty much every cop assigned to the Four-One was permitted inside. Cops from neighboring Bronx commands patrolled our precinct that day. The rest of the attendees stood in quiet formations outside the church, silent as the ghosts in the nearby cemetery.

There is a protocol for funerals of police officers who die in the line of duty. Every officer, including detectives, those assigned to plainclothes units, and Anti-Crime, wears dress uniform. The ceremony includes a group of bagpipers playing a funeral dirge. Pallbearers from the NYPD Ceremonial Unit usually escort the body at funerals for cops who die in the line of duty as well as those who've retired. There was a special honor guard, composed of Four-One cops in full dress uniforms on the steps of the church, the last tribute to a fallen member of their command as the coffin entered and left the church.

The service was a blur; I don't recall much, and I suspect many others who worked the Four-One had the same experience. We were all still in shock. What I do remember was the coffin, since I was unable to comprehend that Kenny was in it. He was so full of life—how could he be dead?

Everyone was crying, some uncontrollably. Emile DeFoe was a wreck. Not only was he Kenny's partner that fateful night, but he and Kenny were best friends. They were always at each other's homes helping with projects, watching sports, sharing the camaraderie that only men who risk their lives for each other on a daily basis can understand. They loved to go fishing together, but after Kenny's death Emile never fished again. Emile was also going to college on his off-duty time. He quit school.

Both Kenny and Emile received the Medal of Honor, Kenny posthumously, for their actions on December 28, 1974. Emile's conduct was exemplary; he was a true hero by anyone's definition of the word, but we all thought that Emile would never fully understand why he'd been decorated with the NYPD's highest award for an incident in which his best friend had died.

Emile DeFoe was never the same. He received counseling, a lot of it, but the guilt persisted. He retired on a disability pension while still a young man. I hope, these many years later, that he has found some amount of peace. He'll never forget Kenny Mahon; anyone who knew Kenny will never forget him.

I've kept the Mass card from Kenny's funeral, which has his picture on it, on my desk for forty-two years. Kenny's death was a blow from which I'm still recovering.

6

'd been a sworn officer with the New York City Police Department for five years. During that time I'd achieved an impressive record of approximately one thousand arrests, not counting assists. I had taken many guns off the street, prevented an untold quantity of drugs from reaching customers, and placed numerous felons in alternative housing courtesy of the prison system. To put the number of arrests into perspective, I'd say that the average cop with my time on the job had around fifty arrests—very active cops perhaps up to two hundred. No one I know of has ever amassed arrest numbers that approach mine during five years on the job. At twenty-six, I'd also garnered over a hundred departmental medals (I would finish my career with 220 medals and 35 awards from civilian organizations).

I loved what I was doing. Every day I went to work amazed that I was actually getting paid for something I would do pro bono if the city suddenly went belly-up financially (an event that came close to reality several times during the 1970s).

The 41st Precinct's Anti-Crime Unit was my home. I loved doing my part, the cops, camaraderie, and the excitement. I would have gladly stayed there for my entire career, but I also coveted the gold shield of a detective, a lofty goal, but one that I thought I deserved. Still, no promotion was forthcoming.

I was told countless times how valuable I was to the unit, and that got me thinking that perhaps I was too valuable and that my lack of movement might have been a selfish tactic of the area commanders. The thought wasn't crazy, even if it was paranoid. Not only were street thugs out to get cops, but the NYPD bosses weren't above sacrificing a cop or two when some political problem needed a remedied scapegoat. Or, as one cop I know so eloquently puts it, "It doesn't mean you're paranoid if someone *really is* out to get you."

I'd never been political, never sucked up to bosses for favors. I just did my job, whatever was asked of me. If I were in the military, I would have been deemed a good soldier. So it came as a bit of a surprise—just as my hopes were growing dim—when I was told I was being promoted to detective, third grade, not for my arrest record but for the fifteen bribery arrests I'd made since I'd been in the Four-One.

The NYPD's Integrity Review Board was established to reward police officers for their honesty, and there was no better way to gauge that than by a police officer's history of bribery arrests. Fifteen arrests for bribery is indeed a big number, but when you take into consideration the thousands of potential bribe situations I'd been in (every time I made an arrest), the number of bribe offers seems reasonable.

Most bribery collars are pretty similar: I'd arrest someone, and then the prisoner would offer a sum of money, drugs, some kind of stolen swag, sex—you name it—to be cut loose. After the initial proposition, I'd get wired for sound by the Internal Affairs Division and then have the prisoner repeat the offer for posterity. As soon as he did, the charge of bribery of a police officer (a felony) would be added to whatever he was initially charged with. The size and nature of the bribe were irrelevant. I'd been offered anywhere from ten dollars to several thousand dollars to look the other way.

The Integrity Review Board was looking for a poster boy to counteract the bad press the department received during the recent Knapp Commission hearings on police corruption, which had painted police work with a pretty broad brush of systemic corruption in certain units. To my knowledge no cop had ever amassed fifteen bribery arrests, so I became a promising candidate for swaying the public's opinion that all cops were crooked.

I was told that my promotion was imminent and was asked if I would like to remain in the Four-One Anti-Crime Unit as a detective. I was thrilled with the offer, even if I didn't quite believe it. It came as little surprise to me that when I was promoted in a very public ceremony, which was covered by the media, it was announced that I wasn't going to stay in the Four-One Anti-Crime Unit. The NYPD is famous for asking cops being promoted where they wanted to be assigned and then sending them in the opposite direction. My new home was to be the 34th Precinct Detective Unit in Washington Heights. I was being transferred to *Manhattan*? This wasn't good.

The 34th was a very high-crime command, not unlike the Four-One—which was a good thing. But being in Manhattan was going to screw up my system of getting in and out of court rapidly, a system that I'd honed over the years in the Bronx. Most people knew me in the Bronx's criminal justice system, especially the court personnel who worked with me to grease the wheels of justice and get me out of court in as little as an hour.

Manhattan Criminal Court was as far away as one could get

from the 34th. They were located at opposite ends of the island with a nightmare of traffic between. A two-or-three-day wait to see an assistant district attorney and a judge in Manhattan Criminal Court was not uncommon, especially on weekends. Cops would actually bring lawn chairs to court with them and recline while waiting to get through the system. I envisioned my arrest numbers rapidly diminishing; every day spent staring off into space or sprawled on a lawn chair waiting in court would be time away from the street.

I called people I thought could help me get back to the Bronx. No good. A source in the Personnel Unit told me the only way to get back to the Bronx was to get a "mutual transfer." This meant I'd have to find a detective in the Bronx who for some unfathomable reason would rather work in the 34th in Manhattan and trade places with me: a body for a body. Plus the bosses of both respective squads would have to sign off on the transfer.

I set a plan in motion. I spent my first two tours in my new assignment designing and printing flyers requesting a "mutual," then visited every detective squad in the Bronx and posted them. Day number 3 found me in the police academy attending the first day of the five-day Criminal Investigation Course (CIC), which all new detectives are required to take and pass—a sort of Detective 101 to acquaint the newly minted sleuth with a different skill set.

While I was in the CIC the miracle happened: a detective from the 52nd Precinct Detective Unit agreed to go to the 34th, and both squad commanders signed off on the transfers. I was back in the Bronx.

The 52nd Precinct covers the northern portion of the Bronx and was considered a medium-crime precinct. I was born and raised in the Fordham section of the Five-Two and knew better; crime was everywhere in New York City in the 1970s. You just had to know where to look.

It had been a neighborhood of Irish, Italians, and Jews when I was a kid; it was now slowly changing to an area of immigrant Albanians, Hispanics, and blacks. As the older generations died off, their children were choosing to seek opportunities elsewhere. As with any recently arrived ethnic group from a foreign country, the Albanians tended to keep close and retain the customs of the old country. Many of the males sought employment in the upkeep of residential and commercial buildings as superintendents, janitors, and porters. The women mostly stayed home and raised the kids. A hardworking lot, the supers and janitors of yesterday became the landlords of tomorrow. Arthur Avenue, known as the Little Italy of the Bronx, would, by the early 1990s, be inhabited mostly by Albanians. When the Italians began to depart, the Albanians bought and continued to operate most of the Italian restaurants in the area.

Albanian gangs began to proliferate. Like the Italians, they were highly structured and exclusionary crime families (outsiders need not apply). Disputes were settled with guns—many Albanian men in the area carried them and weren't afraid to use them. It was about this time that I arrived on the scene and made it my mission to take as many guns off the street as I could. As eager as I was to begin my mission, I first had to ease myself into my new home: the 52nd Precinct detective squad.

I was well known in the Bronx, but I didn't want it to appear that I was going to be a lone wolf who didn't listen to and respect authority. My dream was reality: I was an NYPD detective and was very proud, not only for what I'd accomplished but because I was now part of the best group of detectives in the world. However, with this promotion came some trepidation. I began experiencing separation anxiety after leaving the Four-One, which had become so much a part of who I was. I believe that Fort Apache was unique among the seventy-seven precincts that make up the NYPD. I'm certain I learned the job faster in the Four-One than I could've anywhere else. The Four-One was intense, not only for the mind-blowing crime and poverty problems but also for the bond created among the police officers assigned there. Cops depended on each other no matter where they worked, but it was always my suspicion that the Four-One created the strongest friendships in the city, not unlike infantry soldiers who face death on a daily basis and form connections that last long after their service is completed.

In many respects the Five-Two was the opposite of the Four-One. Because poverty and crime weren't rampant in the command, I was going to have to acquire a new set of social skills when it came to dealing with the residents.

Then there's the question of my own competency. I was a very good street cop, but I was not yet familiar with being a detective. My area of expertise was making arrests on the street, usually for crimes I'd observed in progress. Did I have that ability to reason, deduct, and carry a case through from beginning to end? I'd find out soon enough.

I knew a cop who got promoted to sergeant, and he told me that walking into his new command as a boss was one of the scariest days of his life. This, coming from a Vietnam combat veteran and excellent street cop.

"One day you're a grunt, working the street with your buddies," he's said, "and the next day you're a boss supervising a group of cops just like those you were working with the day before. All sorts of doubts fly through your head: Am I good enough to do this job? Can I come up with answers when asked for advice? Will I be a good sergeant, respected by my peers and subordinates?"

I had similar feelings, the fear of the unknown.

There were nineteen detectives assigned to the squad, and we were under the command of Sergeant Stephen Cantor. Cantor was a former cop with the Tactical Patrol Force who had the reputation of being a fair-but-no-nonsense boss. He was in his early thirties, young for a sergeant at the time, and very young to be a squad commander. Most of his subordinate detectives were older, but they all respected him.

All he knew about me was that I was twenty-six years old, had made over a thousand quality arrests, and earned numerous departmental medals. He was going to control me from the start and make me realize who was boss. I had no objection to what I knew was coming; I'd do my job just as I'd always done, prove myself, and then earn the freedom to really make a difference.

The mere fact that I was transferred to the North Bronx slowed down my high-voltage adrenaline flow to a trickle. There was going to be an adjustment period, but the blood and death that naturally came with policing the streets of the Bronx in the '70s would resurface, and shortly my adrenaline stream would catch up. I caught my first case a few days after my arrival.

"Ralph," Cantor said, "take care of this." He handed me a complaint report.

I read the details, in disbelief that handling it required a detective. Two women in their eighties had gotten into a verbal dispute that had changed course when one of them hit the other one with a hairbrush. The victim wanted the hairbrush assailant locked up for assault. A detective surely wasn't necessary for this bullshit—patrol could've handled it! But I was being tested to see how I followed orders and to get a clear understanding of who the boss was.

Sergeant Cantor probably expected me to complain, but I didn't. I smiled, nodded, and said, "I'll get right on it." His expression was one of thinly veiled amazement. I was going to play the game until the good sergeant realized that I could be a team player. Once he understood that, I'd go about doing what I wanted to do (with the improved results).

I went with Detective Cortes, who was instructed by Sergeant Cantor to let me conduct the interview with the two women in order to see how I'd handle myself. Both ladies were still highly agitated, and the victim had a black eye. She insisted that I lock up her attacker for "ferocious assault." Normally, when an assault victim with an obvious injury wants an arrest made, a police officer has to comply. In this case, I was damned if I was going to march someone's grandmother into the Five-Two in handcuffs so every cop in the house could have a good laugh.

I used my discretion and deemed Hairbrush Lady a person in need of psychological evaluation. Instead of a paddy wagon to the slammer, she got a ride in an ambulance to the nearest hospital psych ward. They'd probably look her over, then send her home. No jail, perp and victim happy, and me not looking like a clown.

Back at the command, Sergeant Cantor called me into his office as soon as he saw me. "Where's your collar, Detective?"

"The perp was obviously in need of psychological help, Sarge," I said with a straight face. "She was transported by ambulance to Jacobi Hospital." I smiled. "Anything else?"

Cantor stared at me for a moment, and I could see the look of grudging admiration on his face. I'd outsmarted him, and he approved of it. Detectives think on their feet, make decisions based on expediency and what's good for the squad. I was beginning to like Sergeant Cantor; his main concern was what was good for the job. I knew I hadn't seen the end of the ball breaking, but he knew I could take it. I'd have to pay my dues before I became a trusted member of the team. I didn't know what was coming next, but I didn't have long to wait to find out.

Cantor gave me my first homicide case a few days later. The deceased was a squirrel, the victim of an alleged gunshot.

I played it with a straight face. "I hope he didn't suffer, Sarge."

"Well, Detective, that's what you're going to find out. A parking lot's being constructed at Fordham University. One of the crew found the critter DOA, looked like it'd been shot. The squirrel could've been a person . . . someone taking target practice . . . or we could be dealing with a serial killer, just warming up, so to speak. Get right on it, okay?"

"Absolutely."

A fucking squirrel murder. I couldn't believe it, but you would never suspect it to look at me. The boss wanted an investigation, and he was going to get one.

A backhoe operator pointed the "victim" out to me. "I almost ran over the fucking thing . . . just lying there in the dirt. Looks like someone shot it . . . right?"

"Yes, sir, that's what it looks like." The animal was almost blown in half, the bullet long gone. "Did you hear a shot?"

He looked at me quizzically. "This is the Bronx. I always hear shots. I sort of tune them out, but this was close to home." He pointed at the dead squirrel. "Coulda been me laying there."

"Yes, sir." I was taking this seriously—as seriously as Joe Friday from *Dragnet.* I wish I'd had the presence of mind to bring chalk with me so I could outline the body. "I'll take care of this from here, sir. Squirrel lives matter. Thank you for reporting it."

I scooped up the remains with a piece of cardboard, put it in the trunk, and headed for my next stop.

Sergeant Cantor dropped his pen. "You did what?"

I was back at the house reporting in. "I took the body to the ASPCA"—that is, the American Society for the Prevention of Cruelty to Animals—"to get it autopsied . . . had to ascertain the cause of death, you know. Tried the morgue first, but they told me they only autopsy humans. ASPCA said definitely a gunshot, but the round passed through the beast and wasn't recovered."

I was going all the way on this one. If I did everything I was supposed to do, I'd inundate Cantor with paperwork for a week.

Sergeant Cantor knew when he was beat. He leaned back in his chair and sighed. "Whaddaya say we call this a suicide and close it out?"

"You know, Sarge, you may have something there. Some people in the neighborhood said the squirrel looked depressed."

Sergeant Cantor never busted my chops again, and we became very good friends, a friendship that endures to this day. He even saved my life once—but more on that later. I'd found a home in the Five-Two detective squad and would become even more productive than I'd been in the Four-One. Another plus was that I lived only a quarter mile beyond the precinct border, just over the city line in Yonkers.

Roger Cortes became my first partner. He was a second-grade detective and about seventeen years my senior, the old man of the squad at age forty-two. For over twenty years he'd been an active cop—you don't get promoted to second grade by being a slacker— but after his transfer to the Five-Two squad he slowed down. Roger was far from lazy, but he was more centered on his family. He had seven kids, five of them daughters, and he lived to be with them. He'd also had a run-in with a boss a few years back and had gotten himself transferred to a detective squad on Staten Island for nine months. For a cop who lived upstate, getting assigned to Staten Island was the equivalent of an FBI agent being banished to North Dakota.

I liked Roger from the outset, but he needed a fire lit under him to rekindle the days when he was my age and eager to do the job. It didn't take long. We started cracking down on the area's problem of illegal gun possession, stopping cars and relying on our gut feelings. Back then, making an arrest relying on street smarts with nothing more than a "feeling" that an individual was up to no good was considered good police work. While there was a chance that some of the arrests would be tossed due to lack of reasonable cause, we still accomplished our goals: guns off the street and the people who carried them in the crosshairs of the NYPD for future reference.

In today's climate such arrests are forbidden and could result in departmental charges. The closest the job came to resembling the old days was the stop-and-frisk program under Police Commissioner Ray Kelly, the present PC's predecessor. Thousands of illegal guns were seized yearly and violent crime took a nosedive. This policy of stopping and frisking random individuals was deemed unacceptable with the new administration because cops were mostly stopping African American and Hispanic young men, and the strategy was halted. While it was true that the NYPD was targeting those ethnic groups, it is also true that the strategy was effective. Now imagine how effective it would be if police were getting guns out of the hands of white perps too! Time will tell if additional guns on the street will have a significant lasting effect on crime statistics, but since Kelly's policy was halted, homicide rates and other violent crime has risen.

Back to the '70s. I'd take the collars, and Roger got the assist. He was happy with the arrangement because he didn't have to spend time in court and could go home to his family.

We'd taken so many guns off the street that someone had circulated my picture among the community so the people with guns could spot me coming. My photo was also circulated at JFK Airport. Given that so many of our arrests were Albanian, newcomers arriving from the old country would immediately be made aware that I was to be avoided at all costs.

For Roger it was like getting back on a bike after many years; he was into the swing of things and felt like a productive detective again. He thanked me numerous times for rejuvenating his outlook. He even mentioned setting me up with one of his daughters, thinking I'd make a fine son-in-law. After a year working together, however, and by then having insight into my social life, he would tell me, "If you ever go near any of my daughters, I'll shoot you myself."

Most detective units in the NYPD have an unofficial suit-and-tie dress code. Detectives have a tendency for trying to outdress each other, making the detectives of the NYPD arguably the best-dressed sleuths in the world.

I was never comfortable in business attire, preferring jeans, boots, and leather jackets. I'd occasionally throw on a sport jacket if I had to testify in court, but mostly every day was casual Friday to me. I wanted to fit in with the street people, who could spot a detective a mile away. The bosses never said anything about the way I dressed because I was bringing in numerous quality arrests, thereby substantially increasing the clearance rate for reported crime—numbers of arrests for reported crimes—in the Five-Two.

I had made 125 arrests after my first year in the Five-Two detective squad, compared to 38 arrests for the *entire* squad of nineteen detectives. Don't get me wrong: the squad had a fine bunch of detectives. I was just a bit more compulsive when it came to the hunt. Plus, the other guys spent lots of time in court, while I had my trusty system. I could have shown up in a football helmet and a dress and the bosses wouldn't have made a peep.

Another benefit of the job was free transportation. I was using department cars and would take them home to Yonkers with me every night. Many cops would do this with unmarked autos, but I'd also take marked radio cars back and forth to work, parking them out of sight in my building's underground garage. For gas I was using the NYPD pumps allocated for department autos. When the oil embargo hit the country and there were gas lines snaking around city blocks, I never had to wait to fuel up.

While not exactly permissible, the bosses looked the other way because of my arrest numbers. I was making the Five-Two look good.

The more time I spent in the Five-Two, the more I localized my efforts on problem areas that remained for the most part unaddressed. The Purple Gang was a perfect example.

The Purple Gang migrated from Detroit in the 1930s after the end of Prohibition. They originally specialized in running booze, but after alcohol became legal again, these hardened gangsters branched out to the usual array of enterprises favored by organized crime, changing their specialty to murder for hire.

The current crop of gang members mostly constituted the male children of members who were either dead or in prison. Truly a family business. Mostly in their twenties and thirties, these junior gangsters were looking to make names for themselves, just like their dear old dads and grandpas before them. Their goal was to either get inducted into one of the five New York Mafia families or gain enough street cred to make crime a lucrative career on their own.

While I couldn't make it my life's mission to follow these punks around 24/7, I could make their lives miserable. Gang members had a hangout on Jerome Avenue, just south of Bedford Park Boulevard. They'd park as close to the location as they could, which meant on sidewalks, in crosswalks, in front of fire hydrants. To launch my operation I did what no other detective in the NYPD ever did: I began carrying summons books. Detectives don't write summonses—that's something left to the uniform contingent. I broke new ground by writing tickets for every Purple Gang parking violation I saw (to the tune of over twenty-five summonses a day). In addition to costing the gang members thousands of dollars in fines a week, I was gathering information to pass on to the NYPD's Intelligence Division, compiling massive lists of license plate numbers and physical descriptions of regulars and associates. I also pulled them over in their cars and made numerous gun collars, recording intel along the way. I did this for years and was recognized by the Intelligence Division for supplying valuable intelligence.

On January 20, 2016, Police Commissioner William Bratton published an op-ed for the New York *Daily News* in which he wrote: "We want to develop well-rounded, highly skilled police officers, not arrest machines." Under Bratton, stop-and-frisk confrontations were down 96 percent from their level in 2011, when he took command. Bratton was training his cops to sharpen their "problem-solving skills," which means fewer arrests.

While my time on the job occurred in another era, it's difficult to see how implementing reactive responses will lower crime rates in the long run. Homicides were up 6 percent in 2014 (the last fully reported year), and, at the time of writing, the first month of 2016 has already seen a jump.

My consistent harassment of the Purple Gang by peppering them with summonses and making arrests proved highly successful in intelligence gathering and showing career criminals that they were constantly being monitored. In today's NYPD the term for what I was doing is profiling—but I did not profile based on race. I profiled based on behavior because that's what good cops do. The Purple Gang members were mainly ethnic Italians, yes, but if their gang members were known to carry guns, they got searched. If gang members violated the law, even if they were minor violations such as traffic infractions, they got slammed with tickets.

Quality-of-life violations such as illegally parking, harassing motorists by cleaning windshields with squeegees, jaywalking, and congregating (especially by youths) were targeted under previous administrations and proved effective in preventing more serious incidents. In my opinion, losing these tools and doing away with the stop-and-frisk technique will eventually affect the law-abiding public. But cops like to look good—and, in one form or another, that's nothing new.

A detective's job is to investigate crime, but that didn't stop me from making pickup arrests; I'd still go out on the street and bust people with guns and drugs. When there was a sudden spike in robberies, I was asked if I wanted to work with the Robbery Investigation Program (RIP), a unit of Five-Two cops from Anti-Crime whose sole job was to work out of uniform and make robbery arrests, I jumped at the chance. I'd be the only detective in the ranks. We'd be working the street, and I wouldn't stand out from the other men in my street garb. Who says you can't go home again?

I began riding with Timothy Kennedy, a highly decorated RIP cop, originally from the 45th Precinct, with four years on the job. We were similar in many ways: both bodybuilders and looking to clear the streets of people who shouldn't be there. He also looked vaguely familiar when we were introduced upon my arrival in RIP. It turned out that we did know each other. A few years back, I was within the confines of the 45th Precinct when I got involved in an off-duty arrest. I apprehended a man with a gun, one of two armed men, while the other had gotten away. After cuffing my prisoner, I called 911 to provide transportation to the Four-Five station house and who do you think responded? Tim Kennedy. He took my prisoner, and I was supposed to follow in my private car.

As Kennedy approached the command with the prisoner, he got a call from the dispatcher to respond to assist an off-duty officer with an arrest. When he heard my name, he told Central that he'd already responded to that job and was already transporting my prisoner.

"There's another arrest—same cop . . . Friedman," the dispatcher replied.

On the way I had spotted the second perp from the first arrest and disarmed and cuffed him. When Kennedy came back to pick me up, he said he wanted to be just like me when he grew up. I was pleased to be working with him in RIP. While not a full-time assignment, it was satisfying to see instances of robbery plummet in the Five-Two.

We began piling up arrests for street robberies. Victims would ride along with us in some instances, and we'd cruise the neighborhood looking for the person who stuck them up. Invariably we'd find them hanging around a street corner bragging to their friends about their score. They never even had the presence of mind to change clothes to muddy the identification.

I always had a good relationship with the uniformed cops. Patrol is the lifeblood of the job, and without the rank-and-file cops, the city would dissolve into anarchy. Some elitist detectives talked down to cops, but I found this attitude to be wrong on many levels. For one thing, there were only nineteen detectives in the Five-Two, but there were a couple hundred cops, who were a wealth of intelligence. It made sense to pick their brains and treat them with much-deserved respect. And eventually one of them brought me one of the most rewarding cases I ever handled as a detective.

Patrol cops came to me often with information on criminal activity, garnered though their day-to-day interaction with the community.

I was in the squad room processing a collar and catching up on paperwork when a young cop, whose name I've since forgotten, showed me a complaint report he'd just prepared.

"Check this out, Ralph," he said. "Thought you might be interested."

It began as a standard report of domestic abuse. A woman

named Jacqueline Karlan called 911 to report that her former husband, Eli Morton Gorin, had shoved her against her apartment door and threatened to "break every bone in her body." The two responding officers took the report and advised her to call if he showed up at the apartment again. As the officers were leaving, Ms. Karlan said, "Oh, by the way, my ex is wanted by the FBI."

This detail was added to the victim's complaint report. The cop who brought me the case figured if he didn't notify someone before he handed in the report, it would be mixed in with the copious other paperwork being processed that day and the most important part would be overlooked.

This was hot! I thanked the cop and began doing some preliminary research.

Eli Gorin had been an upstanding citizen who'd never been arrested for anything until he lost his job and seemed to go off the deep end. He held up a bank with a gun, was caught, and was sentenced to thirty years in prison, where he was deemed criminally insane. In the mix of it all, his wife divorced him.

After seven years, he escaped from Lompac Penitentiary in California and made his way back to New York, vowing to anyone who'd listen that he was never going back to jail. He'd been a fugitive for about eighteen months when we got our lead, during which time he had been tried in absentia for the escape, convicted, and sentenced to an additional six years. But someone would have to catch him first, and so far the FBI had no results.

I requested his photos and got all his family information.

I went to see Sergeant Cantor and laid out the facts. He understood how big this case was. After contemplating a few seconds, he said, "You think you can get this guy, Ralph?" I knew what was running through his mind: the FBI hadn't had any luck, so why should I?

"No doubt, boss." The FBI didn't know the Bronx like Roger Cortes and I did.

"Okay," Cantor said. "You and Roger are off the chart. Get him."

An NYPD detective handles many cases at once. A load of fifteen cases at a time, or more, isn't rare, unlike detectives in the movies, who handle one case and devote all their time to it. The FBI works that way, but not us. The Gorin case, however, would be our sole focus, and we would work off the traditional work schedule.

As I turned to leave, Cantor said, "And I want to be involved. When you're getting close, let me know."

"Sure, boss," I said. In the time to follow, Cantor would work the case with us most of the time while still managing to run the squad in his usual efficient manner. Steve Cantor was sharp: after a distinguished career with the NYPD, he became an attorney and is still practicing law today.

The next day, Roger and I interviewed Gorin's mother at her home in the 44th Precinct. She told us that her son had stopped by but hadn't been there lately.

Later that day, Special Agent Corliss of the FBI called me and advised that Gorin was to be considered armed and extremely dangerous.

We interviewed Gorin's ex-wife, Jacqueline Karlan, who was scared shitless and was very helpful. "I want that bastard caught before he kills me," she said.

She told us that Gorin had come to New York and was due to attend their son's bar mitzvah. The ceremony was to be conducted at a local shul, followed by a reception at a catering hall. Roger and I both attended, accompanied by Sergeant Cantor. We tried to blend in by wearing yarmulkes, but we stuck out like three sore thumbs, this despite the fact that I am Jewish. I did concede to wearing a business suit, which probably made me look even more awkward. Sergeant Cantor pretended he didn't know me.

"I like the suit," he told me. "You look like a hit man for the local Hadassah."

Gorin didn't show at the shul; we hoped he'd make it to the reception. We split up at the catering hall, mingling and eating some food that was so good it made me regret I wasn't more in touch with my Jewish roots. Roger, completely forgetting he was undercover in a yarmulke, exclaimed with surprise, "This shit's great!"

Gorin didn't show at the reception either. It was time to do the tedious part of detective work.

We interviewed the ex-wife again to see if she remembered anything else she could tell us. No luck. While the ex-wife was obviously on our side, we couldn't be sure about Mom, figuring her natural instinct was likely to be to protect her boy. But when we talked to the super of her building, he told us basically the same thing she had: Gorin had stopped by to see his mother but not lately.

Roger and I canvassed the neighbors next. Most were helpful to the extent that people who don't really want to get involved with the police are helpful. Most denied ever seeing Gorin. Those who admitted observing him around the building were vague about time and frequency.

We sat on the building for a few days, hoping to get lucky. No Gorin. We returned in the early evening to talk to those neighbors we'd missed during the day. We got lucky, at least as far as finding a woman who said she'd seen Gorin and was willing to go the extra mile to help us. She was single, around thirty-five, and seemed to have taken a fancy to Roger, which was probably why she agreed to keep an eye out for Gorin and write down his license plate number should she see him again. We also alerted the 44th Precinct detective squad to be on the lookout for Gorin. I had twenty pictures of the fugitive printed and had them delivered to the 44th detectives and the A/C unit.

Three days later, bingo!

The female neighbor had seen Gorin briefly the day before getting into a car in front of the building, and she wrote down the plate number. I ran the plate, which gave us the address of an apartment building on Shore Road in Long Beach, which was right over the New York City line in Nassau County, a continuation of Rockaway Beach in Queens. The car wasn't in Gorin's name, and since it hadn't been reported stolen, we figured he had borrowed it. The owner's name was Audrey Glazer, whom we located by tracking down the real estate agent who managed the apartment building. She lived in apartment 5L. She was clean—no criminal record.

Roger and I staked out Audrey Glazer's building the next day for a few hours. We didn't see Gorin, so we decided to talk to the super, who was cooperative. He told us that Glazer had been a tenant for a while, kept to herself, and worked during the day, though he didn't know where or at what. He also recognized a picture of our fugitive, saying that he had begun living with Glazer recently. He added, "Oh, yeah! He's got a dog as big as a fucking Buick. I think it's a German shepherd . . . really big. Don't look too friendly neither. He don't go nowhere without that dog."

Great.

"Either of them home?" Roger asked.

The super shook his head. "After she leaves for work in the morning, he goes out . . . with the dog. Sometimes he's gone for days."

"You know the dog's name?" I asked. We might have to calm the animal after we collared Gorin.

"Don't know, man. Never asked him. He don't seem like the friendly type. You know what I mean?"

"Listen," I said to the super, after giving a conspiratorial nod to Roger, "we need to get into Glazer's apartment. Urgent police business." We had no right to enter the apartment without a warrant, but I doubted the super knew that. He didn't and handed over a master key without comment.

I opened the door to apartment 5L after knocking and receiving no answer. I made enough noise, assuming that if the dog decided to sleep in that day, he'd hear me. No dog. Audrey Glazer's one-bedroom apartment overlooked the ocean. It was neat and clean. We went into the bedroom and found men's clothing in the closet. Under the bed was an unlocked attaché case that contained two revolvers, a few boxes of ammunition, and a ski mask. After a brief discussion, Roger and I decided to leave everything in place. We would have had a tough time explaining how we came into possession of the case and its contents, since we had no right to be in the apartment. After making sure we left everything exactly as we found it, we drove back to the Bronx to confer with Sergeant Cantor.

Sergeant Cantor, Roger, and I held the strategy meeting in Cantor's office.

We were dealing with a state-certified crazy escaped felon who had sworn never to go back to prison or be taken alive. A lot of cons say that, but in this case we felt Gorin meant it. At six foot four, 250 pounds, and likely armed, he could be major trouble if we didn't take him right. If we fucked this up, we might have a major war on our hands.

We agreed that busting into the Shore Road apartment would be a mistake, primarily because we didn't know if Gorin was going to be there and because cornering him didn't seem like the smart thing to do. Audrey Glazer might wind up a hostage; even if Gorin was alone, the situation might degenerate into a nasty standoff. It was April, and the weather was getting balmy after a long, hard winter, so we decided to keep canvassing the area. We figured we'd get him walking his dog.

"I'll notify the Nassau County cops and the Long Beach PD," Roger said. It was protocol to advise the local police if you were going to be working on their turf. Both departments had jurisdiction in Long Beach.

"Not a good idea," Sergeant Cantor said. "They'll need to know why we're going to be there, and we'll be obligated to tell them. You think they'll leave us alone?"

Cantor was right. The local cops would not only want to be there when the arrest went down, they might want to take command and lock up Gorin themselves. After all the work we'd done, that wasn't going to happen. Additionally, given Gorin's status as an insane fugitive with no desire to go back to the can *and* given that he was likely heavily armed, the cops would want an overwhelming presence in the area. Gorin might be a lunatic, but he wasn't stupid. He'd be on heightened alert and would spot a large number of police officers no matter how dressed down they were. Like cops, criminals, particularly those who are looking at numerous years behind bars, have sharp observational skills.

"Let's sit on the Shore Road address tomorrow, see what happens," Cantor said. He got the necessary permissions from Bronx Area to venture into Nassau County, even though we'd been working there for a while already. We needed the job's okay to cover ourselves when we nabbed Gorin.

Spring doesn't last long in New York. It always seems to come and go in less than a week, and then the humidity wraps us up until September.

The three of us were sitting up the block from the Shore Road building waiting for Gorin to materialize. About 150 feet to our right, the boardwalk was crowded with people taking advantage of the weather, strolling casually and gazing at the ocean. We heard the surf and could smell the salt water. If we weren't there on intensified alert, I would've called it a relaxing day.

Then I spotted Gorin, and I didn't have to be a supersleuth to see him: he towered over most of the pedestrians on the boardwalk. I elbowed Sergeant Cantor, who was seated next to me in the front seat, then pointed to the boardwalk. Cortes perked up.

Gorin was wearing a black leather jacket and jeans. His right hand was in his jacket pocket and his left held a leash, at the end of which was a very big German shepherd. The super wasn't kidding about this dog's size. We watched Gorin for a while. He seemed to have no interest in the dog; all his attention was focused on the people around him. We knew this wasn't a good sign. We all thought the same thing: he's holding a gun in the jacket pocket.

Cantor said, "We should spread out, approach him from three different sides. Ready?"

Roger and I said "yep" simultaneously, and the three of us exited the car.

There had to be over a hundred people in Gorin's immediate vicinity, which was good for our concealment but bad if things went poorly. If he indeed had a gun, there could be collateral damage.

We split up: Sergeant Cantor increased his pace to get in front of the target, Roger went left, and I went right. As we walked, we kept narrowing the distance between us and Gorin. When we were within about five feet of him, we drew our guns and Cantor whirled to face him. As soon as Cantor did that, we all yelled, "Police, don't move!"

I caught Gorin's right hand in a death grip before he could take anything out of his pocket and stuck my revolver in his ear. Roger did the same to his other ear. Cantor jammed his gun in Gorin's mouth, and the three of us forced him to the ground with enough power to take down a water buffalo. And the Hound from Hell? He sat down and watched his master being arrested. Maybe my tattoos scared him

Pedestrians started screaming and running away from us.

Gorin was grunting from the knockdown but otherwise remained silent. I reached into his pocket and extracted a fully loaded .357 revolver containing hollow-point ammunition. He was also carrying loose rounds for reloading. The three of us hustled the fugitive into our car and drove back to the apartment, where we recovered the attaché case, ski mask, and guns still inside. The pooch went docilely with other cops to a local pound. Then we headed back to the Five-Two. Gorin took his right to remain silent seriously; he didn't utter a word.

Now that we had Gorin, we had to figure out what to do with him. He was eventually handed over to the FBI under the For Other Agency (FOA) policy, meaning the arresting officer simply handed over the prisoner to another agency for prosecution.

Special Agent Corliss of the FBI, astonished that we nabbed Gorin, was very generous with his praise. The special agent in charge of the New York office would send a congratulatory letter to the police commissioner, which would go into our personnel files (commendatory letters are a big plus when being considered for promotion).

Alcohol, Tobacco, and Firearms (ATF) had me fly down to Virginia to testify against the person, a cabdriver, who bought the guns for Gorin—known as a straw buyer. A straw buyer is someone who legally purchases firearms for the purposes of reselling them to an unauthorized buyer. The ATF agents treated me well, putting me up at the best hotel in the area and taking me to some great restaurants.

In the end, Gorin went back to prison, which he said he would never do. He had the time he still owed for the bank robbery, plus the extra six years for the escape and a few more for the guns. The woman who harbored him while he was on the run, Audrey Glazer, wasn't prosecuted because it couldn't be proven that she knew Gorin was a wanted fugitive. Gorin will be well into his seventies by the time he gets out of prison, if he gets out.

7

I keep odd hours. Since I worked mostly nights for so many years, my internal clock is the opposite of most people's. Even when I was off duty, I generally adhered to my owlish schedule; it was the way my body worked and the way it continues to work thirty-four years after leaving the NYPD.

I'm up all night and sleep during the day. Six or seven AM is normally the time I go to bed. I get up in the middle of the afternoon. On the rare occasion when I can't put off doing something until the evening and I'm forced to conform to most everyone else's schedule, I do so grudgingly.

Detectives don't spend much time on patrol; we're too busy juggling a multitude of cases or catching up on the river of paperwork that never dries up. Occasionally, however, there were lulls in the craziness, and Roger and I would tour the command in an unmarked car. We'd be looking for crime, but sometimes we also backed up the uniforms on dangerous jobs.

Patrol was a nice respite and brought me back to the not-too-distant past. One of the nice things about going on patrol as a detective was that when you got tired of it, you just went back to the squad room. As a uniform in a sector, your ass was attached to that seat for the entire tour.

While on patrol one day, Roger and I heard a radio run to be on the lookout for a car seen leaving the scene of a burglary. A license plate number was supplied. The crime had been committed in another section of the Bronx, but, as luck would have it, the wanted vehicle was right in front of us with what appeared to be two individuals in the front seat.

We gave the car a short blast of the siren, the universal signal to pull over, and the driver complied. Neither of us could get a clear view of the driver and passenger from inside our vehicle, but we were about to get the surprise of our lives.

Roger and I exited our auto and assumed our tactical positions, with me (being the operator of our vehicle) approaching the driver's side of the car, while Roger (the recorder) positioned himself to the right rear of the suspect car, observing the occupants and ready to take action should I be fired upon.

The driver lowered his window as I came abreast of him. I was about to ask for his license and registration when he shouted, "Get him!" and a very large Doberman pinscher, which I had mistaken as a passenger, leapt over the driver and through the window as I instinctively took several steps backward. The dog, snarling and baring its teeth, bounced off the pavement and jumped for my throat.

I fired my gun, which I had unholstered as I approached the suspect vehicle, striking the beast in midair. The dog dropped face-first to the ground, a bullet in his front right leg.

We subdued the driver, and then I turned my attention back to the dog, who had regained his footing and was limping away. He made it a few feet, curled up, got back on the ground, and began whimpering.

It's no secret that I love dogs, and I felt bad that I had to shoot this one. The dog had obeyed his master's command and went into protection mode when ordered to do so. For me, that is totally different from shooting someone who fully intends to hurt you.

NYPD policy dictates that police officers are required to call Animal Control in any situation when an animal needs help. I knew if I did that, the dog would stand a good chance of being put down. I wasn't about to let that happen.

With Roger tending to the prisoner, I slowly approached the Doberman, who was in pain and crying. Cornered, defenseless animals are apt to attack, and this dog was looking me right in the eye when I shot him. I was hoping he had a short memory.

I knelt down and pet him. He wasn't hostile, which surprised the hell out of me. I decided to take a chance; I gently put my arm under him and very slowly lifted him to my chest. This dog, which a minute ago was ready to rip my throat out, now trusted me completely and let me carry him to my car. I placed him carefully in the backseat, which he took up door to door. This was one big pooch.

I called out to Roger, "I'm taking this dog to the animal hospital in Manhattan."

"Do what you gotta do, man. I'm good here." I heard sirens approaching in the distance. Our prisoner was in no shape to resist or try to escape, so I felt okay about leaving.

One of the best animal hospitals in the country is located on the Upper East Side, and I made it there in record time, lights and siren all the way. The dog let me carry him into the hospital, and I stayed with him until he went into surgery.

The Doberman survived. His master went to prison.

My love of dogs was well known in the squad, so when I had to shoot yet another dog during a major drug bust, the detectives in the squad decided to have some fun with me. Cops can have a wicked sense of humor.

The dog in question was a German shepherd that was guarding a drug den. Roger and I broke through the door with the aid of a battering ram, backed up by the Bronx Narcotics Unit. Armed with shotguns, Roger and I were the first cops inside the apartment. The dog took one look at Roger, saw lunch, and charged him from across the room. Roger was caught unawares and was slow to take out the dog. I pushed him aside and unloaded a round into the animal's chest. The dog was dead before he hit the floor. Once again, I felt bad about the shooting—really bad!—but I rationalized my actions by telling myself I'd ridded the world of a canine career criminal. You tell yourself what you have to.

As with any shooting, a huge amount of paperwork is required. When I'd returned to the squad room the next day, there was an official NYPD communication on my desk (known as a U.F. 49). This is basically a boss's report (in this case from a borough deputy inspector) assessing the shooting and determining whether it was justified. As I read it, my jaw dropped.

The dog I'd killed was a certified Seeing Eye dog with many years of service and had also received numerous awards and citations for visiting terminally sick kids in hospitals around the city. I'd killed the Mother Teresa of the dog world!

I felt terrible. I was flabbergasted. The other detectives in the squad room were no help. They broke my balls unmercifully.

"Hey, Ralph, how many kids are gonna cry themselves to sleep tonight because you whacked friggin' Rin Tin Tin?"

"Yo, Friedman, I just heard some blind guy walked off a subway platform and got splattered by the downtown IRT because you clipped his Seeing Eye dog."

And on it went for about an hour until I finally caught on. Someone had forged the U.F. 49 and invented the deputy inspector.

Cop humor . . .

I was becoming accustomed to doing investigations, a skill that took time to acquire. I couldn't pin down the average length of time I spent on a case with any accuracy, but I'd say about a week, from assignment to completion, is a good guess. Catching Eli Gorin, the escaped convict, had taken a bit longer, though time passed quickly on cases of that size. What I wasn't prepared for, however, was one that was coming my way: it involved a phony home-repair scam, a slick con man, and the makings of a cat-and-mouse game that would ensnare me for over a year and a half trying to arrest the guy.

On a brisk April day, an elderly woman arrived at the squad office claiming to be the victim of a confidence scam. She told me that she'd given one Anthony Alessandro of the Alessandro Home Improvement Company in Pelham, New York, two thousand dollars to make repairs on her home on Decatur Avenue.

"The son of a bitch took my money and never did a goddamn thing," the complainant told me. She went on to say that she'd phoned Alessandro numerous times and had never received a return call.

The case seemed easy enough: visit the contractor's place of business and lock him up. I told her I'd be in touch, scooped up Roger, and went to Alessandro's listed business address, 175 Wolfs Lane in Pelham, located just over the Bronx border in Westchester County.

The Alessandro Home Improvement Company, no longer at that address, was replaced by a real estate business. We interviewed the agent, as well as the proprietors of several businesses in the area, but no one knew the current whereabouts of Anthony Alessandro. According to most of the people we spoke to, Alessandro had moved from the Wolfs Lane address "months ago."

Okay, so perhaps Alessandro's arrest wasn't going to be a slam dunk. Roger and I figured this to be a mere speed bump on the Highway of Justice. Everybody leaves some sort of a trail.

We began with the obvious: phone directories. There were many Alessandros, but no Anthony.

A visit to the Pelham Police Department was next on our agenda. The cops in that department told us that Alessandro hadn't been on their radar. Running down the subject's business phone number proved useless too. It had been disconnected months ago. The Bureau of Criminal Identification (BCI) also had nothing. BCI did give us a guy with the same last name who had been collared a few times, but we checked him out, and he wasn't our Anthony, nor did he know the subject. We reviewed records at various post offices for change-of-address forms, also with no results. The Postal Frauds Bureau had never heard of the guy. We managed to find the name of a former business partner of Alessandro's, but only an old address. Checking with the current residents of that address proved that the partner was just as much of a ghost. We were beginning to think that our boy had beaten customers out of money before; he had all the traits of a serial con man who was trying to get lost and stay that way.

After a few more weeks of old-fashioned ground pounding, we came up with a handful of witnesses who had known Alessandro at one time but had lost track of him. It was these folks who suggested various addresses in Yonkers, Bronxville, New Rochelle, and the Bronx where he was known to hang out. We visited all of these locations and staked them out. Again, nothing. Alessandro was beginning to piss us off. It took us less time to catch Eli Gorin and he was an escaped bank robber wanted by the FBI.

A few days later, Roger took an anonymous call from a man who claimed to know where Alessandro might be found. We went to the two Yonkers addresses that Mr. X provided, and we left with nothing more than information from a neighbor at one of the addresses indicating that the perp "may" have frequented the building in the past.

We contacted Con Edison. Even deadbeats need electricity, right? A spokesperson for Con Ed said that Mr. Alessandro had stiffed the utility by not paying his bills and that they'd like to find him too. I told him to get in line.

I was learning the tedious side of detective work.

We called the original complainant and asked her if she had any additional paperwork from the Alessandro Home Improvement Company. The only thing she had shown us the first time around was a receipt for the money she paid Alessandro. We got lucky; she found promotional material with numerous phone numbers on it, plus the company's business license number.

Roger went to the Consumer Complaint Bureau (CCB) in Lower Manhattan and pulled a picture of Alessandro from a license application. Our complainant verified that the picture was of the elusive subject. Additional paperwork from CCB provided an address in New Rochelle in Westchester County. We were able to locate the subject's ex-wife through the New Rochelle Police Department. The former Mrs. Alessandro was very cooperative, stating that her ex wore a well-styled wig and liked expensive, flashy clothes. She thought he currently drove a Lincoln Continental. And, no, she hadn't seen him in at least six months. We checked with DMV and came up blank; no Lincoln or any other vehicle was registered to the subject.

At about this time Anthony Alessandro began phoning me at the Five-Two squad room.

"Hello, this Detective Friedman?" a male voice asked.

"It is," I said.

"This is Tony Alessandro. I understand you're looking for me."

I feigned indifference, although a month of looking for the guy made me want to reach through the phone line and grab him by the throat. "Yeah, I am. Just need some questions answered. Want to come in?"

"I dunno. Maybe."

Now I'm thinking perhaps someone's playing a joke and whoever's on the other end must be a cop trying to bust my chops. Cops are known to do that—weird senses of humor. "What's your business license number?" I asked. He rattled it off.

This guy was no idiot; he knew exactly why I wanted to see him. "You wanna come on in, Mr. Alessandro? We have a complainant says you owe her some money."

"Yeah, you know, I was thinking of turning myself in. I'm tired of hiding out, you know?"

Was it going to be this easy? "You can stop in now if you like . . . clear this matter up."

"How's tomorrow?"

We agreed to a time the next day. He never showed. The caller wasn't a cop playing a joke, but he was definitely having some fun.

The bullshit phone calls continued for over a year, several times a month. Every time Alessandro called, he'd say he was going to turn himself in, which he never did. He just enjoyed trying to get on my nerves. He was succeeding.

We continued handling the myriad of other cases NYPD detectives handle concurrently, but getting the slippery Anthony Alessandro was always on our minds.

In the meantime, Roger and I continued the hunt, visiting fashionable men's shops on White Plains Road and other areas throughout the Bronx. When that didn't work, we began visiting shops that sold and maintained men's wigs and toupees. Success! Finally.

Alessandro went to a few of the hair places we visited, but he had more of a personal connection at one called Fine Hair in New Rochelle. Not only was he a customer, but he conned an employee's sister out of six thousand dollars. Like many victims of con artists who are embarrassed, she never reported the theft to the police.

The fine people at Fine Hair directed us to Ranger Building Products, the owner of which had lent Alessandro fifty thousand dollars that was never repaid. We felt we were getting closer to the elusive Mr. Alessandro, but closer didn't put him in handcuffs. We needed to get lucky.

And lucky we got. I received another anonymous phone call and was given a phone number where the mysterious Mr. Alessandro could be reached. I ran the number, which came back to a Mrs. Ann Alessandro, located on Parsons Boulevard in Queens.

Roger called and left a message on the answering machine for Anthony to call back. Roger didn't ID himself as a cop and left a number that no one but him would answer. The plan was to have me listen in when Alessandro called back because, after dozens of phone calls with him over the last eighteen months, I heard the sleazebag's voice in my sleep. Apparently, Alessandro saw through that bit of bullshit because Roger got a call from an attorney instead.

After introducing himself as Mr. D'Angelo, and without pre-amble, the lawyer got right to it. "Listen, I represent Anthony Ales-sandro. He wants to give himself up."

Where have I heard this bullshit before? But it turned out that the lawyer was on the level; Alessandro did indeed want to surrender this time. I guess he really was tired of running and realized I wasn't going to give up.

Elapsed time from the beginning of the case until the prisoner in cuffs: nineteen months.

On January 15, 1977, and accompanied by his lawyer, Anthony Alessandro surrendered to Roger and me. Roger took the collar. Alessandro was arraigned on numerous larceny charges and released on bail. Nearly a year later, he made a deal, pleaded guilty to all charges, and was sentenced to multiple years in prison.

Why recount this rather mundane, if not frustrating, case at all? To make the point that this case could have been handled efficiently today with the assistance of technology.

Detectives in the modern NYPD have computer databases at their disposal—programs that make tracking down people much more manageable. The National Crime Information Center (NCIC), a database that catalogs criminality, is used by nearly every law enforcement agency in the United States. Enter a name and any other information available on an individual and the database provides up-to-date police records almost instantaneously. Cops can not only retrieve criminal convictions but also access arrests. Only law enforcement personnel can obtain arrest information, which often leads to the offender's current location. In addition, Social Security numbers are stored, as is credit information, DMV files, and other identifiers that can make life much easier when looking for an offender. There are also numerous other databases, listing every incarcerated prisoner in the country, offering instant identification of fingerprints, facial recognition software, and other useful tools. What's more, practically everyone has a cell phone. As long as the phone is powered up, it can be located using GPS. It all sounds common today, but in my time it was science fiction.

What took many months of footwork to find Anthony Alessandro could have been accomplished in one or two days today. Of course, access to so much data can be abused. This is why cops use proprietary passwords when retrieving information from computer-based sources. Cops are thus accountable for what they download, and police officers accessing law enforcement databases are held accountable for their searches; all must be police-related.

Another case that required determined detective work and a team effort involved a homicide in which a victim was stabbed to death on the street. Solving the crime looked pretty simple at first—we had several witnesses—but a remarkable twist in the case hampered arresting the killer for several weeks.

The victim, a male Hispanic in his late twenties, was found faceup on a residential street, cause of death being twelve stab wounds to his torso and neck.

Neither Roger nor I caught the case. That honor went to Detective Anthony Mosca, a very good investigator with many years in the Detective Bureau. Although there were people on the street who had seen the deceased getting stabbed, the few who would cooperate with us couldn't even give an accurate description of the killer. After two weeks of dead ends and seemingly foggy-brained eyewitnesses, Mosca was understandably frustrated. I decided to help.

While Mosca was a good detective and excelled in clearing cases, he dressed like a detective and therefore didn't have the cooperation of street people. This is where I came in. I had many informants on the street that trusted me—dressing like them gave me that extra edge that cops who looked like cops didn't have.

I should mention that while this was Mosca's case, it wasn't unusual for any detective in the squad to pitch in to help another detective. It's like this throughout the job; cops help other cops. If an arrest is made with the assistance of another detective, the original detective who caught the case gets the arrest and credit, while any detective who helps gets credit with an assist. The object is to get the job done.

The victim wasn't an upstanding citizen, in fact far from it. He had a long arrest record, mostly for burglaries, but contrary to what some people might think of cops, we viewed every victim as deserving of justice. Everyone's life matters.

I started talking to my informants on the street. Some informants are more valuable than others, their track record of supplying accurate information being the gauge of how good they are. But when you talk to a few and most come up with the same information, you listen with more interest.

What I was hearing put an entirely new spin on the case. Apparently the "victim" had been caught in the act of raping a woman while burglarizing the apartment she shared with her husband. The husband, so the story went, had come home early and found the soon-to-be deceased beating and raping his wife. Justifiably incensed and fearing for his wife's life, he grabbed the closest weapon available, a four-inch steak knife. He and his wife's assailant went toe to toe in the bedroom, the rapist getting stabbed a few times, none of the injuries serious. The bad guy broke loose and ran from the apartment with the husband in pursuit. After a four-block chase, the husband overtook the rapist, stabbing him repeatedly until he collapsed and died. Then the husband fled the scene.

It didn't take long for the word to spread. The neighborhood rallied around the husband, and everyone clammed up. This was the Bronx, where crime was reaching epic proportions and good people were fed up. What the husband had done, in most people's estimation, was a brand of street justice, New York style: one less rapist on the street to victimize another woman. If the neighborhood residents could've thrown hubby a block party, they would've done so. The next best thing was to forget they saw the husband kill his wife's rapist. Those who spoke to Detective Mosca had given him false descriptions to throw him off the scent.

Our job was complicated. First, we had to verify the story as it was told to us: that this crime was an offshoot of a man protecting his wife. Whether it was a justifiable homicide was up to the courts.

Roger and I began systematically canvassing the neighborhood, backtracking from the crime scene and creating a timeline as it related to where the witnesses were when they either saw the chase or the homicide. The witness who first saw the pursuit could reasonably narrow down the location of the apartment building from which the pursued and the pursuer emerged.

Detective work doesn't take a Sherlock Holmes to navigate your way to a crime's solution. Logic remains paramount: What's the best way to find the bad guy? If you're lucky, a fingerprint match or other forensic wizardry does the work for you. We didn't have any of that, and extracting DNA wouldn't be on the horizon for another fifteen years. The only things that would solve this case were logic and footwork.

After a few days, Roger and I figured we knew the general area where the chase had begun. It boiled down to a two-square-block radius. We could either begin knocking on doors, and there were hundreds, or talk to more confidential sources, this time in the target zone.

We got steered to a building where the killer was supposed to live, a five-story structure, five apartments to a floor. The best way to find out what goes on in a building is to talk to the superintendent: they know everything.

The super was a little Hispanic guy who initially said he didn't know anything. *Stabbing? What stabbing?* The first thing you pick up as a cop is being aware when someone is lying to you. As time goes on, your bullshit meter is honed to a degree that you can tell a liar before they open their mouths. A good detective can recognize a liar as soon as they walk into a room. Some might think that's a great skill, but analyzing people before they say anything can take a toll on the wonderful mysteries of life, especially when your skill activates when you're not working.

The super was a good guy, a hardworking man who wanted to do the right thing. It was our job to convince him that identifying the man who was protecting his wife (using the word "killer" in this setting wouldn't be helpful) wasn't ratting; it was setting the story straight. If the street gossip was accurate, Roger told him, we could help, maybe even see that no charges were brought. Yes, a bit of a stretch, but we wanted to clear the case, and, truth be told, if the street talk we heard was true, we'd make sure the DA knew we believed it. Eventually the super identified our killer, a man in his midthirties who lived on the third floor with his wife.

We identified ourselves through a locked door. When he opened it, we saw defeat and sorrow written all over him. He gave us his name, and we shook his hand. Just by his demeanor we knew this guy wasn't a killer as we knew them; he was a man who acted on instinct to save his wife.

We talked for an hour. He admitted what he did and explained that he originally jumped the bad guy to help his wife. When the perp broke loose and ran, he said he "lost it" and took off after him onto the street, catching up after a short chase. A ferocious struggle ensued while the husband tried to hold the rapist until the police arrived, during which he ended up knifing him to death.

This was an ordinary guy who worked hard, had never so much as gotten a parking ticket, and loved his wife. For him to get caught up in what he'd experienced was a nightmare.

"You mean you ran after him to apprehend him, right?" Roger said. "He fought and was getting the better of you; you had no other choice. You could've been killed."

Our suspect looked at Roger then to me. I just sat there stone-faced.

"Yeah," he said, "I guess."

"Don't guess," I said. "Neither of us is telling you what to say. We're here for the truth."

He agreed that was what happened.

"Why'd you take off? Looks like you were justified with what you did. It was self-defense," I said.

He shrugged. "I was scared. I don't know the law. I was scared no one would believe me."

"We believe you," Roger said, "and so does everyone in the neighborhood. Where's your wife?"

We waited until she got home from work, at which point she recounted the break-in and rape. She said her husband saved her life.

Putting the cuffs on this guy broke my heart, but it was procedure.

Roger and I spoke up for the prisoner with the DA and anyone else who would listen. He and his wife had been through hell.

A grand jury is convened whenever someone takes a life to determine if a crime had been committed or the killing was a justifiable homicide. Generally, the public is unaware that all killings are homicides, but not all homicides are crimes. In this case the grand jury voted no true bill, which means no crime had been committed. Our killer, whom I haven't identified on purpose, went back home to his wife.

I did not often get emotional satisfaction from police work. The job really has little to do with directly helping people the way you see cops in Norman Rockwell paintings. Certainly, we help greatly by taking criminals who prey on innocent people off the street, but those who get into police work because they think they'll always leave a smile on the faces of citizens are dreaming. If we're not locking someone up, we're giving them bad news, issuing them summonses, or otherwise ruining their day. In fact, I find that those who enter the job because they think they'll be successful at solving society's problems don't make the most productive police officers. The reason is that when they find out ridding the city of crime is an unrealistic goal and that many of the citizens we protect have no use for cops, they become bitter and cynical, which can result in a cop who decides that doing his job isn't worth the trouble.

But just when you think the world is full of assholes and criminals, along comes a guy like the one who protected his wife. It makes you realize that what it means to help people can come in many forms.

8

When I came to the Five-Two I'd expected a calmer, more civilized precinct than what I'd been used to in the Four-One. At first glance, the crime statistics indicated I was correct, but as time went on things began to heat up.

I'd caught a simple domestic case in which a woman's ex-boyfriend had returned to the apartment they shared and stolen every piece of furniture. How did she know it was her ex?

"Because the son of a bitch told me!" she exclaimed. "He called me up and said, 'I got your furniture, bitch.' "

She described her ex as fifty-five years old (eighteen years her senior) and connected to the Mafia. In the years I'd been on the job, I'd come to realize that most people lie to some extent when dealing with cops. Complainants tend to exaggerate what happened to them and make the person who did them wrong out to be a modern-day Jack the Ripper. I doubted her description of her ex as a mob guy, but I ran his name and, sure enough, he had ties to a Genovese crew, the street soldiers of the parent Genovese crime family of the America Mafia.

"And he's violent too. Both him and his psycho son . . . cut from the same cloth," she added.

I got the ex's address and drove there with another detective, Timmy, upon leaving the complainant. The son met us at the door. He greeted us with a sneer that dripped insolence.

"What the fuck do you want?"

He was in his late twenties and dressed like a mobster wannabe: jeans, black silk shirt, highly polished black boots. He also had a swept-back ninety-mile-an-hour haircut, enough gold chains to weigh down a dead body, and the obligatory pinky ring.

I told him we were looking for his father.

"He ain't here."

His old man might've been in the apartment, but we didn't have a warrant and the crime he was accused of wasn't at the level of forced entry. First of all, we still needed to verify the complainant's story and make sure she wasn't lying to get back at her ex. Furthermore, we figured we might be able to settle the dispute without making an arrest just by talking to the former boyfriend. Breaking down a door would be counterproductive.

"He's accused of stealing some furniture from his ex-girlfriend," I said.

This kicked off a string of curses describing the girlfriend. We waited patiently until he was through.

"He's gonna get arrested if he can't clear this up," I told the son in a calm voice.

"Oh, yeah, motherfucker?" sonny boy said. "You come for my father, you're gonna have to deal with me. You ain't taking my dad."

I sighed. I didn't like the way this was going. The accusation was relatively minor, and I wanted to end this with as little turmoil as possible.

His parting words before slamming the door were, "Well, fuck you. You come for my dad and there's gonna be a problem."

Truer words were never spoken.

Over the next few days we found that the ex-boyfriend did in fact take the furniture and that he had it stored in a warehouse. So we returned to his apartment. I figured we might have a problem with the son, so we got our nightsticks and slipped them up the sleeves of our jackets.

His son opened the door again, but I spoke before he had a chance to tell us how much of a badass he was.

"Okay," I said, "we're here to lock up your father." Then I gave him my standard warning: "We can do this the easy way or the hard way. Your choice."

He didn't budge from the doorway. At this point the father appeared behind his son, and we told him we were there to arrest him.

The son swung a punch that narrowly missed my head. Timmy and I drew our nightsticks and stepped away from him, thinking he'd cool down upon seeing the menacing batons. Apparently he didn't give a damn, though, because he came at us again, fists flying.

We overtook the jerk in less than a minute, but he kept on fighting, or at least trying to. His father was screaming curses at us but kept his reaction to the verbal kind. His son may have been stupid enough to try to protect his dad, but evidently that street didn't run both ways. What he did do, however, was clutch his chest, grunt, keel over, and collapse to the floor. We were too busy with his son to pay too much attention to what we thought was a desperate attempt at distraction. His son kept on swinging, and we did likewise. When he finally surrendered, I cuffed him while Timmy attended to the father, who was rolling around on the floor. *Great actor,* I thought; *looks like he was having a real heart attack.* Turns out he was.

Timmy used the apartment phone to call an ambulance. "And put a rush on it," he said.

The ambulance came and scooped up the dad (who had remarkably regained the strength to yell nasty things about our mothers), and we took the son to the squad room to start the arrest paperwork. He looked as if he'd taken a direct hit with an artillery round and was very docile and quiet now. But he still had the swagger of a wise guy as we led him to our car for the ride to the squad.

Sergeant Cantor heard voices from his office and came to see what was up. He took one look at our prisoner, pointed to the floor, and said, "Jesus fucking Christ. What the fuck is that?"

I heard Timmy exclaim, "Holy shit!" I whirled and saw my partner staring wide-eyed at the floor. One of our prisoner's fingers had fallen off. Off! As in totally detached from his hand.

This was perplexing. The only thing I could figure was that while he was throwing punches back at the apartment, one or more of our nightstick blows must have connected with the finger joint and broken it. The finger was probably hanging by a thread of skin, and came off when we got to the squad room. I looked at our prisoner. He was sitting in a chair like nothing had happened. He'd never said a word. Talk about stoic.

The handful of detectives present were staring alternately at our arrestee and his finger, probably trying to imagine what could possibly have happened. We were doing the same. A simple complaint had morphed into a heart attack victim and a son who, if looking for a Mafia nickname, could now and forever be known as "Fingers."

Sergeant Cantor took command of the situation, pointed to the finger, and said, "Get that fucking thing out of here." Then he turned and went back into his office.

Father and son wound up in adjoining beds in Jacobi Hospital's emergency room. Dad would make it, the heart attack being of the mild variety. Doctors attempted to reattach the son's finger. I don't know if the surgery took, but the next day he was in court looking like the Invisible Man. He had bandages everywhere.

The presiding judge looked over the top of his reading glasses at my prisoner.

"What happened to the prisoner, Detective?"

"He resisted arrest, Your Honor." I responded in a clear and authoritative voice.

"Hmm," the judge said. Then to the prisoner he said, "Were you mistreated in any way, sir?"

The mummy couldn't speak very well, but he managed to squeak out a "no."

I had to give the guy credit; he was a true believer in the mob dictum *omertà*. He had made the choice to take on two cops and paid the price, sucked it up, and moved on. Maybe he'd make a good gangster after all.

During my entire career I never raised my hands to a civilian unless they chose to fight. Some, like our budding mobster, knew the consequences of attacking a police officer and lived with them. Others didn't and availed themselves of the Civilian Complaint Review Board to file charges. I've had 205 civilian complaints lodged against me. And I don't mean for it to sound like I'm boasting about that number; all were thoroughly investigated and found to be unsubstantiated.

Some people take issue with the use of a nightstick, or with two cops restraining one prisoner. Police officers have one rule, which is to survive. Once the person either gives up or is subdued, the fight is over.

———

On February 16, 1977, I got involved in an incident that was to have a profound—though delayed—effect on my life.

I was near the end of my tour and Roger had left for the day. I was processing an arrest in the squad room when one of my confidential informants came in and told me about a guy he knew who was trying to sell a gun.

"What kind of gun?" I asked.

"I dunno . . . just a gun," my informant said. "He's looking for a buyer all over the neighborhood."

I went to see Sergeant Cantor and related the CI's story.

"He reliable?" Cantor asked.

"Gold."

We made a plan: Cantor would work with me in Roger's absence. We would send the CI to buy the gun, and after the sale we'd lock up the salesman. Of course we'd go through the pretense of arresting my informant so he wouldn't get made as a snitch. He'd be released later.

The deal would go down on the roof of the seller's building. The CI had some cash, so we didn't have to go through the mountain of paperwork to request buy money from the department. Talk about everything falling into place. Cantor and I would be a few buildings away observing the sale. Then, after the CI had possession of the gun, we'd run across the adjoining rooftops and take our prize.

"Sound good?" I asked Sergeant Cantor.

He shrugged. "Yeah, sure."

We positioned ourselves on a rooftop five buildings away and waited for my CI to make an appearance with the perp and the gun. We didn't have to wait long. But when he showed up we realized that there would have to be a slight change in plans; he had a partner. There were *two* bad guys. Cantor and I felt we could still handle the operation. After all, we had the advantage of surprise. However, the surprise, we'd soon find out, would be our own. We couldn't hear what was being said, but we saw money changing hands and saw the gun, which turned out to be a rifle, a 30-30 Winchester from the looks of it—a very powerful weapon.

Instead of a simple business deal, the guy with the rifle, a Hispanic man about thirty years old, walked to the edge of the roof with the weapon. He took aim at the street below and started pumping out shots. Apparently, he was showing our CI that the gun worked.

What we had was something bigger than the gun sale: a crime in progress. And one that had to be stopped before the nut killed someone. It was cold, so there weren't too many people on the street. But there were enough to litter the area with at least a dozen bodies.

Cantor and I ran for the shooter, identifying ourselves as police officers along the way. As soon as the rifleman heard "Police!" he whirled, aiming right at us.

I fired as I ran, emptying my revolver. I hit him in the thigh and hip. He went down. My informant hit the deck. Cantor was right beside me but held his fire. The second man took off and ducked out of view behind a kiosk.

"I'll go after the other guy!" I yelled to Cantor, who went to the downed perp and kicked the rifle out of his reach. I drew my backup revolver and slowly made my way to the kiosk. These extensions are on almost every tenement roof and usually include dumbwaiters, elevator shafts, airshafts, and pipes. They were about seven feet high, big enough to provide cover and concealment. I had no sight of the second man; I assumed he was behind the kiosk, but I couldn't be certain.

As I rounded the corner, he materialized with a raised knife, already practically on top of me. In that fraction of a second I knew he had me; I was going to get stabbed . . . bad.

I heard a shot. Cantor had appeared out of nowhere and shot the attacker from behind, who promptly went down. Sergeant Cantor had saved my life, no doubt about it.

The perp was on his back and didn't appear to be conscious. As I neared him to take the knife from his hand, he quickly sprang to his feet with the blade extended in my direction in an overhand grip. I instinctively fired a round, hitting him in the stomach, killing him instantly.

The rifleman was in custody, and our CI was ceremonially handcuffed for effect. The man with the knife I'd killed was identified as Manny Rivas, a small-time hoodlum with several arrests to his credit. Back then I thought the encounter with Rivas was the closest I'd ever come to dying—until the day I actually die, of course. But I would be proved wrong.

This was the fourth person I'd killed. I was cleared by a grand jury of any wrongdoing in his death; my actions were deemed justifiable, and life went on for me. It was, however, a surreal incident and made me understand that regardless of my excellent training and physical shape, a random series of events could cause my death. I had made over two thousand arrests, assisted in four thousand more, and was injured numerous times. The number of times I'd been shot were few compared with the number of arrest encounters and other violent incidents I'd experienced. I deplore having to shoot someone and did everything humanly possible to avoid the use of deadly physical force. I've lost count of how many armed adversaries I've disarmed without firing a shot—the preferred way—but when it came down to my life or someone else's, it was going to be his.

A *New York Post* article titled "New NYPD: Think Twice and Be Nice," dated February 22, 2016, reports that Commissioner Bratton asked his commanders to read several news articles before attending a seminar on the NYPD's new guidelines for the use of force. One of the guidelines calls for police officers to "weigh whether the general public would view their use of force as proportional to the threat posed" before taking action.

I find this suggestion unrealistic. When threatened with the use of deadly force against them, cops have little time to consider how their actions look. The New York State Penal law requires that a police officer's actions need only be *reasonable* when using physical force. And a fraction of a second is sometimes all the time that's available to determine that. What could anyone—civilian or otherwise—possibly *think* was the last thought that would occur to me as Manny Rivas moved to stab me in the head. The *Post* article further states that "when engaging a person with an edged weapon, an officer should sometimes pull back to keep a safe distance."

Many studies have shown that knife attacks that occur within a distance of twenty-one feet or less are usually harmful if not fatal to police officers, who at that distance do not have time to draw weapons and successfully incapacitate attackers. Thirty percent of people attacked with knives are killed; knives don't have a line of fire like a bullet, don't run out of ammunition, and take little if any skill to use effectively. And an attacker with a knife gives little warning about his intentions. So how far are police officers to "pull back" before the officer, who is sworn to uphold the law, is in full retreat?

The helplessness I felt when Rivas had the drop on me was a sobering experience, one that I alone could do nothing to prevent. How, in pursuit of a perp who may or may not have been armed, could I have "pulled back"?

Sparing a life is always better. An incident where I could afford to chose life over death occurred on a chilly November day. I was on patrol in an unmarked car with Detective Joe Sahlstrom. We were about thirty minutes into the tour when a call came over the radio that a man was shot at 2400 Sedgwick Avenue. We were a few blocks away and told Central we'd respond. There was no description of the shooter, but that's not unusual. Whoever called 911 left a brief message and hung up when asked for his name.

We'd driven about a block and a half when I observed a male walking north on Bailey Avenue. There were other pedestrians on the street and nothing unusual about this one. Except for the blood on his coat.

Joe pulled up behind the guy, and we quietly exited our unmarked car, coming up behind the suspect with our guns drawn. When we were within fifteen feet of the suspect, Joe and I both hollered, "Police, don't move!"

The suspect whirled around, throwing back his knee-length coat, and leveling a sawed-off 12-gauge shotgun.

If there was ever justification to use deadly physical force, this situation was certainly it. There's no fiercer personal weapon that a shotgun, particularly one of the 12-gauge variety. Loaded with double-ought buckshot, one pull of the trigger would unleash anywhere from eight to twenty-seven steel ball-bearing-like pellets in our direction. We were close enough that he wouldn't even have to aim; one blast would take us both out, and it wouldn't be pretty.

We stood our ground for five of the longest seconds of my life before the gunman dropped his weapon. My finger had been pressing against my Colt's trigger. One more moment of hesitation on our suspect's part would've found him riddled with bullets.

When a police officer takes a human life, it's a measure of last resort that none of us welcomes. It's a matter of survival. I would spare many lives over the course of my career, including that of a robber who pulled a knife on me after I chased him down. He didn't want to take a life any more than I did.

These are just two of the hundreds of times I chose not to shoot.

We breathed a little easier when the man with the shotgun was handcuffed and in the backseat of our car, but just then a brown Volvo shot past us down Bailey Avenue. Since the Volvo was coming from the direction of the Sedgwick Avenue shooting, we figured there was a good probability that the Volvo was somehow involved.

Our minute's respite over, Joe and I jumped into our car and took off in pursuit of the Volvo, which was doing at least 75 miles per hour on side streets. It lost us quickly, so we proceeded to the Sedgwick Avenue scene.

With our prisoner secured in the car, Joe and I talked with units who had been at the shooting scene for a while. Turns out, the shooting emanated over a dispute between drug dealers. No surprise there. While we were talking to some cops, I noticed a blood trail leading to a building down the block. We followed it to an apartment, where we found a male shot up pretty badly, plus guns and 627 glassine envelopes of heroin.

The shooting victim and our prisoner would later accuse each other of attempted murder, saying they each shot back in self-defense. It was a typical excuse and one that we had heard so many times it would mean the prisons were full of innocent people if it were true. We would let the courts figure out who did what to whom. We never looked for the Volvo; by the time we took our prisoners and the evidence from the scene, the Volvo could've been miles away.

Other incidents were equally upsetting but not life-threatening. A 911 dispatcher received an anonymous call about a man with a gun at 2665 Grand Concourse, apartment 7F, a very familiar address. I'd grown up in that very apartment with my family. My father had died in that same apartment.

I was working in an unmarked car when the call came over the radio. Initially, and only for a brief moment, the address didn't register. Thousands of radio runs are broadcast daily and locations blur. And then, to my dread, the memory hit home.

I arrived at the building just behind the local sector, my heart beating just a bit quicker than normal. I'd been on many gun runs so that's not what had me worried; it was that whoever moved into my old apartment had possibly destroyed the sanctity of the place that held my fondest memories.

Crime was rampant in the old neighborhood now, the intimacy of the community a thing of the past. It pained me to see the region degenerate into a high-crime area. When I was boy, everyone felt safe.

The gun run turned out to be unfounded, as many such radio runs are. That in itself was comforting; however, knowing that the incident could have been real was disconcerting. Times change and neighborhoods change too, but trying to wrap my head around the possibility that a violent incident occurred in my childhood home was upsetting.

In order for our criminal justice system to operate efficiently, the innocent must be exonerated and the guilty punished without delay. But rarely do the wheels of justice keep up with the high volume of cases passing through it in a large city like New York. It's not unusual for the most serious crimes to meander in the pipeline for years before a case is adjudicated.

I can think of only a handful of exceptional cases in which justice moved as it should.

One of them begins in my customary position: in the squad room scaling a mountain of paperwork. In the office with me were Michael Fox, a detective, and Clement Krug, a police officer who was awaiting a promotion to third-grade detective. Sergeant Cantor had recently retired on a disability pension because of a job-related back injury. Replacing him was Sergeant Michael Harris, a good boss out of the Cantor mold and, like Cantor, in his midforties.

Two uniforms came in looking for me. I was the go-to detective in the squad when uniformed cops needed help or had an involved case that was growing into something larger. I always took the time to listen to what the sector guys had to say.

The cops brought a civilian in with them, a Hispanic man in his twenties who spoke no English.

"This guy's got a story, Ralph," one of the uniforms said. "Something about a homicide in Manhattan."

"Tell me more."

"The perp lives in the Four-Four. On Nelson Avenue," the cop replied.

He had my interest. I found a cop who spoke Spanish and had our newest informant relate his tale.

He said he had been at his girlfriend's apartment at 1114 Nelson Avenue the day before when her brother, Pablo Vega, came home. Pablo may have had a few cocktails in him and was talkative. What he talked about got the interest of our informant.

It seems Pablo had had a busy night. Before he went to his sister's apartment, he had been in Manhattan sticking up a guy on the subway platform at Sixth Avenue and Forty-Eighth Street.

I interrupted. "He had a gun, knife . . . what?"

"Nope," the interpreter got from the informant. Pablo stuck the victim up with a cigarette lighter.

I asked the informant to elaborate.

Apparently, Pablo doused the victim with an accelerant, probably lighter fluid, and threatened to "light him up" if he didn't hand over his money. The victim complied, but Pablo flicked his Bic anyway and the poor guy erupted in flames. Pablo thought this hilarious, watched the human torch burn for a few seconds, and then took off.

In twelve years on the job, I'd witnessed or heard about all kinds of depraved indifference to human life and other cruel things, but what I'd just learned surprised even me. While the informant sounded credible, I had to check to make certain the incident had in fact occurred.

The location of the crime was within the confines of the Midtown North Precinct. I called and spoke to Detective Hart, who confirmed the story. The victim had died.

"You know the guy who did it?" Hart asked.

"Maybe," I said, and related what I'd just been told. I told Hart we'd check out the informant's story and get back to him.

I sat outside the sister's apartment house with Sergeant Harris and the informant and waited for Pablo Vega, aka "Luchy," to show up. Detective Hart from Midtown North in Manhattan joined us later.

Patience is a trait you either need to have or acquire if you desire to be a successful detective. If you're not sitting at a location, you're wading through paperwork or spending hours in court waiting to testify. After several hours, our informant pointed to a guy walking down the block toward the apartment building.

He gestured wildly and spat forth a barrage of Spanish. Apparently it was our human flamethrower.

Vega was placed under arrest, offering no resistance. ADA Paula Van Mitten charged him with homicide and robbery. Total elapsed time from the murder to arrest: sixteen hours. So swift was justice in this case that at the time Vega had been arrested, the victim still hadn't been identified.

Our informant held up his end and testified in court, and Vega was convicted.

Sometimes the creaking wheels of justice are greased.

I've been training with weights most of my adult life, so working out at 2 AM to me is normal. It was May 4, 1981, during one of these workout sessions, radio blasting, that I received a phone call that gripped my heart with a fear I'd never experienced, not even when Kenny Mahon was killed.

My brother had been shot.

Stu was still a New York City transit cop. It was 1:30 AM and Stu and his partner, Thomas McGurl, had been knocking back a few in PC's, a club on Westchester Avenue in the Bronx. PC's was widely known as a cop bar but had oddly also attracted its share of street thugs, drug dealers, and other troublemakers. This eclectic crowd, surprisingly, is not rare for a cop bar. It's said that New York City is a melting pot, which is a truism that extends to gin mills too.

On this particular night, an altercation occurred just outside the bar between the doorman and a young white male who had been refused admittance because he lacked proper attire. This guy must have been wearing a jock strap and earmuffs or something similarly offensive, because PC's was no fashion mecca.

The argument had been loud enough to attract Stu and his partner's attention over the din of the music inside the club, and they went outside to investigate. They intervened, and the patron got in his car and left, pissed off. Stu and his partner decided to leave PC's at that time, a fateful choice. They got in Stu's car and began to depart the area.

Stu wasn't out of first gear when they encountered the guy they'd dealt with, who was driving the same street in the opposite direction. He slowed down, pulling alongside Stu. They were now driver to driver, less than a foot separating them.

In the blink of an eye, the driver pulled a gun, leveled it at Stu's head, and fired. My brother, who was sober and alert, saw the pistol in time to raise his left arm in a reflexive, defensive maneuver to protect his face. The round entered Stu's triceps muscle and lodged there. Stu veered off to the side of the road while the shooter made good his escape. The bullet was never removed for safety reasons, and since then it has inched incrementally into his chest, where it remains, thirty-six years later, still too dangerous to extract.

I got the phone call from a boss at the scene of the shooting.

"Your brother's been shot—hit in the arm, looks okay—get your ass down here to PC's ASAP."

My knees went weak, and my thoughts immediately brought me back to the night Kenny was killed. Both incidents were separated by only a few months, and I'd been doing the same thing, lifting weights. I just hoped it wouldn't end the same way. The sergeant who had called me made certain to emphasize that Stu had been hit in the arm, what would seem like a non-life-threatening wound. But after years of seeing gunshot victims, I knew even the most seemingly benign wound could take a fatal turn. Bullets can hit major arteries or there can be internal bleeding, not to mention that a bullet entering the body could bounce around and wind up anywhere. This is particularly prevalent with .22s, often considered an ineffective round, but one that travels at tremendous speed and can wreak havoc in the human body. I once saw a guy shot in the leg with a .22, creating what appeared to be a minor wound, only to have the bullet travel to the victim's heart and kill him. I had no idea what caliber bullet had been used on Stu. The upper Bronx was Purple Gang territory, and they favored .22s for their assassinations. Too many thoughts were racing through my brain; I had to get to the scene.

I repeated my movements on the night Kenny was shot: I grabbed both .38s and my shotgun and was out the door in less than a minute. The drive to the bar from Yonkers was a little less than the distance to the Four-One, so I was there in less time than it took me to get to Kenny. I was thankful for that: too much time in the car thinking wasn't productive, and the longer I was driving like a maniac, the more likely I'd wind up in a wreck.

My car, tires smoking, literally screeched to a halt in front of PC's, sliding within inches of a radio car. There were at least twenty marked and unmarked cars from the NYPD and Transit PD parked at odd angles blocking the street. There was a crowd of cops and civilians outside the club.

Talking to some cops at the scene, I was directed to the bouncer who had been in the argument with the person thought to be the shooter. I identified myself and got right to the point: "You know who shot my brother?" Bar bouncers are usually a wealth of information because they often see the same patrons night after night. While he might not know for sure who the shooter was, he might have an idea or be able to direct me to someone with more information.

The bouncer, a mountain of a guy, wouldn't make eye contact with me. I was certain whatever came out of his mouth was going to be a lie. He said, "No, man. Never saw the guy before. First time he's been here."

I punched the bouncer in the face, and he went down like a dropped anchor, having no time to react or show surprise. Within a nanosecond, bosses of all ranks were attempting to contain me. I was livid and tried to break loose and get back at the bouncer, who was now struggling to get to his feet.

Two sergeants dragged me away. "You gonna calm the fuck down?" one of them asked. A group of cops gathered around us, and the bosses looked nervous. While I wanted information about the shooter, fighting with bosses didn't seem productive. I regained my composure, but that didn't stop the several high-ranking supervisors at the scene from getting into a debate about whether I should get arrested for assault. The deliberation became moot because the bouncer didn't seem inclined to press charges. Guys like him were used to getting into brawls. It's part of the job description, and having me charged with hitting him would create a shitload of new enemies—for starters, the entire NYPD and Transit PD. The very least that would happen is he'd never work again as a bouncer anywhere in the city.

In the commotion, someone in the crowd—I never found out

who, and I didn't much care—gave up the shooter's license plate number. The plate came back to a female in Suffolk County, out on Long Island. My gut feeling was that the female who owned the car had lent it to the shooter. However he came to possess it, I needed a name; time was of the essence. The more time that passed, the more distance between me and the shooter. And I wanted him badly.

There were two overlapping investigations in progress, one by the NYPD that was proceeding by the book—seasoned investigators and brass interviewing witnesses while being courteous and professional—and mine, which consisted of volunteer cops from the Transit PD and NYPD. Ours was a scorched-earth inquiry. We were going to do everything we had to do to get answers, and none of those things would be pleasant for anyone withholding crucial information.

A bar patron knew the shooter's father, Carmine Zizzo, a bookie, but didn't know the son's name. It didn't take us long to identify him through his dad's criminal history as Joseph Zizzo. Then the Bureau of Criminal Identification (BCI) came back with his rap sheet. He had ties to organized crime, including the Purple Gang.

I went to Jacobi Hospital to check in on Stu. He was up and around but a little groggy from whatever meds they gave him. A doctor assured me that my brother was in good condition and would probably be released the next day. Our mother hadn't been notified of the shooting, so I called her. It took me a while to calm her down, and then I refocused my attention on catching the scumbag who shot my brother.

The next day, Stu's partner, Tommy, called the Photo Unit and was able to get numerous copies of Zizzo's mugshot, which we distributed to every cop in the area. I was in tunnel vision, my only thought being how to find Zizzo and extract revenge. I would not rest until he was located.

I had plenty of help looking for this guy; many off-duty cops from both departments volunteered their time to help me track him down. We tore up the neighborhood for two days with no luck. Zizzo was in hiding and had been savvy enough to keep his mouth shut and not confide whereabouts to anyone. His father was being watched too, but his son was staying out of touch.

I got word from street sources that Zizzo had found out whom he shot and that I was Stu's brother. He was scared and had every right to be. There wasn't a street thug in the Bronx who didn't know what I was capable of.

After two days, Joseph Zizzo's attorney contacted the NYPD. His client wished to surrender but had conditions: the surrender was to be made at the 43rd Precinct detective squad office to a member of the NYPD who was not Ralph Friedman. Additionally, the NYPD had to guarantee that said Ralph Friedman wasn't to be within three miles of the agreed-upon surrender location.

Initially, I balked at these demands, in fact *any* demands. Zizzo had shot a cop—worse yet, my brother—and he had no right to dictate how he was going to turn himself in. I wanted to be the one to book him, and if he didn't like it, he didn't have to give himself up because I'd find him anyway. It was just a matter of time. I was exhausted, surviving on adrenaline and rage, but kept going under the belief that there was nowhere for Zizzo to hide.

Then I willed myself to calm down and think rationally. If I didn't agree to the demands, Zizzo would eventually walk into a police precinct in another borough and surrender. I'd have no way to get to him, anyway. I relented, agreed to the conditions, and Joseph Zizzo gave himself up.

I tried to figure a way to get near him in central booking or a precinct holding cell, but I'd have had an easier time getting into the White House and hitting the president of the United States in the face with a pie. Screw it. I went to see how my brother was doing instead.

Joseph Zizzo got six years for shooting Stu and my undying hate of anything Zizzo. I made it my mission to drop intelligence reports on his dad Carmine's bookie operation every chance I got. There was some comfort in knowing that every time the Organized Crime Control Bureau shut down the elder Zizzo's book, he probably cursed his out-of-control son.

That's not the end of the family drama, however, and incidents didn't always wrap up so neatly. I was in the squad room clearing up paperwork when I got a call that a "woman" had been mugged. The woman turned out to be my mother.

My mom had been going into her apartment building when she'd been surprised from behind by a purse snatcher. My mom tried to hold on to her purse, which is never advisable, and was punched and knocked to the ground with a black eye. My mom was fifty years old and in decent shape, but still no match for the robber who got away. Roger officially caught the case; the job dictated I couldn't be involved because of the familial relationship. But Roger and I both knew we were going to work it together, anyway.

I got to the hospital as my mom was being released. Seeing her banged up made my blood boil. Here I was again, on another heated mission of blind rage.

Eyewitness identification is unreliable at best—and disastrously misleading at worst—because the average person isn't trained to observe, particularly in a stressful situation. In my mother's case, she was focused on saving her purse, was hurt, and did not concentrate on her attacker. She gave us a vague description and perused pictures of known purse snatchers, picking out a possible suspect. He turned out to be the wrong guy. We followed a few more leads, but they went nowhere. Everyday cases like these are difficult, if not impossible. This one ceased being "everyday" when it involved my mother, but that didn't make it any easier. We never cleared it. I realized I couldn't solve every case I worked, but letting this one go was particularly bothersome. While my mom wasn't hurt badly, that wasn't the point; the bad guy had won, and that's a concept I can't accept.

Roger Cortes and I had been working together for a few years, and the partnership had worked out well. There came a time, however, when Roger was made an offer he couldn't refuse.

He had been a second-grade detective for eight years and was looking for that bump to first grade, the pinnacle for detectives in the NYPD. A legendary rank, first graders are the elite. So when he was offered a position in the newly formed Felony Apprehension Unit, it came with the expectation of a grade jump after a short time in the new assignment. Naturally, Roger leapt at the opportunity. It was the best thing that could happen to him. We'd had had a nice run, but now I was without a steady partner.

9

I began working more with the Robbery Investigation Program. I was the only detective among a handful of very good cops, one of the best being Timothy Kennedy, whom I'd known since he provided transportation for two off-duty gun collars I made in the 45th Precinct a few years back. Now, as partners, we would make many hundreds of arrests for drugs and guns together.

While I had always worked the South Bronx, Timmy was essentially an East Bronx version of me. Very active in the arrest department, he gave the job all he had. He was also a bodybuilder and lived a healthy lifestyle. But the similarities ended there; he was married with two kids, and I was still playing the single game. He was also fair skinned with dirty-blond hair and sported a thick mustache, while I was bearded and tattooed and, as I often told Timmy, much better looking.

The incident that I'm about to relate may seem unusual to those who aren't police officers, but it is not uncommon on the job. Timmy and I had a fight, a real fight, not a schoolyard pushing-and-shoving match. If there was anything unique about this battle, it was its length . . . the brawl lasted thirty minutes.

What brought about this epic encounter might sound trivial, but taking contributing factors into consideration, it was the perfect storm of two guys who were having a bad day and taking out their pent-up hostilities on each other.

As I mentioned, Timmy and I were both bodybuilders, and as such had a friendly rivalry. We'd good-naturedly bust each other's chops periodically—nothing malicious; it's just what guys do.

On the day in question, I was at my desk attempting to clear up paperwork. I was not in the best of moods, but bad days come with police work. Timmy just chose the wrong time to get on my nerves. He silently approached me from behind, grabbed my arm, and said, "This isn't so fucking hard," referring to the size and strength of my bicep.

A few things shouldn't have happened here. One: sneaking up on a cop from behind isn't recommended; we tend to overreact out of instinct. Two: grabbing a cop by surprise is basically seizing an alligator's tail while he's sleeping. And three: insulting my bicep is just begging me to show you how well it works. My immediate response was to grab the bulky Underwood typewriter I was using, whirl on Timmy, and hit him in the chest with it. This made sense to me at the time.

Timmy went down with me on top of him swinging away. Every detective in the squad room froze, then went right back to what they were doing. Taking a lesson from the many witnesses we'd all interviewed in the past, the five detectives didn't see a thing. Fight? What fight? Sergeant Harris briefly came out of his office to see what all the commotion was about, rolled his eyes, and went back in his office.

We were both in it to win it—punching and kicking. Eventually, we spilled into the hallway and to the brink of the second-floor staircase. Statistically, this is when the fight should've ended. Most fights last a minute or two, rarely three minutes. With the energy we were expending, that should've been it.

Not only did neither of us call the fight—a draw at that point—we took it to the next level . . . literally. We rolled down the stairs to the main landing, still spitting, kneeing, head butting, and cursing.

There were numerous cops and bosses on the main floor, plus a smattering of civilians reporting crimes or otherwise looking for advice from a nice, stable policeman. What they saw were two out-of-control cops who seemed hell-bent on killing each other.

The civilians started a chorus of gasps and screams. The cops? They didn't give us a second thought once they saw what was up.

We were now fifteen minutes into the Battle of the Bronx with furniture overturned, chairs crushed, and no end in sight. Then Timmy grabbed me in a bear hug, and we both fell backward through the main doors and into the street.

We were both beaten bloody, but neither of us was willing to give up. After bouncing off the sidewalk and a few department autos, Timmy lifted me off the ground and hurled me onto the hood of a Chevy Caprice Classic. If you're not familiar with the car, it has a sharp, protruding hood ornament, a Chevy logo encased in a metal rectangle, which found a new home in my back.

Did I give up? Hell no! I unplugged myself from the chrome decoration and resumed the fight.

We raged on for ten more minutes, both of us totally exhausted. We were still swinging, but most of the punches were either too limp or our faces too numb. The only way I could see this marathon ending was for both our hearts to give out. We'd be dead, but at least neither of us would have to admit defeat.

Then something happened to end the fight almost as quickly as it had begun. Timmy grabbed my arm, and in doing so ripped off my wristwatch—one that had belonged to my dad. I had inherited it after his death. I pictured it shattering.

"Yo, Timmy . . . Stop!" I said breathlessly. "You got my dad's watch . . . It's my dad's, man."

Timmy stopped cold, watch dangling from his fingers. He knew how much that watch meant to me. All of a sudden, the fight was out of both of us. It was over. We felt every second of those thirty minutes.

One major thing was accomplished: we realized that neither of us could ask for a better partner. And so it came to pass, with Roger gone, that Timmy and me paired up. We stayed partners for the remainder of my time on the job and became best friends. Thirty-five years later, we're still friends.

Before changing the subject, I should add a detail in memory of my friend Roger Cortes. He never got promoted to first-grade. He would hit the mandatory retirement age of sixty-two and be dead of a heart attack within two years.

Timmy and I were summoned to Sergeant Harris's office a few weeks later. Harris was behind his desk with a man in a suit who had "cop boss" written all over him standing by, leaning against a chair

The Suit, whom I won't name here, introduced himself as a retired inspector. He had some trouble and he laid it out for us, but not before giving us business cards for a private security company.

"I own this company," he said. "We have armed and unarmed guards. The armed guys sign out their weapons from the office and go to their assigned site. They can take the guns home after work but are only permitted to carry the weapon to and from the job site. That's it. No off-duty carry permitted, which is the rule as set down by the License Division."

The NYPD License Division is responsible for issuing all manner of pistol licenses, including permits for armed guards. To be in violation of any of the myriad rules involving possession of a licensed firearm means the security company would have *all* their pistol licenses suspended pending a review of the violation. This review could take up to a year, and during that time the security company would lose all their armed-guard contracts, which could easily put them out of business.

Sergeant Harris said, "One of his guards is off the grid with a company gun, a .38 Smith, four-inch barrel."

"How long's he been gone?" I asked.

The Suit grumbled, "Just about a week. It's starting to feel like a problem."

I'll say it was! The gun could be lost, used in a crime, sold, or just vanish along with the guard. Private security guards don't make a lot of money, and this wouldn't be the first one to sell his weapon or trade it for God knows what. I've even heard of guards renting out their guns for hits and stickups. Worst-case scenario, the guard flips out and kills innocent people.

Sergeant Harris gave us the guard's last known address, which was located in another precinct in the Bronx. "Find this guy, but keep it quiet. Do what you do best."

"I sent some guys to that address," the Suit said. "Hard to believe, but it's a doorman building. How a square badge guard could afford the place on what I pay him is a mystery . . . Anyway, my guys had no luck and no cooperation from the doorman. We're private, no juice. I'm figuring you could do better."

We got the subject's description and told the Suit and Harris we'd do our best. There were no photo ID cards for guards back then, and the description could've fit half the male population of the Bronx: male, Hispanic, five foot nine, 165 pounds, brown hair. "There's a time constraint on this too," Sergeant Harris said. "The License Division will be doing their annual gun inventory in two weeks . . ."

"Yeah," the Suit interrupted, "if that gun is still gone by then, I'm fucked."

Timmy and I went to the address, which—just like he said—turned out to a very nice building with a doorman protecting the entrance. The security guard must've been doing holdups with his boss's gun to afford an apartment there.

The first thing we did was talk up the doorman. Cops and doormen get along well, although there has always been a shortage of the latter in the Bronx. Doormen depend on cops for protection, and we need them for information regarding tenants and goings on in the neighborhood.

We identified ourselves and described the tenant. The doorman knew the guy but hadn't seen him all day. We worked out a system where the doorman wouldn't be seen identifying him to us. (There would be nothing worse for our new friend's career path than being known as a rat who helped the cops by fingering tenants.) We would stand away from the building, and if our guy showed up, the doorman was to give us a slight nod.

Hours passed. Several males resembled our subject, but the doorman didn't signal, so we remained in place a little way down the street.

At about 4 PM, a gypsy cab pulled up to the building, and a guy who looked like our boy stepped out. As I glanced to the doorman, I heard Timmy say, "He's got a gun!"

I was on the guy in seconds and held him down so he couldn't reach for the gun, which, by the way, I still hadn't seen. Meanwhile, Timmy was still shouting, "He's got a gun, he's got a gun!"

I gave my perp a half dozen quick jabs as he tried to get up, and then, my adrenaline pumping, I gave him one more and he stayed down.

Timmy was in the mix now, still yelling. This time I heard him a bit more clearly: "He's not the one, he's not the one!"

Which sounded very similar to: *"He's got a gun."*

Now we had a *real* fucking problem. I'd just attacked some poor innocent who was probably coming home from work after a hard day at the office and wound up in the middle of his worst nightmare, all because Timmy and I had had a failure to communicate.

Timmy said, "Jesus, Ralph, what the fuck did you do?" He was looking around for witnesses. Fortunately, other than the doorman, there weren't any.

"Man, I'll tell you later," I said. "Give me a hand with this guy."

We scraped Joe Citizen off the pavement and hauled him to the doorman.

"You know this guy?" I asked while I lifted his head up for a good view.

"Oh, yeah," the doorman said, seemingly unfazed, "he's 5C."

I was praying that he lived alone. The doorman told me he did. I searched his pockets and found the key to his apartment.

Timmy and I hoisted each of his arms over our shoulders and half walked, half dragged him to the elevator. He was coming around.

"What the fuck happened?" he mumbled.

"Some asshole tried to mug you," Timmy said. "You'll be okay."

I kept my mouth shut. Not one of my finer moments.

We got the guy into his apartment and deposited him on a couch. He looked okay, just a bit confused, and his face was beginning to blow up like a balloon.

"Have a nice day," I said as Timmy rolled his eyes.

Back downstairs, we cornered the doorman.

"Who are we?" I asked him.

He shrugged. "You guys? Never saw you in my life."

Doormen, the cops' best friend.

As we drove back to the command, we rewrote history. We felt the doorman was good and would keep quiet about the incident. The story we told to Sergeant Harris was that we couldn't find the subject and didn't think we could.

"It's a dead end, Sarge," Timmy said.

When the sergeant turned his attention to me, I nodded like a woodpecker and mumbled, "What he said."

Sergeant Harris looked at us like we were crazy but was savvy enough not to pursue the matter. If he'd been tighter with the retired inspector, we may have had to elaborate a bit more or, worse, return to the subject's address the next day and continue the stakeout, but our take was that the Suit had walked in off the street and asked for a favor from Harris, one cop to another, knowing he wouldn't be turned down. The thing that continued to haunt me, though, was the thought of that gun out there.

When Timmy and I signed out for the day and were leaving the squad room, I said to him: "He's not the one, huh?"

We looked at each other and couldn't help laughing. I felt awful about hurting an innocent man, and the joke wasn't meant to be at his expense, but Timmy and I both needed a release.

I'd heard some talk that I was about to get promoted to second-grade detective. Actually, I'd been hearing the same scuttlebutt almost since I'd gotten promoted to third grade five years before. I'd received way above-average job performance evaluations right out of the gate, and for those five years led the entire NYPD with the most arrests and medals. I was overdue for the advancement, but the city's financial troubles were getting in the way.

A job freeze had been instituted in 1975 because of New York City's fiscal crisis. The Big Apple was in poor shape financially, and if you were a city worker, you paid the price. So severe was the crisis that for the first time in the city's history, police officers were going to be "furloughed," which is a softer term than "laid off."

Cops with fewer than six years on the job were getting let go with a promise that, as soon as the city got back on its feet, they would get their jobs back. Cops have a cynical streak and not too many believed the promise, but three years later the city kept its word and rehired those they had let go. Those cops that remained and were due for promotion would have to wait seven years for the promotion freeze to be lifted. Everyone who worked for the city would be in limbo until New York City had a few bucks in the bank.

I felt bad for the guys losing their jobs back then, but I wasn't going to be one of them; at the time I had two years additional city seniority, counting my time as a police trainee. My extra time saved me, having been sworn in as a police officer in 1970, which was right on the borderline for layoffs.

You can imagine my confusion when I arrived home from work to find a letter telling me I'd been furloughed. It was a helluva jolt. I called the NYPD's Personnel Department and set them straight. In essence, they told me I was wrong, that I'd never been a trainee.

These were the days before computers, and somehow records

verifying my two years' service as a trainee with the NYPD had vanished. I was concerned but stayed calm. One thing I'd learned about dealing with New York bureaucracy is that if you work for the city, you should save everything, which means every piece of paper issued by the city that has your name on it.

I'd saved all my paystubs, in addition to a mountain of arrest forms, departmental recognition letters, and everything else that had the name Ralph Friedman attached to it. I had to physically go to personnel and show a clerk the stubs to prove that I'd actually been employed by the department as a trainee. They wanted to keep the paystubs. I gave the clerk a you've-gotta-be-fucking-kidding look. No way was this bureaucrat keeping originals of anything relating to my employment.

Those paystubs saved my job. It's been thirty-five years since my retirement, and I still hold on to everything pertaining to my service with the NYPD—literally cartons of material—which coincidentally is serving me well as I write this book, as I refresh my recollections of the good old days.

While *my* job was secure, my brother Stu's job wasn't, as his tenure with the city began in 1974. Ironically, he received his "bye-bye" letter upon returning home from a ceremony where he had been awarded the coveted Combat Cross, the second-highest medal under the Medal of Honor. I felt for him; police work meant as much to him as it did to me.

The promotion lockdown ended for me on April 2, 1982. I made the journey to One Police Plaza to be elevated to the rank of second-grade detective. I wanted to go alone, unlike my last promotion to third grade, when I'd had family and friends attend. The auditorium was packed with those of us who had been shelved for years, waiting for this day to come. It was sort of anticlimactic. All I wanted to do was shake Police Commissioner Robert Maguire's hand, get the photo op with him, and get back to work and on the path to first grade.

I was still single and loving it, not looking to settle down because at that time I was married to the job. Even if I got involved in a serious relationship, I knew from past experience that no woman would put up with being runner-up to the NYPD. Whatever she invested in our relationship was riskier than playing the lottery.

That said, I never stopped looking for my next ex-girlfriend.

I was on patrol in an unmarked car one day when I made eye contact with a lovely young Hispanic girl. Around twenty-five years old, she was gorgeous: around five foot six with long dark hair and a dynamite body. After having spent half my life in a gym, I was naturally attracted to women who were in good shape. I thought I'd seen her around the neighborhood before but couldn't be sure; all I knew was that I had to meet her.

I pulled over, got out of the car, and introduced myself. Cops have a pretty easy time meeting women.

Her name was Lucy Santiago, and we hit it off immediately. She told me she worked for an insurance company in Manhattan, was single, and lived alone. She also had an incredible smile. I was definitely in lust.

Over the next two weeks, we met for dinner a few times and talked for hours. She was nice to be around and wasn't what you might call a "cop groupie." While plenty of people don't have high opinions of cops, there are quite a number of women who gravitate toward the badge. Go to any cop bar and you'll find some women who think we're the best thing since the Lone Ranger. That's not to say I couldn't find nice girls elsewhere. Show me a cop who can't find a girl and I'll guarantee him a place in the Guinness book of records.

I'd have to win Lucy over and I'd enjoy doing it; she was pleasant to be around. After a few dates it was a nice surprise to hear her say, "Why don't you come up to my place Friday after work? I can cook us dinner." My deductive reasoning and her sly smile told me that dinner wouldn't be the main course. She didn't have to ask me twice.

It was Tuesday and I began counting the days until Friday.

Over the next few days a cascade of robberies, burglaries, a carjacking, and assorted assaults and other turmoil kept me busy, but Lucy was always on my mind. When Friday finally rolled around, it didn't arrive too soon.

I was working from 4 PM to midnight that day and planned on taking some compensatory lost time toward the end of the tour to get to Lucy's place as early as I could. As chance (the bad variety) would have it, I got stuck with a late arrest, one that would keep me tied up for many hours. I was pissed, but there was nothing I could do about it.

I thought *I* was disappointed, but that was nothing compared to the way Lucy handled the news.

"You can't come over after you're done?" she asked, the frustration evident in her voice. I fantasized about what I was going to be missing.

I explained how things worked. "I could be here until three, four in the morning, maybe later." It was only 9 PM now. "I don't want to hang you up. How about next Wednesday? I'll take the day off."

She perked up. "You can do that?"

"Yes, no problem, I'll be there." We settled on eight o'clock.

So the clock began ticking again. I convinced myself that good things come to those who wait.

Three days later, I was on the street keeping the neighborhood safe with Timmy when our unit got a "forthwith" to the station house over the radio.

I looked at my partner. "You're not getting locked up are you?" I said, memories of Gus Paulson flooding back to me.

Timmy looked at me like I had two heads. "Huh?"

"Never mind. Let's just go in and see what we did wrong."

There were two unsmiling guys in suits waiting for us in Sergeant Harris's office. The sergeant was nowhere to be seen.

Timmy and I stood there looking like deer in the headlights.

"Which one of you is Friedman?" one of them asked.

Oh, shit.

I raised a finger. They both produced lieutenant's shields. The gabby one said to Timmy, "You can go." Both of them looked like poster boys for the Internal Affairs Division, affectionately known to street cops as the Rat Squad.

Timmy gave me a wane smile and left. The boss doing all the talking told me to sit down. I assumed I was going to be read my rights. Thoughts were racing through my mind, trying to figure out what I could've done wrong to warrant a visit from two bosses. Internal Affairs investigates allegations of serious crimes committed by members of the department. I delved into the recesses of my brain trying to come up with something I could've done that was bad enough to call these guys in. I was coming up blank.

"I'm Lieutenant DiLeo," the same one said, "this is Lieutenant Hummel. We're from the Intelligence Division."

The fear and apprehension that seized me as soon as I entered the room left me in a rush, like a balloon deflating, my trepidation turning to curiosity. I figured they needed information on a case I'd handled.

"What can I help you guys with?" I asked, relief undoubtedly evident in my voice.

Lieutenant Hummel shook his head. "No, it's what can we help you with, Detective."

The other one, DiLeo, said, "You know a Lucy Santiago?"

I sat up straighter in my chair. In a short period of time, my emotions ran the gamut from fear to curiosity and now to confusion. Why did two bosses from Intelligence want to talk to me about Lucy? "Yeah," I said, hesitantly, "I know her."

"You had a date with her this last Friday you didn't keep?" DiLeo said.

"That's right. I had a collar, had to cancel. What's this all about?"

"That collar saved your life," Hummel said.

How was I supposed to respond to that? "Huh?"

DiLeo pulled up a chair and slid it close to me. "Lucy Santiago is Manny Rivas's sister."

He stopped talking and allowed that to sink in.

It's not often I'm speechless, but I was now. Rivas, whom I'd shot and killed on a rooftop six months ago, was Lucy's brother? My head was swimming with images of Rivas holding a knife less than two feet from me and then switched to Lucy and her sexy, captivating smile.

Hummel was talking again and woke me from my reverie.

". . . a plot to kill you."

"What? Kill me?"

Hummel said. "A snitch we were using heard about it and called us. Santiago's invite to her place was for the purpose of killing you . . . avenging her brother. She had two of Manny's friends in a closet, and when you were most vulnerable they were going to pounce and torture you to death."

"Your body would never be found," DiLeo added. He snapped his fingers. "Chopped up and dumped. Bye-bye, Ralph."

Jesus! It was Lucy's plan all along to murder me? I'd been played, and I didn't have the slightest clue what was going on. Like a lamb being led to slaughter. While I was appalled at the sheer viciousness of the plot—Lucy was the last person I'd ever have suspected of something like this—the fact that I'd been completely fooled was the most disturbing aspect of it all. I'd survived for years on the job because I had more street smarts than those who wanted to do me harm. All the years honing my tactical and investigative skills weren't enough to keep me from walking into a trap. Had I begun to lose my edge? While I wasn't old, to survive the perils of the demanding streets of the Bronx, one needs the freshness and speed of youth. As I'd seen in countless B-movie Westerns, there's always someone around who's faster. And I would've been murdered in the most brutal way if it weren't for a nameless informant. Obviously, I never showed up for my date with death, and I never heard from Lucy again. She must've figured I'd sensed an ambush. Lucy couldn't be prosecuted for the plot to murder me. There was no real evidence of the crime, other than the word of an informant, and the only way to get her locked up would be to send me into harm's way and arrest the plotters when they made their move on me. The NYPD wasn't about to set me up as bait in an apartment with no backup right there with me.

Conditional cynicism is endemic for most street cops; we trust very few people we encounter on a daily basis. This distrust of people in general also encompasses cops' personal lives, but we learn to trust the individuals in our inner circle. After the Lucy

Santiago incident I took that mistrust one step further: now I couldn't trust *anyone*. My very existence would depend on my suspecting anyone and everyone. I knew this attitude was unhealthy but couldn't help myself. As long as I was on the job, I'd have to be even more situationally aware than I had been.

I'd gotten a pass from the patron saint of street cops, or maybe my survival had been just a matter of luck. Whatever had accounted for my good fortune, however, I was looking out for myself, and there was much more coming my way.

Nothing angers me more than crimes against children, the elderly, and women. Most cops feel the same way. While crime in general offends our sense of order, these crimes really set us off.

Soon after the Lucy Santiago incident, a rapist began a series of attacks and robberies within the confines of the Five-Two. Dubbed the Williamsbridge Rapist by the media, the attacker committed nine reported rapes and robberies in a five-block area over a two-and-a-half-week period in February 1982. We assumed the number of victims to be even greater because many sexual crimes go unreported for reasons ranging from the victims' humiliation to their disillusionment with the criminal justice system to help in any way. For others, it's the possibility of having to testify at their attackers' trials.

Whenever crimes of this magnitude are committed, and particularly when the press makes a point of keeping the story above the fold, the NYPD forms a task force whose sole job it is to capture the assailant. In this case I was part of the task force. Task force detectives put their pending cases on hold or the cases get reassigned to other detectives.

I'd been searching for the rapist for several days to no avail, as had the other task force detectives. A meeting was held at borough headquarters to discuss strategy. Attending the meeting were the detectives who were doing the footwork, the Bronx chief of detectives, and a handful of high-ranking bosses who would supervise and conduct interviews with the media.

The meeting dragged on and I was getting antsy. Finally, I couldn't take it anymore. Being idle while a pervert was on the loose brutalizing women was nonproductive. A simple "Go out and get this asshole" would've been enough to focus the best detectives in the Bronx on their task, but instead we were forced to listen to endless theories and plans of attack.

"Excuse me," I said to the boss addressing the troops, "shouldn't we be out looking for this guy instead of talking about it?"

The reaction I got from the bosses was enough to make you think *I* was the criminal. An inspector threatened to cite me for insubordination, while others above the rank of captain joined in with calls for my head. The detectives, however, had nodded in approval at my comment, as did the two sergeants present.

I didn't regret saying what I had said. Speaking your mind in any bureaucracy is ill-advised, but I was never concerned with ass kissing.

The meeting was soon adjourned, and we hit the street. As we exited the headquarters building, I heard Sergeant Harris mumble to another boss, "Fucking Friedman," but there was admiration in his tone. Still, I wasn't off the hook; a lowly detective doesn't address a high-ranking boss in the manner I had. Unbeknownst to me, plans were forming to seriously stick it to me.

Saturating the target area had proved fruitless. We had spotted a few individuals who fit the general description of the perp—light-skinned African American, tall, thin, around twenty years old, but none was the correct person.

Then, on the same day as the borough task force meeting, the rapist struck again in an apartment building courtyard on DeKalb Avenue.

We were working with one of his victims, a young woman who had been riding with us and was adamant about helping us catch her attacker. She was smart, motivated, and best of all angry. We would channel that anger into our search for this brutal criminal.

She rode in an unmarked car with Sergeant Harris during the day and with me at night, putting in many hours of focused patrol time with negative results. Criminals usually operate in areas with which they are familiar, generally living among their victims. We figured patrolling the Williamsbridge neighborhood would eventually lead us to the rapist, but I was concerned that our helpful victim would grow weary of the hunt before then. I was mistaken. This was one gutsy, driven woman. She was in it for the long haul, no matter the time involved.

Police Officer Melvin Dodds was riding with me because Timmy was off. I was driving, Mel was up front, and the complainant was in the backseat.

At 7:10 PM we were turning onto Gunhill Road when the complainant grabbed my shoulder. "There he is!"

She was pointing to a tall, light-skinned black man walking down the street toward Rochambeau Avenue. He fit the description of the attacker perfectly.

"Are you sure?" I asked.

"One hundred percent," she said. "That's the guy."

"Okay," Mel said to her, "stay in the car."

I pulled the car to the curb ahead of the suspect, and Mel and I got out and approached him cautiously. We were a few feet in front of him when we identified ourselves. He turned and took off like a greyhound, with us in pursuit.

The good news was that we were sure we had our rapist in our sights. The bad news was he was young and ran like his ass was on fire. I was on the opposite side of the street, keeping him in view should he decide to cross, while Mel was behind him.

After three blocks of a full-wind sprint, the guy was still way ahead of us and widening the gap. I thought, "fuck this" and ran into the street and stepped in front of an oncoming car, waving my shield like a winning lottery ticket. The driver screeched to a halt.

A choice had to be made. I could either drag the driver out of his own car and commandeer it to continue the pursuit (think Gene Hackman in *The French Connection* chase scene) or let the driver do the driving while I directed the chase. I chose the latter because the driver was a young man and cooperative ("What do you want me to do, Officer?"). We took off down the street, picking up Mel along the way.

As we pulled up alongside the suspect, he spotted us and made an abrupt turn to enter the apartment building at 3591 Bainbridge Avenue. We were just steps behind him.

The front door to the building was locked. Gotchya, motherfucker!

The perp, later identified as David Patterson, nineteen, abandoning his attempt to get through the front door, rounded the building and tried to hide in the courtyard, but we were right on him. He put up one hell of a fight, which was expected because, if arrested, he wouldn't breathe free air again until he was eligible for Social Security.

In his possession was an ID card belonging to our helpful victim. He confessed to assaulting her and robbing her at knifepoint. He also had a woman's watch in his possession. When we got him back to the squad room, he confessed to three other rape/robberies and was picked out of a lineup by additional victims. Other line-ups would be held at a later date and he'd be positively identified as the attacker by more victims, who were now coming forward.

The press was all over the story, and Mel and I were at its epi-center. The victim who'd accompanied us wasn't named because sex-crime victims are not identified to the media. The borough bosses who had been devising ways to skin me alive for being a wise ass had to back off given the accolades I was getting from the press. Mel and I were the men of the hour and thereby un-touchable. Not only did we grab the bad guy, we did it the same day as the borough meeting, which made the brass look good too. Hours after the "new strategy" had been formulated, an arrest had been made, which was the story they wanted, even if, realistically, a courageous victim and a bit of luck had everything to do with getting the rapist.

This was a particularly satisfying case, not only because we got the bad guy but also because the level of cooperation from the victim was outstanding. She was one impressive individual, and our focus and intensity was to right the grave wrong inflicted on her and the other victims. To have her with us when we took the guy down was very rewarding.

Not all of my cases were as gratifying. Or they're gratifying in a different way.

Timmy and I had gotten information from various neighbor-hood sources that there were two drug dealers operating in the precinct and nobody seemed to be able to get them. The decent folks from the neighborhood had been complaining. The word was they ran their business openly on the street, selling heroin and weed, so we didn't think we'd have a problem collaring them.

The first day we cruised the area we observed the dealers ex-actly where our sources said they would be: standing on their street corner awaiting customers. These were young Hispanic guys, early twenties, who had an unconcerned air about them. Usually street dealers are extremely wary. Not these guys; they were joking around and seemed as if they didn't have a care in the world. We hoped to change all that.

We parked around the corner and approached them on foot. Before they knew what was happening, Timmy and I grabbed one mope each and began a thorough search. We didn't find anything incriminating.

"Where's your stash?" I asked, not really expecting an answer. I wanted to get a baseline for how they lied to compare with how they told the truth, for example in telling us their names.

They denied everything, of course, but it was obvious they were lying. After the usual threats to cease and desist selling drugs and to clear out of the neighborhood, we left.

The next day we drove past the same corner, and there they were as if nothing had happened. We approached them again. In addition to not having any contraband, they also developed an attitude.

"You can't harass us—we ain't done nothin'."

As we drove away, Timmy and I decided that it was going to be our mission to get these assholes with their goods.

We figured they had identified our unmarked car, so we took to using our own personal vehicles. We watched them talk to nu-merous customers, but from our vantage point we couldn't tell for certain if drugs passed hands. Occasionally, one or both would enter the apartment building they were standing in front of. When the customers departed, we'd swoop in and confront the suspects. Still nothing. To further confuse them, we switched to my motorcycle, me driving, Timmy on the back, with the same results. They were clean every time we searched them. We were beginning to feel ineffective, not a mind-set we were used to experiencing.

We decided to modify our tactics. We would observe them through binoculars from a rooftop a few buildings down. When they entered the building, we'd sprint across the adjoining roofs and down into their building, trapping them.

We were on our roof for hours before our suspects arrived at their designated corner. Like a shop opening for the day, their customers started cycling by. After two hours, their client base slowed, and they went into the building.

We leapt into action and dashed across the several roofs on our way to theirs. One problem: their building was the only one on the block that was unattached. There was a ten-foot gap between the buildings that we hadn't seen from the street because of a fake façade.

"Now what the fuck do we do?" Timmy asked when we came to a sudden stop near the roof's edge.

We could make a running start and take the leap, but it was a sixty-foot drop to the alley and we were weighted down with guns, flashlights, and other gear. Then I spotted the plank.

A board, about twelve feet in length and a foot wide, was lying invitingly on our roof against the stairwell kiosk.

Timmy and I looked at each other, the unspoken words between us saying, "Do we dare try it?"

"Fuck it!" we both said almost in unison and grabbed the plank, placing it between the two roofs.

It seemed sturdy enough and might have been used in the past to make a hasty escape, then pulled out of the way. Why else would it be on the roof to begin with? I was trying to talk myself into making the crossing. I'm sure the same thoughts were going through

Timmy's mind. We didn't have any time to hesitate or our targets would be back on the street or, worst-case scenario, gone.

I went first, shimmying across the narrow piece of wood as quickly as possible. It sagged a bit under my weight but held up just fine. When I got to the other side, Timmy mounted the plank. He was a few pounds lighter than me and, unless a sudden gust of wind blew him into that big precinct in the sky, he'd make it too. He did.

We hustled down the stairs and found our guys on the third-floor landing. They looked at us coming down the stairs and their eyes bulged.

Guns out, Timmy said. "Don't move a fucking muscle." They complied.

I had confused their reaction with being resigned that we had caught them with their supply, but it turned out to be a look of shock at lengths we were going to in order to nab them.

They were clean. Again.

We handcuffed them as we thought about what to do next.

Timmy and I backed off and talked strategy, which basically amounted to a lot of head scratching and cursing. Meanwhile our prisoners got ballsy and started wisecracking, calling us names and saying all sorts of things about our mothers.

Do you beat them up and call it street justice? But street guys can take beatings; they'd be back on the street in wheelchairs hawking their goods. Timmy and I came up with something better (or worse, depending on how you look at it).

We removed the cuffs. Thinking they were in the clear, they took their first steps to freedom. We stopped them.

"You're not going anywhere," I said.

They exchanged glances, confused. "What the fuck?" one of them said.

"Take off your clothes," Timmy said.

They were speechless. Timmy repeated the order. They stripped to their underwear, protesting steadily that they didn't have any drugs.

"This isn't a search," I said. "It's a lesson. Now take the rest off."

They looked at each other but complied. They stood buck naked in the tenement hallway trying to cover themselves.

"Okay," I said, "you can go now."

They both reached for their clothes.

"Without the clothes!" Timmy bellowed.

They begged, cajoled, and promised never to return to the area if we'd let them get dressed.

"Everything stays here," I said. "If we see you even walking through this neighborhood again, this is the least that'll happen." The last we saw of the two dealers they were running down the block to the shouts and jeers of the people on the street. We knew they would never return to the area. They were too macho.

Sometimes things happened this way back then. Today this would never happen, and I'm sure some readers may not believe it ever happened. Let me assure you, it did, and similar incidents occurred quite often. The thinking was that sometimes justice takes many different forms; sticking to the letter of the law often doesn't work. Cops wanted to rid the streets of criminals, and the people from the area where those dealers operated, even the ones who didn't have very nice things to say about the police in general, applauded our actions.

I'd been a second-grade detective for about two years and I'd begun hearing rumors of a forthcoming promotion to first-grade detective. Within months those rumors took a more solid turn;

bosses who knew the system assured me that I'd be promoted by the first of the year, a brief six months away.

I was ecstatic; after only two years in my current grade, I was getting bumped upward because of my stratospheric number of quality arrests and the numerous medals I'd been awarded over the years, that number now passing two hundred.

First-grade detective is the pinnacle of any detective's career. Of the approximately 3,400 detectives in the NYPD at that time, only 115 had attained the rank of first grade.

I looked forward to the day with anticipation. With only fourteen years on the job, I would happily remain a first-grade detective, with a salary equal to that of a lieutenant, for the rest of my career. All the hard work, stress, injuries, and emotional turmoil was about to pay off.

Plans, however, sometimes go awry. For me, my hopes and dreams for the future would end not at the hands of a criminal but by simply being in the wrong place at the wrong time while attempting to come to the aid of a fellow police officer.

10

Monday, August 1, 1983,
4 pm-to-1 am tour of duty

It was a brisk day for August, hovering in the midseventies. The normally scorching month began with a series of thunderstorms that cooled it right down. By late afternoon it was just overcast, the storm clouds drifting off toward Long Island.

Timmy and I had some arrests to follow up: meeting with complainants, conducting a few interviews. We didn't expect a busy tour. Mondays are like that. People are partied out from the weekend, and the junkies wouldn't be on the street to make their buys until close to midnight. But in the Bronx anything can happen and usually does.

My anticipated promotion to first grade was looming, only I didn't know exactly when it would come. To my glass-half-full way of thinking "by the first of the year" could be as early as tomorrow.

I was happy, both because of the looming promotion and because I enjoyed the job. It was nights like these, when things were what passed for quiet in the Bronx, that I had time to reflect on a career that still had a way to go before I would hit retirement age. I was fourteen years in and could retire with a pension after twenty. That would make me forty-one years old, but I knew I'd stay on the job until I was dragged away kicking and screaming at the mandatory retirement age of sixty-two and a half.

I was by now the most decorated detective in the NYPD's history, an accomplishment I was proud of. With over two thousand arrests and another four thousand assists, I was more active than any detective in the city. But I was most proud of the cops I'd worked with over the years. No one could ask for better and more lasting friendships than I had.

I'd been quiet for a while, and Timmy asked if everything was okay.

"Yeah, man, things are great. Just thinking about the job."

"Hard to believe they actually pay us for doing this, right?" Timmy said. We both laughed.

9:15 PM

A cop calling a 10-13—officer needs assistance—spewed from the radio in a rush. The officer sounded like he was in serious trouble and needed help desperately.

Timmy activated the siren, and I stuck a magnetic revolving red flashing light on the roof. Other units from the division responded in a flurry of acknowledgments over the radio. We were off to the scene in a cloud of burnt rubber.

Timmy was driving. Normally I'd be behind the wheel for the entire tour because I liked to drive and Timmy couldn't care less, but I'd just gotten back from a motorcycle trip to Virginia Beach and my body was still vibrating from being wrapped around a Harley engine for several days.

We were hitting speeds up to 75 miles per hour on Bedford Park, heading west and going so fast I had to secure the red light to the roof with my hand.

Our siren was running at a steady ear-shattering whine. The last thing I remembered was our unit approaching the intersection where Bedford Park meets Jerome Avenue. A Five-Two precinct sector car that was heading south on Jerome to the same call for assistance with siren blaring T-boned us on my side of the car as they shot through the intersection. A rookie male officer was behind the wheel with a female officer as the recorder. Our sirens had drowned each other out, and neither unit was aware of the other.

I remember nothing of the impact, its immediate aftermath, or my subsequent removal to North Central Bronx Hospital. Cops who responded to the accident scene would later tell me I was trapped in our car for over two hours. The Fire Department responded and needed the Jaws of Life to get me free of the mangled auto. I was told that cops had crawled into the car to talk to me, keep me awake, and offer support as others fought to disentangle me. I had already gone into shock and would recall none of it.

I would spend my first week in the hospital unconscious from drugs to reduce the pain. On my first night there, my mother and brother were told that I might not make it through the night. As days passed and it appeared as if I was going to survive, doctors upgraded my condition to I'd probably never walk again.

Almost immediately I began to get death threats. It seemed like every punk I'd ever arrested wanted me dead. I was totally defenseless, flat on my back in traction, and these brave souls chose that time to threaten me . . . over the phone, no less. I was placed in a double room, one for me and the other for a contingent of fourteen police officers who guarded me around the clock in shifts.

When I finally started to come to I was told the extent of my injuries: twenty-three broken bones, including my pelvis, which was broken in four places, and a shattered hip. On the plus side, I didn't need surgery. The doctors said my superb physical condition and thick muscles cushioned the vital organs and prevented the broken bones from moving and causing further injury. It would take me years to recover and every day of it was trying, but in the beginning it was torturous. The pain was excruciating and unrelenting. Because I was on by back with my leg elevated in traction for seven weeks, I developed bed sores. My veins began to collapse from getting numerous IVs and injections. I was living my worst nightmare.

I was informed that Timmy had a broken right shoulder, as well as neck and back injuries, two broken fingers on his left hand, and glass in his eyes, with stitches required to repair an eyelid. Police Officer Al Bunis, the driver of the radio car that struck ours, had a large, deep cut to a knee and an almost severed ear. His partner, Officer Cheryl Williams, suffered a broken arm, neck, and back injuries and the loss of her front teeth. When she arrived at the hospital, she had her teeth clutched in her hand, and they were successfully replanted.

All three officers were treated and released within twelve hours. Timmy Kennedy remained on the job and was eventually promoted to detective by the time he retired, a promotion long overdue. Cheryl Williams also remained on the job and climbed the rank ladder to lieutenant. She's now retired. Officer Bunis retired after a successful police career. I would never work as a police officer again.

My mother and brother came to see me every day of my hospital stay, all nine weeks of it. The NYPD was very kind throughout. They provided my mother with round-the-clock transportation to and from the hospital; anytime she wanted to visit me, all she had to do was call the local precinct and they'd have a car to her in minutes.

There was a steady stream of visitors, mostly cops, at all hours, and they never came empty-handed. There was more food in my room than the buffet line at a Howard Johnson's. The cops there with me would smuggle in everything from Chinese food to lobster. When the doctors and nurses took breaks, they came to my room to eat because the spread far surpassed what they had in their lounges.

I recall coming out of my drugged stupor after a week and seeing seven women encircling my bed. At first I thought I was hallucinating, but on closer inspection I realized that I'd been dating these women concurrently over the last year and they all picked the same time to visit me. What are the odds? I feigned passing out until they left, thinking I'd have a lot of explaining to do and might wind up with even more broken bones.

I was dating my current girlfriend, Grace, at the time. I figured she must have a good sense of humor because she didn't give me any grief over the incident. She may have been the most recent woman in my life, but she was a keeper. Extremely kind and generous—and a knockout—she was at my bedside every day, and as I started walking again she helped me get around. Grace is a unique person, completely selfless and devoted. After thirty-five years, we're still together and have a beautiful home.

The healing process was hitting a few snags. In addition to my bed sores, I had contracted phlebitis from the IVs. Following that was a bad bout with pneumonia and a staph infection that could've killed me. I was on an antibiotic drip six times a day for forty minutes a pop. A doctor from the Centers for Disease Control was assigned to me. Years of treating my body like a temple was paying off. Anyone else would be dead.

All the poking and prodding with needles began to collapse my veins. I was about to have surgery to correct the problem when a doctor vetoed the operation at the last minute and instead prescribed warm compresses and massages to rejuvenate the veins. It worked. That success was short-lived, however, when an IV catheter (a device that keeps a vein open) fell out of my arm and a nurse shot me up straight with meds from a syringe, which wasn't supposed to be done. My body was on fire for two days until the effects wore off.

About seven weeks into my hospital stay, it was deemed that I should begin to get around on crutches and use a wheelchair. Easier said than done. Two months earlier I was lifting literally tons of weights on any given visit to the gym; now walking twenty paces down a hallway wore me out.

I was determined to do my best to get back into fighting shape. To that end, the cops who were guarding me went way above and beyond their security responsibilities. These guys would hold me up in the beginning as I tried to navigate my way around the hospital hallways on crutches. They stayed past their tours working with me, cajoling me, giving me confidence, and encouraging me to take one more step. I also had to learn how to navigate between a wheelchair and crutches.

I began to realize that my policing days were over. Initially I went through a phase of denial; *I was going to get better, go back to the gym and build myself back to my fighting weight. I'd get my promotion to first grade and get back on the street. Everything was going to be fine.*

But it wouldn't be. By an ironic twist of fate, a car accident accomplished what literally hundreds of New York's most violent criminals tried to achieve: putting me out of commission.

Denial morphed into anger, then, finally, acceptance. I'd never again be the physical specimen I was before the accident, and there was no denying that. I realized that at age thirty-four, discounting the damage I'd endured, there were bad guys out there half my age that were quicker and more ruthless than the thugs I'd been dealing with for fourteen years. In any other profession, thirty-four is prime, but being a cop in the Bronx ages you quickly. The NYPD would undoubtedly put me out of the job on a line-of-duty disability. I resigned myself to the fact that I was going to be a retired detective and there was nothing I could do about it. It would take a while before that happened, and I was going to concentrate on getting better. I would deal with being a civilian when the time came.

ESU supplied an ambulance for me the day I was released from the hospital and took me home. The Detectives Endowment Association (DEA) provided a maid/chauffeur during the week for three months, and Grace moved in and cared for me around the clock.

I was still pretty much a mess. I was very weak, tired easily, and could barely get around in a wheelchair, let alone on crutches. It would be eight more months before I was totally ambulatory. For now, it was baby steps.

While I was in the hospital, my brother took care of my ten-year-old female German shepherd, Timba, who liked exercising as much as I did. I had to come to grips with the realization that I could no longer care for her. It broke my heart, but I had to find a suitable home for a full-grown dog. My brother knew two young women who lived together and were dog lovers who were happy to take Timba. After all I'd seen and been through, one of the toughest things I ever had to do was give that dog away. I cried and grieved as if a friend had died.

I was chomping at the bit to get back to the gym and did so while I was still confined to a wheelchair. My DEA-supplied maid took me. Initially, I could work only my upper body. My first workout didn't last long; I totally exhausted myself within five minutes. Gym sessions grew incrementally longer after that, but progress was snail-like. By the time I could depend entirely on crutches, I was squeezing out fifteen- to twenty-minute workouts.

November 1983

It was time to think about the reality of retirement. The NYPD provided me with an accountant to advise me on the various options for maximizing my benefits. In addition to health and pension considerations, I was advised to wait until the first of the year (January 1, 1984) to get interviewed by the medical board and submit my retirement papers. That way, it was explained to me, I could take full advantage of additional benefits that would not have been afforded me had I chosen to retire sooner.

The interview with the medical board went quickly. They scrutinized my hospital records and asked me questions regarding my mobility. They reserved a decision, but by the time I got home my phone was ringing. It was someone from the board advising me that I'd been granted a full job-connected disability pension.

It was over. It was my time to decompress, to take it easy and enjoy what life had to offer. What had just become clear was that I would now be a former member of the NYPD.

Epilogue

I hadn't been back to the Four-One in almost thirty years.

Retiring from police work isn't like retiring from a civilian job, primarily because it isn't a job; it's a lifestyle. Not too many jobs in the private sector require that you be on call 24/7. Not too many occupations other than the military and firefighting have you working side-by-side with someone who would give their life to save yours.

Being a police officer is also being part of a culture, one that a noncop can never quite understand. Police officers work in a vacuum; there are cops and there's everyone else. So when you leave the job, you're no longer a part of *us*; you're part of *them*.

That's not to imply that a retired police officer is ostracized by active cops. We still get treated with respect by those on the job. For example, a retired officer or his family can pretty much count on receiving special treatment if there's a family emergency.

But things change, subtle as they may be. You feel as if the secret handshake was changed the minute you pulled the pin.

Then, of course, there's the huge turnover that all police departments encounter. People get promoted, get transferred, retire . . .

die. In a relatively short period of time, most of a precinct's manpower is flipped and those familiar faces are gone.

So your visits become more and more infrequent.

After three decades, there wouldn't be a soul in the Four-One who would recognize me, except perhaps the rats. They seem to live forever.

While I had had strong ties to the Five-Two detective squad, most police officers' allegiances belong to their first command, where they *learned* the job. My heart belonged to the Four-One; that was where I cut my teeth.

As the years passed, I had fleeting thoughts of returning to check in on the Four-One but dismissed them for all the reasons I've mentioned. Recently, those thoughts started recurring with greater frequency. At first I didn't understand why. I couldn't have asked for a more fulfilled life with Grace; I was back to bodybuilding and was in top physical shape. I had great friends and maintained good relations with my family. I also hadn't lost my detective's instinct. I was still constantly aware of my surroundings, so the *sense* of policing was always there. There were times when I'd pull up behind a lone state trooper or local cop conducting a car stop, get out and ID myself, offering to stand by as a backup. The officers appreciated these actions, and I'd get immense satisfaction making myself available in case something went wrong.

After some honest self-evaluation I understood why I was thinking more and more about the Four-One. As much as I'd been fighting approaching old age, it was creeping up, slowly and insidiously. I feel that the fewer regrets we have when we're old or when the end is near, the more peaceable the passing. We all have regrets, but never returning to the place that had the most impact on my life would definitely be a mistake.

———

I made the drive at midnight on a warm June night in 2013. I had never shaken my weird hours; I was still up most of the night and slept during the day. So, with Grace asleep, I made the decision in an instant. I was going to the Four-One.

I lived in the city and made the short drive with some anxiety. So many years had passed. Would I still feel like a cop when I walked through those massive station house doors? I didn't want to go into the beehive and not feel like a bee.

I parked across the street from the station house in a spot designated for cops and tossed my Detective's Endowment Association membership card on the dashboard.

The exterior of the fortress-like structure still looked the same; just as grimy and battle-scarred as when I'd last seen it. The tenements adjacent on both sides were gone, as were other dilapidated housing structures in the neighborhood. Some of the buildings had been replaced by attached private homes, built with federal funds to pretty up the appearance of urban blight. These small houses actually had miniscule yards with grass and immature trees—talk about culture shock! The last time I was in the neighborhood, the only type of grass you'd find was the kind you smoked. Fort Apache was now a lone oasis in a vast wasteland of mostly empty lots, and it would soon acquire a new nickname: Little House on the Prairie, after the TV series of the same name. Barren, flattened surroundings abounded, much like a farmhouse in the middle of nowhere.

I identified myself as a retired detective to the lone cop on station house security and he let me pass. The interior of the building had been almost entirely refurbished, and I hardly recognized it. The only familiar sight was the massive desk from which a boss would direct precinct operations, the same one that was there when the house was opened in 1914. It had been moved about twenty feet closer to the entrance, but other than that, the throwback to another era was still intimidating.

Instead of a boss manning the desk, there was a police officer. Following protocol, I approached the desk and identified myself, and the desk officer, Police Officer Curtis Chambers, welcomed me warmly after I told him I'd worked there back in the day.

We talked for almost an hour, he telling me all about the changes in the area. We traded war stories, as cops do, and I wasn't too surprised to learn that crime had taken a significant drop. There was no housing in the area, and therefore hardly anyone around to raise hell. The newly built homes, Chambers told me, were occupied by law-abiding families.

I went upstairs to the second floor, where the Anti-Crime office and the detective squad room were when I worked there. The floor was now subdivided into offices—several offices: Precinct Detectives, Major Case Squad, Latent Print, the Grand Larceny Unit, and an administrative office—each with impressive etched-glass doors and polished floors. I felt like I'd stepped into the future, and in a way I had. It was unnerving to realize that what once was would never be again. The grime and cigarette smoke carried a lot of personality; now everything seemed so sterile. Try smoking in a city building these days and you'll get castrated.

I went into the detective squad room. Five detectives were hunched over computer keyboards and didn't immediately look up. I fixated on the spot where Detective Picciano had been murdered while fingerprinting a prisoner, which was now desk space where a young detective sat.

The young detective looked up, and I snapped out of my reverie. "Can I help you?"

"My name's Ralph Friedman. I used to be a cop in this command." We shook hands. I will not identify him for reasons that will shortly become evident.

He eyed me carefully. "Not *the* Ralph Friedman? The guy with all the medals?"

I smiled. "You got me."

That broke the ice. We spoke for hours, about the changes in the command, changes in the job, lack of political leadership with balls . . . the usual cop rant.

At one point he appeared wistful. "I bet those were the days. Not everyone just obsessed with political correctness."

"The term hadn't been invented yet. We had bosses who backed us up. City Hall stayed away. Making a lot of good-quality arrests was a good thing. They liked proactive cops. Now . . ." I let myself trail off.

"Not like that anymore, Ralph. Precinct-level bosses are good, but when you get to borough and Puzzle Palace level, they get a ball-ectomy before they get their rank."

The Puzzle Palace was better known as One Police Plaza, aka headquarters, and his complaint was valid if I can believe most every cop I've talked to over the years. According to a recent survey conducted by the Patrolman's Benevolent Association (PBA), morale is at its lowest point in the history of the NYPD. The survey showed that the "dangers officers face are greater despite an influx of new cops and an increase in technology."

The PBA membership online survey, which six thousand responded to, found that 87 percent of the cops surveyed considered the city to be "less safe" since Mayor de Blasio was voted into office and that 97 percent say the mayor has created an environment "where criminals feel emboldened to carry guns and use them against civilians." A remarkable 96 percent of cops felt that the relationship between the job and the public had deteriorated in recent years. The most unsettling response was that 97 percent of police officers "are reluctant to take action for fear of lawsuits or complaints by the public."

City Hall responded by citing lowered crime statistics. Crime stats being down are indicative of police officers doing their jobs despite the fact that a huge number of them have astoundingly low morale.

High morale is extremely crucial in hazardous occupations where the safety of citizens relies on motivated employees. If police officers feel they're being treated unfairly, their job performance will suffer. In today's climate, many police officers are more concerned that doing their jobs will lead to lawsuits, firings, and possible jail time because they get little (if any) support from elected officials. Couple all that with the real dangers that exist every time a police officer goes to work and what you have is an ineffective police force.

I loved being a cop and was very good at what I did. However, it pains me to say that I'd never want to be a cop in the atmosphere that's prevalent today. There was a time when I felt that if I had kids I'd urge them to become police officers because there's no greater reward than keeping the peace. I wouldn't do that today.

I spoke to a few uniformed officers before I left. Despite the difference in our ages, we made an immediate connection based on the fact that we were all cops. Once you put on that uniform, no matter how many years have passed, it seems as if you've known all other cops forever. The eagerness in their manner, their willingness to serve and make a difference brought me back to when I was their age. It made me proud to be in their company. My loyalty to the NYPD remains undiminished, and I bleed blue in my heart whenever a cop is injured or killed.

Before I went home, I made a detour to 500 Southern Boulevard. The building was still there, and the neighborhood eerily quiet, as if out of respect. It was on the night of December 28, 1974, that Police Officer Kenny Mahon was murdered inside that building. I sat in my car for a few moments, engine running, and thought I could still see Kenny, eager, determined, going into that tenement to meet his death.

Tears came for Kenny and every cop who gave his life for this city. I hoped some of its citizens still cared about its police officers.

Grace and I bought a house in another state, some distance from New York City, and are happy in our new home. We have a black Labrador puppy that enjoys the suburban lifestyle as much as we do. I still have my memories. It's not solely about me anymore, as it was when I was a cop with a mission; it's about my relationship with Grace and our combined outlook for the future.

I've designed an homage to the NYPD and my awards on the first floor of our home; part museum, part legacy, part office and den. It took almost a year of painstaking, loving work with master craftsman Billy Butterfield to complete the project. It was worth the expense and hours of labor. It faces the driveway so I have a clear, unobstructed view of anyone approaching the house. Old habits die hard. Late at night when a silence permeates the house and the neighborhood, I go there. It's my best place to unwind. There's a lot of history adorning those walls; a lot of pain, a lot of joy. If, as some say, we're all destined to find peace in our past, then I've found mine.

ACKNOWLEDGMENTS

Throughout my career I was extremely fortunate to have had the privilege and honor of working with the best officers in the NYPD, who were unrivaled by any police officers anywhere. I was immediately impressed by the officers in the 41st Precinct. True professionals, they made a huge impression on me, and I was inspired by their dedication, commitment, and courage.

Among the best of the best were George Widicka (RIP), Richard Biller (RIP), and Stanley Gamb, to name a few who stood out. These were men I was in awe of and who served as inspirations. I was lucky to serve with these men and honored to have had them as partners.

During the course of my career I was also quite fortunate to have had some incredible supervisors: bosses who recognized and encouraged my commitment and dedication to the job. Thomas Walker, whom I had the great privilege to work under when he was a lieutenant and again when he was a captain and returned as commanding officer of the Four-One, was by far the best boss anyone could wish for. There were two other bosses who stood out among the best: Sergeant William "Wild Bill" Taylor and Sergeant

John Battaglia, may they both rest in peace. I want to thank the dedicated and brave officers I had the privilege and honor to have partnered with: Kenny Mahon (RIP), Billy Rath, Mike DePalma, Eddie Fennell, Robert DeMatas, Davy Cohen, Lester Rudnick, and Nat McCain.

I also wish to thank Sergeant Stephen Cantor and Sergeant Michael Harris, who were excellent detective squad bosses. Special thanks to Roger Cortes (RIP) and Timmy Kennedy, my partners with whom I worked for most of the years I spent on the squad; they should have been given the rank of first-grade detectives.

All these men should have the undying gratitude of New York City and its citizens for the selfless work they performed and the sacrifices they made in protecting and keeping the city's residents safe.

I would also like to thank my agent, Frank Weimann, the dedicated and professional staff at Thomas Dunne Books/St. Martin's Press, and, most of all, my coauthor, Patrick Picciarelli, who got inside my head and put my life on paper better than I could have imagined. I'd be remiss if I didn't mention Harry Schott, who introduced me and Patrick and brought us together to write my story. I'm indeed lucky to have such a team on my side.

This book would not be complete or have been possible without the undying love of Grace Rossi, who has stood by me through the worst time of my life, the accident that ended my career and almost ended my life.

Detective Ralph Friedman, NYPD (ret.)
January 1, 2017